For Brian Domonic Muir.
There would be no *Critters* without you.
Rest in peace.

WE'RE HERE FOR THE KRITES: THE MAKING OF CRITTERS
Copyright © 2025 by Matthew C. DuPée
ISBN-13: 979-8-9890130-9-8
http://HarkerPress.com

Book Designed by Dustin McNeill

This book is an independent editorial work of film journalism and not authorized by or affiliated with New Line Cinema, Warner Bros, or any other entity associated with the franchise.

WE'RE HERE FOR THE KRITES

THE MAKING OF
CRITTERS

Matthew C. DuPée

Edited by
Natalie Tomaszewski

Following Page Spread: Effects maestro Werner Pretorius and his Amazing Ape team provided dozens of Krite puppets for 2019's *Critters Attack!* (Source: Werner Pretorius)

TABLE OF CONTENTS

A NOTE TO READERS

Growing up in the 1980s was a remarkable experience for many burgeoning horror film addicts, myself included. Between the rapid rate of high-end horror debuts from both independent and major studios, the introduction of the home video market, and the proliferation of gorier and gorier practical effects, the horror genre reigned supreme during the Reagan era. While slasher pictures-cum-franchises like *Friday the 13th* and *A Nightmare on Elm Street* began to dominate the box office, horror-comedy blockbusters like *Ghostbusters* and *Gremlins* also became a sensation, spawning a cycle of cash-ins and rip-offs. Among my favorites is *Critters*, a meager-budgeted creature feature from New Line Cinema that masterfully blended elements of horror, sci-fi, and comedy with fantastic practical effects and a family-oriented story.

I first watched *Critters* at a slumber party when I was in the third grade, about two years after the film initially graced the silver screen. Amidst a chaotic melee of sugar-high eight-year-olds wrestling, jumping off of furniture and scarfing down a third slice of pizza, I stood transfixed watching red-eyed razor-fanged furballs wreak havoc on the Browns's family farm. The 86-minute run time flew by as I watched on in a hypnotic state of awe. As kids began to crash or settle in playing Nintendo on a separate television, I rewound the VHS rental tape and immediately watched it again. From that night forward, I was hooked. Sketches of Krites, the species of porcupine-like aliens featured in *Critters,* littered my school notebooks, hung on my family's refrigerator, and kept me inspired to devour any and all creature features I could get my paws on. Still, nothing came close to replacing my love and adoration for Stephen Herek's *Critters*, an instant cult classic. *Critters* was followed by a bigger budgeted sequel in 1988 and two additional installments in 1991 and 1992 respectively, as well as a reboot and a separate mini-series in 2019.

Although my first foray into writing books about horror cinema focused on the much loved Christmas horror subgenre in *A Scary Little Christmas: History of Yuletide Horror Films, 1972-2020*, I knew for my second book I wanted to take a deeper dive on a much more focused film or franchise. *Critters*, for me, was a no-brainer.

An early conceptual sketch of the Krites by Charles Chiodo. (Art courtesy the Chiodo brothers)

While there exists a robust literary examination of the making of *Critters* and similar films in the incredibly well-written *Critters: Devoradores del espacio exterior* by Octavio López Sanjuán, the book remains unavailable in English and covers a wider range of monster comedy films alongside *Critters*. I wrote *We're Here for the Krites* in an effort to celebrate the legacy of *Critters* while also capturing the fascinating story behind a risky low-budget independent film production that turned into a commercially viable success. This book is not a critical essay; rather, it's a chronological history of the making of the *Critters* franchise and memorialized oral history from many of the creators themselves.

How did a seemingly forgettable low-budget creature feature become such a commercial and critical success? Why and how did *Critters* evolve into a cult classic franchise adored by fans around the world? This book not only tackles these questions, but offers keen insights and context drawn from over 40 original interviews with many of the masterminds behind the genesis of *Critters* and its five-film franchise. Incredibly rare primary source material, including archival footage lost to history for over 38 years, personal letters, and never before published photographs are used to celebrate the fascinating story behind the making of *Critters* and its sequels.

Writing this book marked a true literary journey and an exercise in patience, as tracking down many of the cast and crew members, some long retired and living off the grid, posed a tremendous challenge. However, time and perseverance reigned supreme, and having the opportunity to speak with the producing duo behind all four original *Critters* films – Barry Opper and Rupert Harvey – was nothing short of incredible. Similarly, the deep insights offered by the effects artists responsible for creating the Krites, the Chiodo brothers and their team, as well as other effects artists like John Naulin and Chris Biggs who designed and built the non-Krite aliens featured in two of the films, was a dream come true. Many others were critical in providing behind-the-scenes photos and illustrations, with a profound thanks to Paul Salamoff, Bradford Plows, Dwight Roberts, John Naulin, Jene Omens, Larry Bock, Frank Ceglia, Charles Austin Muir, Lin Shaye, Dee Wallace, Bobby Miller, Keith Arbuthnot, Werner Pretorius, Tashiana Washington, and of course, the Chiodo brothers. I remain indebted to all of the cast and crew who were generous with their time to speak with me about these films and regret not being successful in enticing the few voices rarely heard in celebrating the history of the franchise, namely Stephen Herek, Scott Grimes, and Terrence Mann, though it was not without trying.

The author with the Chiodo brothers.

It's my sincere hope that this book deepens your appreciation not only for *Critters* but the entire franchise, even the reboot, despite its initial lukewarm reception by viewers. So buckle up and grab your sling-shot, it's time to travel back to Grover's Bend and take a deep look at the creation of *Critters* and its cult classic franchise.

- Matthew DuPée

CHAPTER ONE

CRITTERS

DAWN OF THE 'MONSTER COMEDY' FILM

A new cinematic trend emerged in the early-to-mid 1980s: the 'monster comedy' film. Owing much to classic '50s sci-fi and monster movies pioneered by the likes of Roger Corman, the monster comedy film often featured relatively family-friendly content – balancing its contemporary horror sensibilities with humor and practical special effects – and at times, animatronic puppets. Blockbusters such as *E.T. the Extra-Terrestrial*, *Gremlins* and *Ghostbusters* all inspired a plethora of cheap knock offs like *Ghoulies*, *Munchies*, *Hobgoblins*, and even the Bollywood film *Nukie*.

Along with monsters becoming smaller compared to the threats imagined by cinematic creatures in the 1950s and 1960s, the monster comedies of the 1980s sought to replace the previously large, outrageous monsters with smaller, more lethal threats. The early 1980s also witnessed the emergence of an edgier appetite for darker sci-fi films, many of which featured various alien threats replete with more gore and memorable practical effects. It's as though the baby boomers who grew up during the Kennedy era's fascination with space exploration and technological marvels were now purveyors of neo-noirs like *Alien*, *Blade Runner*, *The Terminator,* and a slew of B-movie knockoffs, like *Trancers* and *Zone Troopers*. But sci-fi and futuristic adventure films with various monsters were also a force to reckon with as movies like *Galaxy of Terror*, *Xtro*, *Krull*, *The Last Starfighter* and *Starman* saturated the drive-in market.

In April 1986, the horror sci-fi comedy *Critters* invaded theaters to critical fanfare and captured a generation of genre lovers's hearts for decades to come. Featuring animatronic creature effects and puppetry designed by the legendary special effects siblings the Chiodo brothers,

Opposite: The Brown Farm. (Photo courtesy Bradford Plows)

Critters ranks among the best monster comedy films ever made. Famed film critics Gene Siskel and Roger Ebert enthusiastically bestowed the film with "two thumbs up" and Joe Bob Briggs, the "King of the Drive-in," dubbed it "the best of '86." Most astonishing, perhaps, the film's box office earnings dwarfed its meager budget by almost fivefold, galvanizing *Critters* as a commercial success destined for a franchise.

THE ROAD TO GROVER'S BEND

Like the making of many other cult classics, the roadmap to *Critters* is an intriguing and remarkable set of circumstances that intersected at Roger Corman's New World Pictures during the early 1980s. In September 1981, a tenacious and crafty 19-year-old named Brian Domonic Muir departed his humble family home in West Linn, Oregon and drove himself to Los Angeles with a dream of making it in the film industry. Among his scant belongings was a handwritten horror-sci-fi script simply titled, *Critters*. Like many similarly-minded cinefiles before him, Brian's exposure to the Los Angeles film industry came via the Roger Corman School of Filmmaking. Brian started out in the mailroom of Corman's New World Pictures before becoming a production assistant on sci-fi cheapies such as *Time Walker* and later serving as a camera assistant on *Space Raiders*. But it was the production of the sci-fi breakout film *Android* in 1982 that paved the road that would eventually lead to *Critters*.

"My brother, Don Keith Opper, was employed by Corman as a production manager and sometimes carpenter," producer Barry Opper explains. "The father of a young child at that time, he was really an actor and a writer but took regular work at New World to support his family. Everyone at New World doing production jobs to make a living, it seemed, were really intending some other career than what they were doing for Roger. At that time I had been involved for some 12 years with two rather notorious theater groups with national and international attention. When a rumor circulated at New World that Roger might be interested in producing a script that could be shot on sets that were already up for *Battle Beyond the Stars*, my brother and a fellow carpenter wrote a script called *Android* for which they got Roger's assistant Aaron Lipstadt to agree to direct and his production accountant Rupert Harvey to agree to produce. Don called me to see if I might be interested to work with Rupert to help raise the 50 percent of the budget Roger was asking for him to agree to pay his half and offer his studio for the shoot. Two young assistants on that production were named Stephen Herek and Brian Muir."

Android, a moral dilemma tale set in deep-space and starring eccentric European actor Klaus Kinski and newcomer Don Keith Opper as an experimental android named Max 404, accumulated a talented crew under Corman's tutelage. The film was produced by Barry's burgeoning company known as Sho Films, composed of his business partners Fred Schwartz, Rupert Harvey, and himself. Rupert Harvey, an experienced British music industry producer, broke into the film industry by serving as a production accountant on Corman's *Galaxy of Terror*, a low-budget riff on Ridley Scott's *Alien*, before partnering with Barry Opper to form Sho Films.

Muir and Stephen Herek, a University of Texas at Austin film school alumnus, also worked on *Android* – Muir as a production assistant and Herek as one of the film's assistant editors. The cinematographer was a young and upcomer named Tim Suhrstedt. Among the film's art department, James Cameron, just a few years prior to his breakout film *The Terminator*, as well as Brian Muir's *Two Guys Who Watch Movies* co-host Mark Pritchard, and Philip Dean Foreman, a British colleague of Rupert Harvey and soon-to-be world class production designer.

Following *Android*, many of the future *Critters* crew worked together on *City Limits*, a dystopian future fantasy film directed by Aaron Lipstadt based on a script by Don Opper, the same writer-director pairing used in *Android*. Once again, Barry Opper and Rupert Harvey served as producers, Tim Suhrstedt as the director of photography, while Muir and Herek served as assistant editors to R.J. Kizer, a Corman regular who also worked with Rupert Harvey on *Galaxy of Terror*.

DID YOU KNOW?

A Texas native, *Critters* director and co-writer Stephen Herek originally attended the University of Texas at Austin in hopes of playing baseball, but didn't make the cut. Herek refocused his efforts on filmmaking and studied under Edward Dmytryk, known for his 1940s noir films and *The Caine Mutiny*. After graduating in 1980, Herek relocated to L.A. and ended up in the editorial department for famed indie pioneer Roger Corman. After *Critters*, Herek went on to make *Bill & Ted's Excellent Adventure* and became a regular at Walt Disney Studios in the 1990s.

THE KING OF CULT!

Roger Corman, born on April 5, 1926 in Detroit, cut his teeth early on in the industry after graduating from Stanford in 1947, first in the mailroom at 20th Century Fox and then as a story analyst. He later sold his first two screenplays in 1952 and started his own production company, Palo Alto Productions, in 1954. Corman immediately proved his merit as a budget-conscious producer able to provide content on a shoestring and quickly. Palo Alto Productions's first feature, *Monster from the Ocean Floor*, was shot in six days for approximately $12,000. His next film, a car chase film called *The Fast and the Furious*, garnered the attention of Sam Arkoff and Jim Nicholson, who would go on to create American International Pictures (AIP). The pair financed Corman to provide a plethora of cheaply made "B-movies" needed to fill time and space for drive-in theaters.

Ever expanding his operations and cranking out numerous pictures a year, Corman eventually left AIP after creative differences and started New World Pictures in 1970. New World's cheapies dominated the 1970s; Corman was crowned "King of the B's" and became the most successful independent film producer in American history. Corman's relentless production output birthed the careers of some of America's most profound directors, including James Cameron, Martin Scorsese, Ron Howard, Francis Ford Coppola, Joe Dante, Jonathan Demme, Allan Arkush, Monte Hellman, and many others. Corman's low-budget, indie film environment continued into the early 1980s and played a major role in pulling together the critical creative components responsible for *Android*, which led to the making of *Critters*. Having produced over 400 films in his career and forever galvanized himself as a maverick indie filmmaker, Corman's indelible mark on American cinema will never be forgotten. Roger Corman passed away on 9 May 2024 at the age of 98.

The camaraderie on Corman's super low-budget sets among the crew led to creative collaborations on personal pursuits and stoked the dreams of making their own low-budget B-movie, particularly among the likes of Herek, Muir, and Patrick Rand, an editor at New World Pictures. "Brian Muir, Stephen Herek and I all worked for Roger Corman at his trailer department down at the 'Lumber Yard' in Venice, California," Rand recalls. "Brian was not actually in the trailer department, he was doing various things and different positions but we all knew each other working for the company. Steve and I both worked in the trailer department in editorial and we all became fast friends and watched a lot of movies together. We shared cinematic world views to a certain extent, anyway. Steve and I were both transplants from Texas. We both went to the University of Texas at Austin and I was a year or two ahead of him but we didn't really know each other until we moved to Los Angeles. As best as I recall, we had all been discussing that we should develop something because we were working on all these Roger Corman films that we felt we could do much better than (laughs). So many people felt the same way at that time (laughs). Brian actually had a story and a completed script for *Critters* that Steve thought, with some work, we could get into shape. The idea always was: Steve would direct, Brian was the writer, and I was the editor. My memory of it was that's how it always was when we started working on it."

EARLY SCRIPT

Although Muir's original hand-written script of *Critters* – rendered on lined three-hole punch stationery, longhand, in pencil during the summer of 1981 – has since been lost to history, Muir explained in one of his last interviews that the original script had a darker tone and delved much deeper into R-rated territory with scenes of graphic violence and bloody mayhem, including some deaths among the story's main characters. But the origins of Muir's writing the initial script comes from an unpublished retrospective essay he wrote prior to his untimely death:

"I wrote the first draft of *Critters* when I was nineteen, still living with my parents, brothers and sister in West Linn, Oregon. But I was already a fan of movies, reading everything I could about them. I made my own Super 8 films and even converted my closet into a little editing room. And as of the early summer of 1981, my plan was to take every penny I had and go down to L.A. to try and make it in the movie biz. Naive, ridiculous, insane; the way of all dreamers.

"I figured it would be a good idea to have a script under my arm when I arrived in town, ready to take Hollywood by storm. Horror films were popular moneymakers (and still are; will always be), and since I loved horror movies and had even made some of my own, I decided to write a horror film. But what kind of horror film?

"I felt back then that the key to any successful horror film was the menace, the monster. What do we think of first when remembering our favorite horror flicks? We remember Frankenstien's monster, the wolfman, the creature from the Black Lagoon. We remember King Kong and Godzilla, Leatherface and Jason. The other characters don't spring first into our brains, not the plots of these horrors, but rather the star monster.

"So what would my monster be? I felt it had to be something that could be filmed on a relatively low-budget, smartly deducing that my first contacts in Hollywood (despite the grandiosity of my dreams) would not be with the big studios with the extravagant budgets.

"I don't recall but I think I came up with the title before the monster: Critters. It was a word that we have all used at some point or another, an all-encompassing word used to describe any creepy-crawly and sometimes even large varmints, but generally it called to mind a smaller creature and smaller monsters are generally scarier than larger ones. They can slither, crawl, creep, and sneak into tiny nooks and crannies; they might move fast and come at you from all angles, whereas a bigger monster, even one man-sized, is more restricted in terms of their movements, speed, and possible hiding places.

"So the Critters would have to be small. I thought for a long time what they would look like and eventually came up with four-legged, furry, and with a mouth full of multiple rows of teeth and always hungry. I knew I wanted the Critters to come from outer space because I was also a 19-year-old science fiction fan and the melding of sci-fi and horror seemed like a good idea at the time (surprisingly, this melding of genres never came up as a deterrent before or during production, but in the years since I've encountered that roadblock on a number of projects). Having the Critters to be convicts from space – not the first visual we think of when we conjure up the image of the convict – was my tribute to 'The Zanti Misfits,' one of the great episodes of *The Outer Limits*."

Nevertheless, the basic story remained the same: a family living on a farm in rural America is invaded by escaped alien prisoners known as Krites and the destitute family must join forces with intergalactic bounty hunters to destroy them before they overrun the town of Grover's Bend. Though never explicitly stated in the early drafts, the town of Grover's Bend was most likely set in Texas – no doubt influenced by Herek and Rand, both of whom were from Texas – before later being changed to Kansas.

Brian Domonic Muir on set of one of his many self-produced Super 8mm short films made with friends and family in West Linn, Oregon before relocating to Hollywood, California. (Source: Robert Epler)

"Brian was just like a 16 or 17-year-old kid, and he had this idea of, instead of all the big monsters in movies, to do something with smaller monsters," explains Charles Austin Muir, Brian's younger cousin and close friend. "He had, even for a film professional, a monumental encyclopedic knowledge of films. And he was really into monster horror, of course, but he had this idea, back then, because small monsters weren't as much of a thing yet. When he wrote this, it was way before *Ghoulies* and *Gremlins* and so he came up with this story about this family that's kind of like him and his family. Now, they didn't live in a rural area like the Brown family, but it was that solid middle class kind of family. And the bowling, one of the things that the Muirs and the extended family, we all had this annual bowling tournament… Every year, I mean, people would dress up and there were teams with weird names, just all this ceremonial stuff. I would go every year and Brian made it to a couple of them. Bowling was big in the Muir family. So that bowling scene, in *Critters*, I don't think, I mean this is my own idea, but I don't think that bowling scene would have been in the film, there wouldn't be those gifts if there wasn't the Muir family bowling tournament. So that's just to give you an idea of the flavor of it. You know, from his own growing up. And he loved *Twilight Zone* and *Outer Limits*. And me and him used to geek out all over all this obscure old stuff. Anyway, one episode he was particularly fond of was 'The Zanti Misfits,'" which is about a ship full of tiny, extraterrestrial prisoners being sent to a penal colony that ends up in crash landing on Earth and gobbling up a small town. How about that?"

Muir even sketched early depictions of the flesh-munching Krites, designed a proto-movie poster, and solicited then-burgeoning storyboard artist Len Morganti to contribute early design ideas for both the Krites, Warden Zanti, and the bounty hunters. (Morganti would ultimately be hired to storyboard the shooting script for *Critters* a few years later.)

It was Muir's pairing with Rand and Herek that eventually reformatted the story to include more commercial sensibilities akin to a Steven Spielberg production, a formula that had reshaped Hollywood's studio output in the early 1980s with films like *E.T.* and Richard Donner's *The Goonies*. "I had no idea what kind of acid trip he was on, but he [Muir] had come up with a bizarre little story," Herek recalled to *Fangoria*. Despite being written years before both *Gremlins* and *The Terminator*, Herek claimed several rewrites were required to avoid any controversy. "The *Critters* script was around a long time before either of those movies were made, but we had to rewrite because much of the script was similar to what was in those movies. We knew people would say we ripped them off, so we changed some things around," Herek told *Fangoria*.

"Reworking the script involved some fairly big changes. All that was really kept were who the characters were and the basic idea of the script – the critters coming from outer space and the problems that they would cause once they got to Earth," Rand explains. "Originally, Brian had written it so that the bounty hunters were just bounty hunters. I came up with the idea that the bounty hunters should be shape-shifters... My thought was, we could make the bounty hunters be able to turn into anything. They land on Earth, and say, he turns into Rodney Dangerfield, or who knows what (laughs). We thought it could be really funny. And that is when the script started to take on more humorous tones beyond the critters being funny. I think that is something that Steve was very strongly promoting – the dark humor aspect, but dark humor is something that Brian was all about as well… I would never describe Brian's humor as mean spirited, but he liked going dark, that's what he found to be funny. Steve was good in overlaying a little more commercial sensibility to the script, and more of a commercial sense of humor to it."

Critters

EARLY DESIGNS

Early sketches of the Krites by Len Morganti featured armless bipedal aliens as were described in Brian Muir's earliest drafts.
The description of the Krites in all variations of the script changed very little over time.
(Source: Brian Muir courtesy Daniel Griffith of Ballyhoo Productions)

Brian Muir paid homage to 1950s and 1960s sci-fi television programs, movies, and even the 1938 radio broadcast of *War of the Worlds* when he wrote *Critters*. Muir undoubtedly sought inspiration from the 1953 film *Invaders from Mars*, which features an adolescent protagonist who witnesses a flying saucer crash near the rural farmhouse he lives on with his parents. He uses a telescope and later sits on his roof to get a better glimpse of the UFO just like Bradley Brown's character in *Critters*. The rural farmhouse even has a similar white picket fence as seen at the Browns's family farmhouse and the main Martian is a "butthead" alien floating in an orb similar to that of Warden Zanti, which of course pays homage to the "Zanti Misfits" episode of *The Outer Limits* first broadcast in 1963. The town of Grover's Bend in *Critters* is also a nod to Grover's Mill from Orson Welles's *War of the Worlds*, a realistic radio broadcast that featured hostile aliens landing on Earth and attacking local residents, the general plot of *Critters*.

"I can tell you, [*Critters*] is a thematic mix of *Gremlins* and *The Terminator*," a slightly scruffy but laid back Stephen Herek explained with a chuckle, "I've been preparing for the shoot by drinking four margaritas a day, and a joint or two in the afternoon." Herek's largely unseen interview appeared on a long-forgotten 1985 episode of *Two Guys Who Watch Movies*, a public access television show hosted by none other than Brian Muir and his co-host and fellow cinephile Mark Pritchard. The short segment, which appeared on the show's 16th episode in the spring of 1985, also included an exchange in which Pritchard announced that Muir also had a role in the upcoming production of *Critters*. "I think now we have to reveal you are also involved with this [*Critters*]," Pritchard said to Muir as the camera switched back to a master shot. "Let me just fill them in a little bit real quick. When *Two Guys* started about 2 years ago, we thought, '*Hell, anyone can do that*,' a cable access show. But I think you had a similar approach on a script, '*Ah, look at these B-movies, anybody can do that* [a B-movie].' So, you did it." In an extremely rare occasion, Muir speaks publicly, albeit briefly, about his role in writing *Critters*. "I wrote it, and Steve co-wrote it with me." After a self-deprecating joke about why Muir agreed to allow Herek to direct, to which they all laugh, Muir explains that *Critters* should be in theaters sometime in early 1986, but not to worry, as *Two Guys Who Watch Movies* would be tracking the development closely. The segment is abruptly closed out after a producer alerts them it's time to run the trailer for *Mad Max Beyond Thunderdome*.

Barry Opper, a talented producer who also hailed from the Corman era of independent filmmaking, recalls first reviewing the script for *Critters*. "Steve Herek and Brian Muir brought us a script they had been working on, Rupert [Harvey] and I liked it, developed it with them, and

STEVE'S IN LOVE

First time director and Texas-native Stephen Herek goofs around with the infamous giant critter suit at the production's office on Sunset Boulevard. (Source: Larry Bock)

quickly were about to do a deal with New World to make the film at a very low-budget, which is all we could get from Roger [Corman]. However, before we signed a deal with Roger, Rupert and I went to Milan, Italy to MIFED [Italian acronym for the International Market for Cinema and Multimedia] to help sell *Android* internationally and there we met Bob Shaye of New Line Cinema. While in Milan, Bob told us if we ever had a project he might like, he'd be interested in doing a movie with us. So, several weeks later, we met him in his room at the Chateau Marmont in Los Angeles on a Friday, and by the next Monday, we had a contract to do *Critters* with New Line. It was twice the budget that we would have had with Roger. Also it gave us a two-picture deal."

"As far as script development is concerned, to Bob and Sara [Risher] at New Line, I was giving them pretty much a – it wasn't a finished script – but it was a well-advanced script," producer Rupert Harvey says. "I don't know how dark it was originally intended to be, but what

I reacted to and viscerally responded to was not exactly a family film, but it was very much an entertaining film. It wasn't light, but it certainly wasn't dark. I didn't feel that it was a horror film. I seem to remember something about some of the family members dying in the original drafts, but I don't think that lasted very long. I think that one of them was killed in the very first draft I read, but I do remember that it was intended to be darker and it was not the movie which I wanted to make. And it wasn't the movie that really was pitched by Steve the first time. I think that might have been a bit of a bone of contention. Knowing Steve's sensibility of what he pitched, I suspect that darkness had already been lightened by Steve quite a bit before it came to work.

"Our perspective was very much engaged in the world that we lived in and produced in at the time. What I was reacting to was a story with a lot of Americana on it, in it, about it… The whole sort of Midwest countryside world and the farming family and the archetypes that the family represented were really what was appealing to me. It was, '*Let's invade this incredibly well-known archetype with aliens from outer space*.' So here is the invasion of that world. You know the famous painting which we used in some of the ads, the "American Gothic" painting by Grant Wood, it has the wife standing with her balding husband who's holding a pitchfork. Well, that represented the myth of the American family, and I reacted instantly and viscerally to the idea of something so sacrosanct and stable and normal being upset by nasty little critters from outer space… And then we continued to do other drafts and things and Don Opper, being a writer himself, was very good about the way in which he participated in and tried to guide Steve and Brian in the right direction. So, Don had a lot to do with it. He wasn't at all heavy-handed. It was very well done the way it should be, just asking all the right questions and being a very experienced and a very, very good writer himself. A talent he unfortunately never was able to really put on full display. But the script was pretty much developed in-house by ourselves at Sho Films. It wasn't developed enormously after we'd done a deal with Bob… So we were in a strong position as far as changes to the script were concerned. We weren't particularly having to make changes to get New Line on board."

With a completed script and a two-picture deal with New Line Cinema on the books, Barry Opper and Rupert Harvey began pre-production work in May 1985. The script's ambitious creatures and visual effects would require an equally audacious team to pull it off on such a tight production and preparation schedule as well as a minuscule budget, all things considered.

PRE-PRODUCTION

With New Line Cinema financing the picture, the task of hiring special effects teams to handle the wide range of practical effects, animatronic puppets, alien creatures, and pyrotechnic explosions got underway. The decision was made to hire two specific special effects teams for *Critters*: one team would handle the special makeup effects, designing the alien creatures and essentially all other non-Krite work, while the second team would only work on designing and puppeteering the Krites.

To handle the non-Krite effects, the producers tapped John Naulin and his teammate Anthony (Tony) Doublin, two special makeup effects artists who had just come off the award-winning and commercially successful horror film *Re-Animator*. Naulin recalls receiving a call by Smart Egg Pictures in New York to consider working on *Critters*, to which he agreed. Smart Egg Pictures, a pornography production house on the east coast, eventually transitioned into commercial cinema, partnering at the time with Bob Shaye and his then-incipient production company New Line Cinema. Having worked with Doublin on *Re-Animator,* the pair would once again collaborate on *Critters*.

"Because Tony Doublin had brought me in on *Re-Animato*r – he was actually working with another makeup artist, but they had had kind of a fight, not a physical fight, but they were not getting along – he invited me to do the makeup part of *Re-Animator* and we ended up winning all these awards and all that sort of stuff," Naulin notes. "So when I got *Critters*, you know, he helped me, I helped him. I invited him to come and work on *Critters* with me and do the physical effects of the physical props like the weapons and all of those efforts. Tony had worked more with the Chiodos than I had, but when we had a shop down in Hollywood, we had done some work with the Chiodos on, yes, Pee-Wee Herman, the TV show."

Doublin had first met and worked with Stephen and Charles (Charlie) Chiodo on projects in 1981, including the "Jews in Space" segment for Mel Brooks's *History of the World Part I* and a short while later, the first feature-length project for the Chiodos, a film called *Flicks* (a.k.a. *Loose Joints*) that was never released theatrically. "I worked with Stephen and Charlie on their first job in Hollywood," said Doublin. "Stephen was my sculptor and Charlie was my art director. We did creatures, mechanics, miniatures, visual effects – the whole nine yards. So we've been friends ever since 1981." Another *Flicks* alumnus, a special effects fabricator and skilled camera operator named Jene Omens who worked at the Magic Lantern effects house, would also go on to enjoy a long-standing working relationship with the Chiodo brothers. "I graduated in 1979 and began working in the industry soon after," says Omens. "Tony Doublin, Bill Hedge, and Bob Greenberg were all part of the Magic Lantern. That's where I got my start, working on "Jews in Space" with the Chiodo brothers."

Stephen and Charles, the eldest of the Chiodo brothers, had relocated from New York to Los Angeles in October 1980 just prior to landing work on the Mel Brooks segment. "Most of what we did during that time was *never* released," Charlie told *Fangoria* in 1986. "But we were working with people, new material, and learning all the time. The wealth of filmmaking information was amazing because we knew very little about the technical side of what we were doing."

The Chiodos proved resolute and soon landed their next big gig on Albert Pyun's *The Sword and the Sorcerer* designing and fabricating a crypt lined with slimy, blood-drenched faces reminiscent of the gooey effects later implemented by special makeup effects icon Screaming Mad George in films like *Society*. With a growing portfolio of credits to their name, Stephen and Charlie worked on the award-winning Disney stop-animation short film *Vincent*, directed by Tim Burton, who would later employ the Chiodo brothers shortly thereafter to do a claymation segment for *Pee-wee's Big Adventure*. Albert Pyun followed up *The Sword and the Sorcerer* with a dystopian sci-fi feature called *Radioactive Dreams* and once again hired Stephen and Charlie. This time, the Chiodos were tasked with designing a large-scale, fully operational robotic mutant rat. Instead of suggesting building miniatures or using hand puppets, Charlie sketched conceptual art depicting a 14-foot animatronic rat, much to the producers's delight. At this time, Stephen and Charlie were joined by their youngest brother Edward and his newly-wed wife Linda who relocated to Los Angeles from Long Island, New York in April 1984.

The ambitious endeavor for *Radioactive Dreams* teamed the brothers up with fabricators and mechanical wizards Dwight Roberts and Peter Chesney, and over the course of 3 months, the team constructed a fully operational 14-foot mechanical rat complete with snarling lips, and a movable tongue, arm, and paw. Despite their momentous efforts, the film's chaotic production schedule and dwindling finances prompted the producers to scrap shooting additional sequences using the giant rat and ultimately the film fell into distribution limbo. However, the production fiasco offered valuable technical lessons to the brothers and strengthened their resolve despite working hard with little to show for it in terms of completed productions.

Charlie Chiodo touches up the giant 14-foot mechanical rat used in
Albert Pyun's *Radioactive Dreams*. (Source: the Chiodo brothers)

Dwight Roberts, a mechanical genius who would go on to work with the brothers for decades to come, recalls constructing the giant rat and ultimately what led to *Critters*: "The Chiodos came over and said, '*Hey, we have this job building a 14-foot rat.*' The thing was all air-operated and had to be strong enough to pick somebody up in its arms or mouth. Charlie and I did all the sculpting and painting on it and then we all did the mechanics. I had this row of valves that probably took like seven people on it to operate this thing. Everybody had different control functions. It wasn't like any kind of electronic animatronics. We worked on this project for about a year. The Chiodos's younger brother, Edward, was coming out from New York so I got him a job at ISS making props and doing some electronic stuff, blinking lights for *The A-Team* and stuff like that. And then after a while, his brothers got this job, I think it was *Sectaurs*, it was a movie that was going to be featuring giant insects, guys riding giant insects. I was talked into leaving ISS, which was an awesome job because they had benefits and insurance, and after about two weeks we were searching for a shop where we were going to do this *Sectaurs* project and then we learned the producers pulled the plug on it. So there I am. No job. No benefits. Thankfully, the Chiodo brothers landed *Critters* not soon thereafter."

Although New Line showed interest in hiring special makeup artist Kevin Yagher to design the Krites, Yagher was tied up working on *A Nightmare on Elm Street 2: Freddy's Revenge* and he instead recommended the Chiodo brothers to be considered for the job. Yagher had worked as a special makeup artist on Pyun's *The Sword and the Sorcerer* and knew well what the Chiodos were: a capable and endlessly creative force. After securing an interview and reading through the script, the Chiodo brothers made their way to the producers meeting in such a hurry that they forgot to bring their portfolio and highlight reel. Charlie, however, did bring conceptual sketches of the Krites, and the trio followed up the next day with their complete portfolio and highlight reel to cement the deal. "I don't remember really a prolonged negotiation," Edward Chiodo recalls. "You know, based on Kevin's [Yagher] recommendation, he wouldn't recommend somebody that couldn't do the job that wasn't qualified. We had that meeting and I kind of got the feeling we were working on it right then and there."

"I think Charlie sketching right there in the meeting, showing what he had done, I think impressed them," points out Stephen Chiodo. "And the dialogue, that's what it is. I mean, you talk and you start brainstorming there with them and they get a sense of the collaboration immediately if you're in line with what they're thinking by the words you use and the things you suggest. And I think that's where we kind of hit it off... For the design, they didn't want to make it look like there was a human in a costume. So all the appendages were reduced. So it couldn't be a person there, a big wide gaping mouth that opened up out of a pile of fur. And as we were brainstorming about it, we would think, '*Okay, what is something similar out there?*' And I think it was Charlie who came up with the Tasmanian Devil, the Warner Bros. cartoon character, which is just a very tapered down, upside down triangle, or a cone with a giant mouth. And I think that was like one of the first takeoffs that he started doing. But he had a four-legged one like a dog. He had a lot of variations."

According to a pre-shooting script dated May 9, 1985, the first description of a Krite appears on page 46 during the scene when Jay Brown encounters one of the furry creatures hiding on a rickety shelf in the basement. The script denotes the Krites being "covered with bristly black fur, two small luminous red eyes, a large mouth filled with shiny ivory incisors," and the ability to "raise itself on four stubby legs."

"The way they [Krites] were described in that first draft of the script remained true until we shot the film, and the Chiodo brothers realized them exactly as I had first pictured them in my mind during that hot summer of '81 up in my old bedroom," Muir reflected upon in his unpublished essay. "The additional – and definitive – detail of their ability to curl into a ball and roll from place to place was a Chiodo invention. That for no other reason proves they were the perfect guys to bring these beasties to life."

Despite having several initial variations, time was of the essence if the Chiodos were going to pull it all off. The trio had just under 10 weeks to muster a team, design, *and* construct all of the puppets needed for the production. To do so, the Chiodo brothers shared a workshop with John Naulin and Tony Doublin, working together inside a small warehouse located around

Western and Sunset Boulevards in Hollywood. Interestingly, the warehouse was rented from musician Frank Zappa, who maintained a small recording studio and soundstage in the front of the facility at the time.

"We got this little space in Hollywood, turned it into our shop," remembers Dwight Roberts. "But it was a shop with nothing, you know, no tools, just hand tools. So all the animatronics, everything was done with just tools out of your tool bag. No machining, nothing sophisticated. Very primitive." The respective teams began in earnest building props, including the cannons used by the intergalactic bounty hunters "Ug" and "Lee" and the non-Krite alien masks and prosthetics, including "Warden Zanti" and his floating pod. Charlie's early design sketches were quickly approved by the producers and the process to create the puppets began in earnest.

The producers quickly agreed to Charlie's Tasmanian Devil-inspired bipedal design for the Krites,
a design kept for the sequel as well, as depicted in this sketch. Variant designs included a four-legged Krite,
which also featured a pronounced tail. (Source: the Chiodo brothers)

BUILDING THE BEASTS

Designing and constructing the two dozen puppets required for the production would be a testament to the skill and creativity of the Chiodo brothers and their team. The team would go on to include Dwight Roberts as lead mechanic; Gene Rizzardi, who built special props including the hero critter puppet that eats a firecracker and explodes; Jene Omens, who assisted with mechanics and eye sockets; Mike Jones, who assisted Stephen Chiodo with sculpting duties; Deborah Galvez and Ans Ellis, both of whom were responsible to plugging the hair and fur onto to the puppets; and Mitch Bryan and Bradford (Brad) Plows, both of whom were then-CalArts students and assisted with shop duties.

"We had to lock the design down as quickly as possible, so the first critter was sculpted and cast the first week," Charlie told *Monster Land* in 1986. "We created twenty-four puppets. Of these, the four main characters were fully articulated hand puppets with front and side snarl, eye-rotation, eye-blink and remote controlled brow mechanisms, cable controlled hands and the ability to be plugged into a walk cycle with rods. The other twenty puppets were specialty puppets."

With the design of the Krites locked down, the Chiodos went to work sculpting, designing, and building the puppets and experimented with various mediums to achieve the "animalistic" aesthetic desired by the producers. The Chiodos and their team set about building a plethora of stunt puppets for specific gags, including remote-controlled rolling puppets capable of rounding corners, puppets that could bend into a ball, puppets capable of shooting air-powered quills, more specific one-shot puppets, and a larger 27-inch puppet (used to attack Bradley Brown's bicycle).

"We just jumped into this thing," explains Stephen Chiodo. "They said, the producers and Steve, they said they wanted the critters to have more of a quill-like quality, not fur, but a quill-like quality to their pelts. And so we found antelope fur, we found all these things, and moose pelt had this quill-like quality that was really great. We knew nothing about taxidermy at the time. We should have stripped off all of the hide, or at least laminated it with oils to make it more flexible. We were pretty unaware of all of those techniques. So we just put it on. It was flexible in the beginning, but as it got used over time, it got stiffer and stiffer. And my hand was inside most of the time, and boy, it was really tough to puppeteer those guys… I think the original critters are more realistic because you could just tell the patina, the way the light plays off of the fur, it just feels a lot more real than the subsequent ones, which I think look more like puppets."

Fabricators Ans Ellis (left) and Deborah Galvez (right) used real moose pelts to dress the Krites, a challenging endeavor given the thickness and stiffness of the pelts. (Source: the Chiodo brothers)

The Chiodo brothers experimented with a variety of real furs, including yak, rabbit, antelope, and others before settling on moose pelts, which had to be acquired in Canada at the time, to create the authentic and iconic look of the Krites. As it turned out, moose pelts had the proper balance of coarse, quill-like follicles as opposed to the less desirable, fluffier furs that would have diminished the sinister aesthetic of the Krites. "I mean, because there was an undeniable reality – because it was *real*," says Edward Chiodo. "The luster of the sheen of the fur, the quill, the pile, it was real. Where, you know, synthetic fur is synthetic. Some of it looks really good. It's far more flexible, but it just doesn't have quite the same look."

To amplify the menacing look of the Krites's burning gaze, a highly reflective Scotchlite paint was used on the back of the eye socket, which allowed a more authentic, animalistic glow to the eyes compared to an internal light source. "I came up with the idea," says Jene Omens. "The best way it worked, and I don't remember if they did it or they cheated it, but the best way that that system worked is that the actual camera, to get the most reflectivity out of it, there's a half-silvered mirror in front of the lens. So off to the side of that camera is a light pointing into a 45-degree, half-silvered mirror bouncing straight into the puppet's eyes, and it returns back. They did some of the shots that way, and they did other ones just by putting the light as close as they could to the camera. I had to find the right tint, the red tint, the right red tint so it wouldn't block out too much of the light reflection. So that was an art in itself. It didn't come from the light. We actually did put a coating, a very light coating, on the actual eye surface. So too deep of a tint could have destroyed the effect."

Director Stephen Herek commented on the efforts to amplify the glowing eyes to *Monster Land*, noting "The only thing that makes them look different are the eyes. It's better than having a light source inside the head which doesn't look as good and is a pain to rig. We could've put a red light bulb inside the head, but that's exactly what it would've looked like. The original concept for the eyes was that they were to glow yellow, and when they got mad, they turned red. The only way to do that was to use the Scotchlite, but they finally decided to keep the eyes red throughout the film."

In an attempt to further realize the glowing eye effects, cinematographer Tim Suhrstedt designed a beam splitter rigged to the camera's matte box that focused a direct light source into the puppet's plexiglass eye sockets. However, the rig proved cumbersome and difficult to finesse, limiting the amount of footage used for the effect and never fully realizing its full potential.

"The eyes posed a challenge because they wanted to do this special idea that the Chiodos had about trying to get a natural reflection in the eye when a light would hit the eyes," Dwight Roberts explains. "It would bounce back and you'd see that reflection that animals have when the light hits it. So we used clear plexiglass balls and dipped half of it in Scotchlite paint. It was a paint on these little brass cups that I soldered a little arm to, and those cups would be glued onto the Scotchlite so it wouldn't actually penetrate the eyeball. Because when light went into the eye, it reflected straight out, and you couldn't have anything, you know, in there to pivot on or anything. The whole back surface of the eye was like a reflector mirror. Which didn't go over real well with the cinematographers because they had to set up a beam splitter that was thrown together so that they could shoot a light sideways into the beam splitter, which was mounted right in front of the lens. Essentially the light would bounce straight out from the camera lens.

Fabricator Jene Omens (top) works on an assembly for the eye socket of a Krite. Omens was instrumental in fabricating the eyes and Scotchlite technique along with Dwight Roberts (bottom).
(Sources: the Chiodo brothers (top) and Dwight Roberts (bottom))

So it was an ordeal to set that up every time. So I don't know how much realism they actually got out of that."

"I guess the big beef we had, and this goes throughout all of these *Critters* movies, (laughs) was we wanted to get that kind of red eye reflection out of the critters," recalls Stephen Chiodo. "Like when you shine a light on an animal at night, how it kind of, the retina reflects back, like a stop sign. And we had designed that effect for *Critters*. And it entailed taking these plexiglass balls, putting Scotchlite paint on the back edge. Scotchlite paint is the kind of reflective material used for stop signs. So when you shine a light on it, it kicks back the light towards the source. And it was beautiful. The puppets from *Critters* all had that capability. But in order to get the maximum effect out of it, you had to put a beam splitter in front of the taking camera, the production camera, so that a light that was flashed into it would reflect back on that nodal point of the lens and actually kick back and shine brightly. Well, Tim Suhrstedt did not want to put a piece of glass in front of his lenses, and Russ Carpenter, (laughs) no fucking way was he gonna do this! This effect was never utilized to its full capacity. What they compromised was that they would put a light near the lens, like above the lens or around the lens, and it would shine towards the eyes and kick back a little bit, but never the full amount."

"Tom Callaway tried really hard on *Critters 3* and *Critters 4*. I mean, Russ [Russell Carpenter] and Tim [Suhrstedt], they were for it in concept, but again, we didn't work with them," assesses Edward Chiodo about the Scotchlite beam splitter effect. "Very rarely did we do a first unit shot with Tim or Russ. It was always the second unit, and we never had the time to finesse this technique. It's funny, in the first *Critters* movie, when the dad, Billy Green Bush, goes down into the basement with his flashlight, and he shoots the flashlight across the shelf and you get the flash of the critter's eye. You get this white flash that comes back because it didn't have a red gel on the light, so it's a cool little thing, but it's still not the 'Critter effect.' It's the unfiltered Scotchlite effect kicking the light back. It had a great effect. It would have added this dimension and a realistic aspect to the character that was never utilized."

The Krites designed for *Critters* revolved around the base model – paltry 13-inch puppets – a cramped space for both the puppeteers and mechanical fabricators. Jene Omens, who fabricated puppets's arms and legs, explains some of the challenges. "We had to cram a lot in there. It's like how much, you know, the saying *'How many pounds of poop can you put in a little bag?'* Well, we put as much stuff as we could inside a very little, little teeny, tiny little space.

Stephen Chiodo takes a short break on set after a sequence puppeteering the remarkably small critter puppet which just topped 13 inches, a design choice the Chiodos came to regret. (Source: the Chiodo brothers)

DID YOU KNOW?

Before earning an Oscar on James Cameron's *Titanic*, cinematographer Russell Carpenter served as still photographer on *Critters* and as cinematographer on *Critters 2*. Though better known for his work on films like *True Lies, Titanic*, and *Avatar: The Way of Water*, he also served as cinematographer on such genre films as *The Lawnmower Man* and *Pet Sematary Two*.

And it worked. And it came to life. We made all different kinds of critter balls, and different sizes. Some would get thrown, but others were slightly more innovative. For instance, we had one kind that was this plastic sphere and we took a remote-controlled car and chopped it up to fit inside the sphere. We were basically driving an RC-car inside the ball to get it to move. That is how the critters that moved around corners were done. As the car was trying to drive forward it would move the critter ball around. We could get it to turn left and turn right. Dwight [Roberts] was really good. He was a really good engineer."

The Chiodos remained hellbent on delivering practical effects that delivered an outsized production value and specifically wanted attributes that would set the Krites aside from other productions, particularly the bigger-budgeted *Gremlins*. For instance, the Chiodos designed a unique cable rig and specialized mechanical rotating-leg puppet to simulate a Krite walking on its own behalf, a gag that even the crew on *Gremlins* failed to pull off. For it to work, the puppet was attached to an overhead dolly using wires while a small motor inside the body initiated movement in the legs. Although the puppet's feet would remain slightly above the ground surface, when shooting with a high enough angle, the illusion of the Krite walking would be achieved. The specialty rig and puppet were ultimately utilized and a segment of the walking Krite gag appears in the final cut when the Krites attack Bradley and April upstairs. A similar walking Krite gag was achieved in the barn scene and featured a more conventional puppeteering approach. Puppeteers worked the legs and arms of the Krite underneath a wooden rig (covered in hay) that had a slit cut out down the middle for a guide arm that fulfilled the illusion of the Krite walking on its own power. Proving to be ingenious innovators, the Chiodos were tapped by producers into figuring out how to design and fabricate an unexpected demand by Bob Shaye: a giant critter.

BOB SHAYE WANTS A GIANT CRITTER

Approximately half-way into the production, Bob Shaye insisted on a late script change and wanted a giant critter, much larger than the 27-inch medium-sized critter, to attack the family through a closet during the film's second act. In the 9 May 1985 version of the script, the Krites grow marginally after eating, particularly after a critter devours Chewy, the Brown family's cat, a scene that was ultimately excised before principal photography began. But the largest Krite mentioned in that script comes at the end, when a trio of critters drag April Brown across the field and into the spaceship and the description of the large critter is only the size of a "large dog." Still,

Shaye was insistent on introducing an even larger, man-sized Krite. Begrudgingly, the team took the challenge head on, but warned the producers and Herek that the suit, both aesthetically and functionally, would have limitations.

"Later on, Bob Shaye decided he wanted a big monster at the end, a big version, something we did not want ever to do because the critters were designed never to be a person in a costume – but the only way to do the large critter – was a person in the costume. So we had to design, re-engineer the whole look for it. It never quite worked. But Ken Hall came on and headed that team for us," remembers Edward Chiodo. "We started building it when we were closing our shop and getting ready to move to location. So we started it in the shop, but then we finished it on location. It was horrible working in that heat and a trailer, a construction trailer. It was terrible."

"The Chiodo brothers couldn't devote their full time to creating the suit when they were on set," says Dwight Roberts. "Plus, it takes a lot of work to make a little tiny costume that somebody can fit into. So you have to have the dimensions of the person to actually sculpt and work off of. So all that's gotta be done while you're working on set. I'm sure the Chiodo brothers, mainly Charlie, were going back and forth from the trailer to the set. Charlie was probably not too happy because he didn't get to be on set quite as much as he would have liked."

Although not entirely thrilled about the last minute inclusion of a giant critter, the Chiodos agreed with Shaye's thought process in principle. "I mean, I'm an advocate for having your monsters turn big at the end, to have some kind of a big boss," explained Stephen Chiodo. "So I think it was a great idea. But the design of the characters doesn't work when you blow it up. The scale of proportions [...] was like a garbage can that opened up like, like a lid (laughs)." The Chiodo brothers jokingly referred to the giant critter suit as "the Kool-Aid Kid," given its overly large hinged mouth, stubby legs, and wide body.

"Bob's instinct was correct," relents Edward Chiodo. "In a way, you needed to top it because we had the small critter, then we had the medium critter and you do things in three. You need to take that next step. So he was right by instinct, but again, it just was not the creature to do it with and then to change the design to accommodate that technique. It's not what we do. It's just, it was bad. That's why you don't see it very much."

By many accounts, director Stephen Herek and co-writer Brian Muir were opposed to the Krites growing larger the more they ate and were vehemently opposed to a man-sized Krite suit being used for the finale. "If I had to do it over again, I wouldn't have made the critters grow as big as they do," Herek told *Fangoria* during production. "But the executive producers felt it would be interesting to let them get real big. How the big one will look at this point is an ongoing question. It's a cinch that the role of the big critters will be made in the editing room."

Perhaps among the most effective scenes involving the large critter involves Nadine van der Velde's character April Brown being attacked through a barricaded door frame. The large critter's arm explodes through a dresser propped up against the doorway and gropes and rips at April, who screams in sheer terror. "Nadine was great too," recalls Stephen Chiodo. "I remember one scene that I did with her, this is when the large-sized critter attacks her, and we had a critter glove, and it kind of breaks through the wall or the drawer or something and grabs her hand. And we did that. We did it for real. I grabbed her and was kind of fighting against her and she kind of freaked out. It kind of, it really struck her. She got frightened and she really reacted as if it was this real thing happening to her. And that was a really interesting moment for me, you know, just being a puppeteer and working with actors that closely. But she was great."

Stephen Chiodo (left) and Dwight Roberts (right) tinker with a 27-inch Krite puppet, the largest of the puppets to be made until Bob Shaye's insistence on making a giant critter as seen with Charlie Chiodo (opposite page). (Source: Bradford Plows)

Despite reservations about using the large critter suit, Herek, an experienced editor, planned to edit around the sequences involving the suit, inserting close-ups and silhouettes of the large critter in action. Given the limited time to use the critter suit, fewer mechanical resources were devoted, though the suit did have eye movement mechanics installed, but little else.

Several stuntmen, including not one but two little people, as well as the Chiodo brothers and their teammate Deborah Galvez, would all go on to play various aspects of the giant critter. "When we built the large critter suit, a little person was inside it, to animate it," explains Ans Ellis, one of the Chiodos's effects artists. "Dwight [Roberts] said, '*Okay, try and stand up for me,*' and we heard this faint voice coming from inside that said, '*I am standing up!*' (laughs) The suit was just so heavy, the little person could not get it to move."

"It's a funny way of how I got the part," stuntman and actor Kevin Thompson says. "They had cast a littler person, a smaller person than me, to squeeze into the outfit. But the mouth on the suit was so freaking big and heavy. The entire weight of the suit was in the mouth apparatus, so I actually had to bend backwards to operate the mouth. When I first put it on, I understood why the little person who they first cast fell over wearing the suit, he was so light. So he couldn't do it and the stunt coordinator was standing right next to him and he looked at the director and he goes, '*I got a guy.*' (laughs) I just worked with him on the Ewok movies, like *The Battle for Endor* and *The Ewok Adventure*. Now, of course these are the days way before cell phones, so he calls me and I just happened to be home. I mean, had I not been home, he probably would have called another guy. I was living out in the Pasadena area and he called up and asked '*How fast can you be in Valencia?*' That's how many times you end up getting the gig, just being available.

"So I got there and it's in the middle of what is now called Stevenson Ranch. We filmed at a farmhouse that was built and later blown up. These days that area is mostly built up with housing developments, but back then it was empty land not far from the Magic Mountain theme park right off the I-5 freeway. I get there and he leans over and whispers to me, '*Don't complain and you'll get three weeks of work.*' So I put the suit on, I was like, '*Son of a bitch.*' You know, this sucker's heavy. I weigh 95 to 100 pounds and the suit weighs around 65 pounds, maybe more. So there I am, sitting down and putting this suit on and the mouth is down – it's laying down because it's heavy – and they say, '*Okay, can you bring the mouth up?*' I bend backwards to get the suit to move like they need and the mouth opens up and they say, '*Perfect!*' This is what the other guy they had originally cast was not able to do. So I ask them, '*What is this monster, is it like a big dumb character type-of-thing?'* And they say, *'Oh no, no, no, you have the agility of a cat.'* I was like, *'Whoa.'* (laughs) And so that's how we started. That's how I got the gig."

Although Kevin Thompson wore the suit for many of the sequences involving the giant critter, a few segments involving cut away shots or close-ups of just the feet, involved Chiodo crew members like Deborah Galvez and even Charlie Chiodo, who performed the stunt when the giant critter leaps through the Browns's second floor window after attacking April.

"I remember the little person working in the big critter suit took off after lunch, one day," remembers Deborah Galvez. "We couldn't find him, and there was a scene that was up. And so I was the smallest one, so they put me in the bottom half of it. So I was just like the legs. I just wore that, and they shot from the legs down. I was walking in the spaceship. That was me. So the scene where the big critter is walking on the spaceship and you see just the legs and feet, that's me. It was fun to do and it was definitely funny."

Fabricator Ans Ellis designs an appendage for the giant critter (left) while Deborah Galvez and Dwight Roberts work the jaws of the giant critter. Once completed, the giant critter suit weighed almost 70 lbs.
(Sources: Bradford Plows and the Chiodo brothers)

BECOMING THE BOUNTY HUNTERS

Two intergalactic bounty hunters who possess the capability to transmorph into other beings to better blend into their operational environment became an essential trope of the *Critters* universe. In the film's intro, two such bounty hunters, "Ug" played by Terrence Mann, and "Lee," played by a variety of actors the bounty hunter morphs into, are shown traveling from deep space to earth in pursuit of the escaped Krite prisoners.

John Naulin and his team designed the faceless voids of the bounty hunters and the blobulous Warden Zanti, but Chris Biggs was later brought in to work the transformation gag and additional close-up work for Warden Zanti. "We were working on what we called the pre-morph bounty hunters, which had a translucent silicone mattress on it," remembers John Naulin. "In order to make this thing, we call that level of the metamorphosis, we call them the 'Q-tip heads'. When they're wearing the silicone mask as the Q-tip head, it's got two little tiny, maybe 3/16th inch holes that line up with the pupil and that's it. That's the only opening in those masks to see out. That's why they look good because the camera basically, if you're off angle at all, that material doesn't look like there's any visible opening in it. The day before we're set to shoot this sequence, they realized that Terrence [Mann] was as tall as he is. And the person that they had hired to stand in as the Q-tip head was not. And I said, well, you can't establish this character at like 5'10" and then suddenly have him be 6'1.5" or 6'2". He's not morphing that way. This is before he morphs, he's got to be 6'2", roughly 6'2". A friend of mine named Konrad Williams was available. I brought Konrad over and he dressed up in the costume. I said, '*Come out. You're going to only have two little tiny holes to see out of. As long as you keep everything lined up and look straight forward, you'll do great.*'"

"When Konrad – and I do not remember who the other gentleman was – but when Konrad and the other guy walk through coming towards the fog down below and they're coming towards the camera, they walk through kind of an archway," Naulin explains. "And that's how they made the hallways look really long; they made what are called pilasters. They made just the archways. There was nothing in between them. It was a perspective shot. When you line them up, they go in and in and in and in. And it looks like a long hallway. Your mind puts the walls in there, but there are no walls. He's just basically walking down a straight corridor towards this opening. He is 6'2", and it is curved. If you look real carefully, he runs right into the opening. He kind of bounces off, and tilts his head and goes the rest of the way. Again, it was the nature of this shoot.

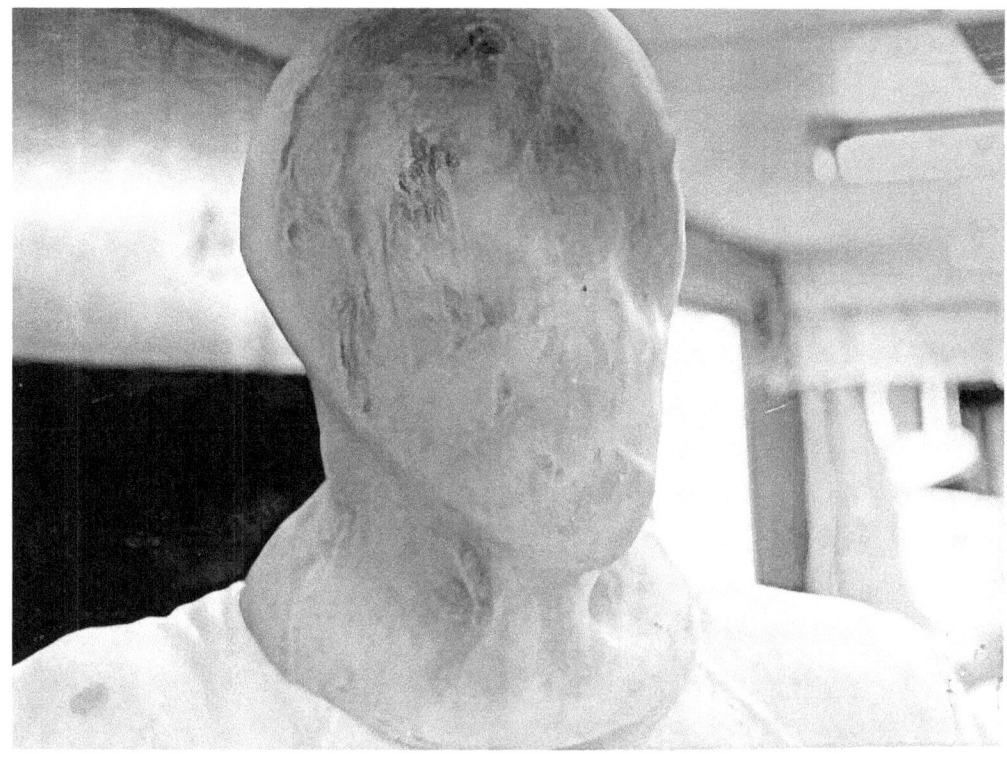

The "Q-tip head" bounty hunter would become an iconic trope in both *Critters* and *Critters 2*.
(Source: John Naulin)

They didn't do another day. So that's what they had shot-wise, and that's what's in the film – that's the take they used."

The look of Warden Zanti played by Michael Lee Gogin was inspired by a comic book villain known as the Mekon who appeared in the British sci-fi series *Dan Dare*. The Mekon, like Warden Zanti, had a smooth, oversized "melon" head and moved around using a levitating chair. Producer Rupert Harvey credited British sci-fi comics, particularly *Dan Dare*, as an early inspiration on his work, and considers Warden Zanti an homage to the Mekon and a nod to the universe of British sci-fi comics he grew up reading.

"When doing the hover pad used by Warden Zanti, they didn't want to go with it on wires," remembers Tony Doublin. "So we did that. Once I hired the little person [Michael Lee Gogin], we got his weight and size, and that's what developed that. And then they didn't want to go with wires, so we had some long shots that were coming down that hallway. So we actually built it, there was a machinist that I was working with on some other stuff. We designed and built

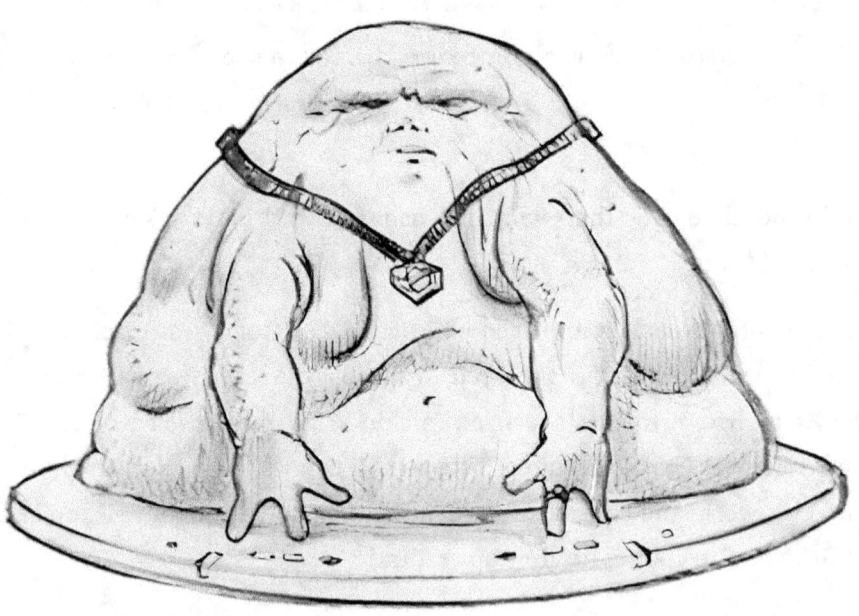

Early sketches of Zanti by Len Morganti depicted a rather shapeless blob on a hovering chair.
(Source: Sketch provided by Brian Muir courtesy of Daniel Griffith.)

a rig to extend a Chapman crane arm 16 feet. This allowed us to put the crane in the back of the hallway that comes down and basically had a drape or a hole or something like that. That way we could drive the crane down the hallway, which would be blocked out, and it would look like the Warden was floating on the chair. We had to figure out what our load was and then balance. So we worked with the grip department and of course the door we told them we needed had to have a truck door, a shipping door. They weren't shooting in a studio; they were shooting in a warehouse. We said we need to have a large door that we can run that dolly through with our rig on it. And, of course, they got one that had a truck ramp outside. So we had to block all that up and that was a real clusterfuck. And then they cut out of that hallway. We didn't get a chance to check and make sure there wasn't a freaking shadow. So they ended up cutting out a shot early. You know, sometimes their appetites get too big, their eyes are bigger than their budgets."

In pre-shooting versions of the script, Warden Zanti was actually an assistant warden who accompanied another character, Warden Krull. Both were described as strange beings, short, and solid blobs of some undefinable fleshy material. They had two arms and a face with humanoid features but no legs. Instead, they were propelled about by small circular pads upon which they sat. In a scene discussing the next steps needed to track down the Krites, Warden Krull and Zanti confer inside an office where Krull keeps an alien potted plant, described as a long stem topped with what seems to be a huge unopened bulb with lips. When Krull pets the bulb, it makes an "appreciative mewling sound." Although both Warden Krull and the alien plant were listed on the April 29, 1985 Special Effects Breakdown as well as a May 9, 1985 script, neither would make it into the actual shooting script.

Though Naulin and his team, including John Criswell, were on set during the initial bounty hunter and Warden Zanti sequence, contractually Naulin had to report to his next project, *From Beyond*. "You know, they had this attitude on *Critters* like we could just run forever. '*Well, first of all, you haven't paid me anymore. So no, you can't run forever*,'" Naulin explains. "It's all based on mandates, you know. It's all based on what I need to pay for a crew to be there. We were still shooting the opening, the sequence in the prison. Tony and I had done a day of Warden Zanti and his floating rig. I mean, I literally was there Saturday working on *Critters* and Monday morning I started *From Beyond*."

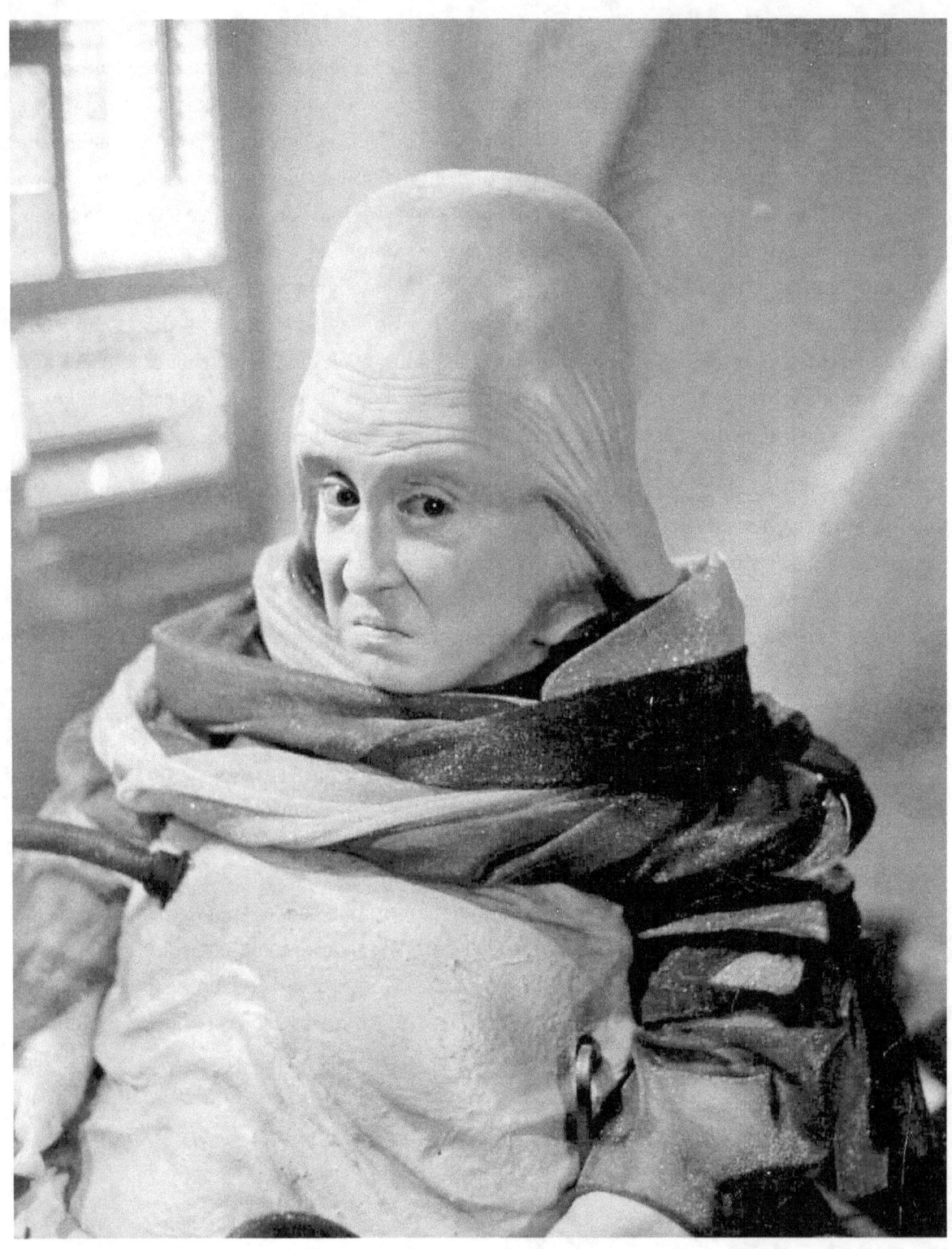

John Naulin and his team worked up actor Michael Lee Gogin with prosthetics and a customized hover chair.
(Source: Photograph of Michael Lee Gogin courtesy John Naulin)

Warden Zanti's chair was mounted to a Chapman crane to give the illusion he was hovering down the ship's corridors.
(Source: Photograph of Michael Lee Gogin courtesy John Naulin)

TRANSFORMING THE BOUNTY HUNTERS

An Interview with **Chris Biggs** (Part One)

(Special Makeup Effects, *Critters* and *Critters 2*)

How did you get involved with *Critters*?

I basically had gone in and worked on a couple of things for New Line. And when they sent me the script for *Critters*, I read it and was like, '*Oh good*.' I did a full breakdown. I didn't realize that the Krites were going to be done by the Chiodo brothers from day one. They actually went to the Chiodo brothers and just said, '*We want you to do this, boom!*' They were given a kind of carte blanche because they were the stars of the movie really. The Chiodos were very practiced at puppets and their stop motion. Their stop motion stuff was always amazing and they have a really, really cool design sense. Their stuff is always great. Charlie, Ed and Steve, they're all great guys. And I never met, the funny thing was, I never met them until probably, I don't know, after weeks of our filming thing.

Can you describe working on the Warden Zanti character in *Critters*?

For the first one I didn't design it, it was just, '*Here fix this, this looks like shit*'. And a guy had basically built it. It was a prosthetic, but he made it out of slip latex and poly foam. So it blended off like a brick wall. I mean, I had to do everything, the transformation of the bounty hunters and the new Zanti piece, in two and a half weeks. I was working pretty much 24/7 and I didn't have time to rebuild Zanti. They'd already shot stuff with him so I really couldn't change the design. The original makeup artist and I took the piece that they had given me, that they had used on set, and I carved off about a half inch of it and then I glued it down to the positive with latex. I mean, the mold was made properly. It's just that they decided to go with poly foam instead of foam latex because they wanted to reuse it over and over and over and over again. And you can't really do that. So we had one day on set with Michael Lee Gogin who played Zanti. He was quite the hoot. We went drinking out afterwards. But we just glued it on and they reshot all the close-ups of it.

Was the new footage mostly for medium or long shots?

Mostly long shots. I think we shot with Michael for one afternoon and the next day we shot the bounty hunter heads and that was quite the thing. That was kind of exciting. It was the first time I'd used gelatin in that way. I'd used it for melting heads and things like that, but never to do it in reverse. It became quite the thing.

So you guys kind of blasted it with heat guns?

I had, I think, four of these turbo heaters. They're for like heating warehouses. Then I had a handheld heat gun that I would go through where there's areas that were not getting enough heat. I'd hold the heat gun just out of camera range and we were shooting this thing. I mean it was about the same time. It was still too fast or it was still too slow when we watched the dailies. I think they went down like a quarter step on it, not all the way, just because they're compressing the footage. And they weren't just chopping out frames, they were actually re-timing it with an optical printer. And it actually made it look a little less stop motion because it blended frames together and they caused a little bit of motion blur and stuff like that. It was actually better that we did it too slowly because when we set it up with the optical printer it looked really good. It was the skin, the muscle, and then the bone, and then the bounty hunter face that was underneath it. So it was three reverses and one forward.

And you said that the entire time that you were brought in was really just two and a half weeks worth of work to get all that done?

Yeah, yeah. It was down to the wire. I had a live cast of the actor and then did a clay press; made it clean. I sculpted that down to the musculature and I made a mold of that. I made sure that on the original head, I had a base that everything registered into so all the pieces would have the same registration on the bottom. That way, they'd all fit in the holes perfectly. And then we literally just cut off the registrations. And I had PVC tubes inside of each head, the fiberglass head that I made. I had a fiberglass of the muscles and two fiberglass skulls because I needed to go over. So we started with human skin on the musculature. I sculpted the life cast down to the musculature, made a mold of that, did a clay pressing of that, and then sculpted the carving down to the skull, so that way everything fit within each other. It was all negative sculpting. There was no positive anything. I had to be very careful what I was doing, so I didn't go too far, because I didn't want to build something up and all of a sudden it's like, '*Oh, it's too thick here. It's too far here.*' So everything had to be negative. Then once I had the molds made, then it was just reversing the process, making fiberglass casts of the skulls. I had to do two of those. One of the musculature, but everything because of the way the base was made, everything fit within each other. All of the molds were silicone. It was the only way to do it. Oh, we did make a bladder mask for the bounty hunter. So when he's starting, we kind of had a couple of bladders going off in a couple spots, but that was pretty basic.

And the idea that I wanted to do was – there was like a very thin layer that was the skin of the bounty hunter, that was kind of yellowish. And then behind that was perfectly clear. I put a little bit of a layer of the skin on the back of the mask, and then I put a little bit of a layer of the skin on the front of the mask, and then behind that was perfectly clear. I melted the gelatin and then I evacuated it to get out all the air bubbles. And then I poured that into the mold. So the idea was, I wanted it to blend so that when the skin melted away, it was completely clear. And it would look like the skull was refining itself. Like it was all stretched out and distorted, and then it was refining itself down to a skull that way. It kind of looked like that a little bit. It didn't come off as well as I'd like, but it was pretty cool.

Oh, that is cool. And you had designed the look of their blank faces as well, right?

No. I came in literally three weeks after they finished principal photography. So I was brought in as a savior, which really pisses me off because I bid on the show and didn't get it. (laughs) I got the next one [*Critters 2*], though.

Opposite: Chris Biggs used a variety of techniques to pull off Ug's transformation from a "Q-tip" head into a replica of Johnny Steele (Terrence Mann). (Source: Chris Biggs)

Do you remember the first time that you saw the final cut? And in your recollection, everything kind of worked?

Oh, yeah, I got invited to the cast and crew screening. It was nice. You know, all the laughs were there and I thought it was hysterical. I mean, I loved the script when I saw it. I was like, '*Oh, this is hysterical.*' It was a comedy horror, you know, and I think that's always the best way to go. And my attitude is, you know, make them scream, make them laugh.

Did Stephen Herek work with you on the Zanti and transformation effects?

Stephen was there when we did the Zanti stuff. The transformation stuff was so technical and so slow. We were there for literally, I think, like 15 hours shooting those. What I had rigged was the costume piece, the jacket that they wear. I rigged that on a fake body, and I had the collar, where the head slid down into the PVC, and it would click into place. It was basically grooves that sliced into the PVC that it was slipping down into and then it had little pegs on them so you could go right in and as soon as they bottomed out it would be the perfect location. It had to hold because it was gonna have to sit there for freaking hours. So I think it took about five hours to shoot each one. These heaters were like frickin' rocket engines. They were like jet engines. They were about three and a half, four feet long and about a foot wide. They had that jet engine front on them where it was sucking the air in and the back end of it was blowing it out. And it had turbines in it, it was spinning. We actually had to turn the fan off every time. It was like we timed it so we turned the fan off just as they were clicking the frame and then we turned it back on again because it was making bits of the gelatin kind of wiggle. Notice on the first head, which was the actor's head, the musculature, it had the least amount of gelatin on it. Of course the other thing we had was a giant drop cloth at the bottom and we had reservoirs, holes in the body so that when the gelatin melted, it went down into those things and just like rolled off the side of the face. It was at about a 40 degree angle. So we had the back, I think there was a headrest. I think we ended up dumping the headrest after the first one because it was like, '*No, this is not working.*' Then I had two of each head just to make sure it worked well. And they said, '*Well, if there's any problems with these, we'll check in with the dailies tomorrow and then we'll be back Wednesday.*'

Did you have enough time to get an impression of Steve Herek or not really just because it was like a time crunch and hectic?

As a director, no, I saw him for maybe 10 minutes. He was directing the actor. He was a nice enough guy. I can't really say positive or negative about him. He was there, doing his job, you know. He wasn't demanding. I was kind of disappointed though when we did the Zanti for *Critters 2* that it was just a little hologram. I was hoping they would go in close because there's a lot of detail on that thing. When you see it, it's like, you can't see a goddamn thing. But that's what it was in the script. I just went with the details. I was actually building it for *Fangoria* magazine, not for a movie (laughs). You know, one of the guys I had working for me had just gotten back from working on *Nightbreed*. I think it was Australia where they shot that one. And I hired him and he's an amazing painter. He painted all the airbrush work on Zanti. And then I kinda came in and did my, one of my favorite things to do is what I call dry brushing. I'll take three or four colors and just sort of dry brush lightly on top of the piece because it shows, it enhances the details in the sculpture. And so it makes the pop on screen a little bit better. Otherwise, it's mushy. Airbrush is great for some things, but it's a little soft and mushy for my taste.

"HOLY SHIT! WHAT IS THAT, A CANNON?"

Another iconic attribute of the bounty hunters, besides the ability to transmorph into host-planet beings, was the telescopic cannons each held attached to a holster rig on their thighs. Throughout the film, the powerful cannons easily destroyed everything from the chapel's pulpit and organ, walls and doors, a toilet, and of course, critters. Perhaps slightly dated by today's standards, the machined aluminum cannons were certainly noteworthy at the time. Tony Doublin, tasked with building the cannons used by both bounty hunters, quickly became frustrated with the production's minuscule budget and stubborn hesitancy to reconsider the impractical cannon designs.

"When it came to the budget, I felt that if you haven't got the money, you haven't got the time when it actually comes to do what you need to do. So it becomes half-assed and it just carries through the whole thing. At least my end of it. Like the guns. They had a drawing of how big this thing was. And it's like, they're supposed to be sitting in cars. They're supposed to be sitting in the spaceship. How the fuck can they sit down with this three-foot gun? I built a mock-up of it based on their dimensions and drawings, just cardboard boxes, cardboard tubes and shit, just something quick and dirty just so they could get an idea of what the size was. Well, they didn't want to shorten the gun, so that's why the gun became an extender… So, instead of building two sets of two guns, there were six guns because there's two bounty hunters. So each bounty hunter essentially had three guns. One was folded up, didn't do anything, lightweight, except it lit up. Another would light up, all matching, and had pneumatics in it so it could extend. Well, it was pneumatic, so you couldn't have a hose going from an air bottle into it.

"I think we ended up having to have a backpack on them because there was nothing we could put under the costume or whatever that would make them free standing. So they put a backpack on them so they would be self-contained. Batteries aren't an issue, but we needed something to give us about 90 psi. We found at surplus stores out here these old air bottles used for pilot ejection seats. These could take 2,000 psi and they were about three, four inches in diameter and a little over a foot long. Well, you gotta put a regulator on it, because you gotta take that 2,000 psi and be able to use it over time and allow you to shoot multiple takes without having to change air bottles. This is why you had to put a regulator on it to get that pressure down. You basically have this mini bottle, we use CO_2 because it's inert, so we had to take those bottles and have them pressure tested and certified for safety. And then we had a regulator that we used. We had air lines that had to go in on the costume. Now also because they had to be flexible as far as being able to get them up in the firing position so the barrels could come out – it was basically a hinge. But it also had a lock in it. And we could change the guns easily from the dummy gun to the expanding gun to the firing gun. We made a belt and modified a ratchet to be the locking mechanism. It was just a regular ratchet setup you'd find in any tool bench or toolbox. There's some of them that have a locking pin to lock the socket onto the wrench and then they have the ratchet so it can go up and then you hit the little switch and it can go down. Instead of having to engineer the whole fucking thing, we just welded it onto a plate and made these special belts. Then we had to make an aluminum plate.

"The chassis of the guns, they all had to be identical. So we had to weld sockets, at least the ass end of the guns which were all aluminum, machined aluminum. Now what I originally wanted to do with this was basically modify a shotgun and put a cover on it – but oh no, '*It's got to have multi shots in it,*' you know, and I said '*You can get two shots out of this, no problem.*' And we just basically, we just build stuff around it. And make it short enough so that we kind of had a gun like James Caan had in *El Dorado*. He's got that really short shotgun that puts out a big wall of flame. Well, that's what I originally wanted to do with this thing. And as long as we modified it so it wouldn't take a standard shell, we figured we could get away with, number one, not having a license or a title guide and number two, not violating federal law. Which was sort of important, but we wanted to get around having a pyro guy and a, well they had fire safety there anyways, but we wanted to get away from having to have pyro stuff. If

An original sketch of the bounty hunters by Len Morganti also depicts an early iteration of the cannon blasters. (Source: Brian Muir courtesy of Daniel Griffith)

it's a gun it could be like a prop guy. But they didn't want to do that. They wanted four shots on this fucking thing. They wanted the length and the size."

"Okay, so the story continues," says Doublin. "Because of the fact it has to move and it has to do this and that, we made it out of aluminum so we could match the six barrels. Now, we had a pneumatic ram inside the gun to make it go in and out. We had lights on it and inside of it. That was in the battery pack, plus a solenoid valve that the actor could trigger down where their gun fired. So we had little switches and stuff like that. It all had to match. Well, then we get into what's it gonna fire when the barrel's out. Because we had to build a special barrel, they wanted four shots. Okay, so we built a special barrel. I was talking to gun builders. I was talking to my machinist. I was talking to people about how we could go about doing this. We ended up building four chambers inside the barrel, that big front end of the gun, with four firing mechanisms all wired to switches. Then they wanted special color flames and stuff. Okay, fine. So I went to a reloading company and we came up with an idea. There was stuff available to us back then that, since 9/11 and some of the other bullshit with airplanes, is difficult to purchase now. They put a lot of restrictions on a lot of the stuff we could buy back then, which we can't buy now. Colored flames and all kinds of pyro things that were not explosives that you've now got to have a pyro license to buy. So we bought this stuff, but what we wanted was something you couldn't shoot.

"We designed the guns so that you couldn't shoot a normal 12-gauge shell in it. We trimmed down like a half to three quarters of an inch off the shell. Then we couldn't have wadding come out, so we used foam. There were these guys who were doing the loading and creating a mixture. We're seeing a test of it. The guy comes out, he's got his big hand covering up his thumb. And this is a professional reloader who did all these special loads and stuff. The test thing he had had a hole in it. He was holding it, hit the cap, the flame went out through the side of the hole and basically blew his thumb apart. You had to take a wrench down there, they were bolted on, there was ways to line it up and key it, you put the four shots in, put it on the receiver, and lock it in. We had to have double, triple safety backups on this. So what we did was, there's four chambers on these guns. And there's four buttons under the guns and also a fifth. The fifth you have to hold with your thumb because that arms the gun. Then you can fire one, two, three, four chambers. And if you don't hold that fifth button in the back with your thumb, they won't fire. Double backup. It's all battery operated, self-contained. There's a switch in the backpack that the actor cannot get his hands on that has to be turned on by me or my assistant before the take. So there's no way, if we didn't turn that on, there's no way that some dumbass fartin' around could shoot off something and hurt somebody as bad as that. We had a double backup on us. And nobody got into that zipper backup but us.

"I had a guy working for me, we went through it, because I was still working on some other stuff for the show, so I couldn't be out on set when you're out in the middle of nowhere at the house. So I had the guys on set, thoroughly trained, doing the guns. There was no way we were going to have an accident. Of course, that gun was rigid, so we had three different guns times two, because there's two bounty hunters. So what I've been talking about is they [producers] were asking for more than I could deliver. We never ever during live action shooting or first unit production fired more than one round. So we get into doing inserts. Well, we think we need to maybe fire multiple rounds. I got in the costume, got the belt on, and we did an insert of me firing all four barrels. That was never used. So they spent all that extra money, and I mean thousands, for nothing. That's why they changed the guns on the second one. If you look at *Critters 2*, the guns are almost like pistols. But when I turned the guns over to them, that's when I started. Because they shot all the location stuff first. And then we did the space station and the space sets and that stuff for the intro in the warehouse. So that was like the last stuff. I was busy in Hollywood at my shop building the platform, getting all that stuff ready to go."

During the production of *Critters*, shot in Valencia from late July through August 1985, the notorious California serial killer Richard Ramirez was actively attacking and murdering his victims across Los Angeles. Dubbed "The Night Stalker" and "The Night Prowler" by the media, Ramirez terrorized southern California between March 1984 and August 1985. On the night of May 29, 1985, Ramirez brutally attacked two elderly sisters at a residence in Monrovia, one of whom died from her wounds a few days later. Tony Doublin, the prop master on *Critters*, lived two blocks away from the crime scene. During filming, Tony and his then-wife, who served as his on-set assistant, could not secure a babysitter for their two school-aged children and Doublin refused to let them stay at home alone with the Night Stalker on the loose. He brought the children to the set on short notice, much to the chagrin of Daryl Kass, the production manager. Tony held his ground, offering a stern ultimatum: either let the kids stay on-set or lose a night of production. Kass relented and the production carried out, shooting the scene where Nadine van der Velde's character April is dragged unconscious up the hillside by the giant Krite to the awaiting spaceship.

Despite Doublin's frustrations, the bounty hunters and their blaster cannons, a potential pitfall for the amount of action sequences required, had plenty of screen time and effectively used a variety of pyrotechnic effects, a staggering amount for such a low-budget production, an effort special effects coordinator Frank Ceglia remains proud of. "We built the stunt toilet out of stearic acid, a substance that's like brittle wax. There's no way you could blow up a real toilet, it would be too dangerous to do and having all that ceramic shrapnel flying around," Ceglia says. "We did a lot of gags like that, almost every time the cannons went off we had these mini explosions ripping the walls and doors apart. For the blasts in the wall, we had a thing called a cable trawl, kind of like a ratchet contraption with air pressure. We made pie-shaped pieces of Lauan to make a full circle. Each wedge had a cable on it that was attached to the cable trawl. When you're ready, the cable trawl pulls and each of the wedges collapses quickly, so it looks like it's being blasted. I remember launching those doors off the bowling alley, too, when the bounty hunters enter. I had come up with a way to yank the doors off with bungee cords and some pyrotechnics. I think it turned out well. We also created a façade for the chapel that the bounty hunters drive the police car through. The chapel is here in Newhall, California. We then used squib packs to blow up the pulpit and piano."

PREPPING THE LOCATION AND CASTING

The tight timeline for preparation impacted not only the special makeup effects team and the Chiodos's work on the puppets, but the art department as well. The entire farmhouse and barn had to be constructed in six weeks, according to Rupert Harvey. "Interestingly enough, it was Philip Dean Foreman, our art director, and the production designer Gregg Fonseca – brilliant guy – who pulled that off. He died not long after, unfortunately. Gregg had worked on *A Nightmare on Elm Street* and *Nightmare 2*, but after the first *Nightmare*, everybody was keen to get him. Gregg's influence was very much on the house and the barn, but Philip was allowed to sort of run loose because it was our baby. Philip was a Brit like me and from the same background. Philip designed the spaceship and stuff like that as our art director… Gregg, as production designer, had an overview on all of the things like the costumes, the bounty hunters's costumes and stuff like that."

The production's crew built the Browns's family farmhouse and barn in an isolated valley in Valencia, California, not far from the Magic Mountain amusement park and the famed Walt Disney Company-owned filming location and backlot known as Golden Oak Ranch. Remote enough at least for the house to be properly blown to smithereens during the film's climactic

The production had a customized house and barn built to represent the Browns's idyllic farmhouse. A rare glimpse of the back of the house depicts its open design for ease of use by cast and crew and for lighting purposes.
(Source: Bradford Plows)

ending. "The location was great," recalls second unit director Mark Helfrich. "It was in the middle of nowhere and it was like our own private location. There weren't any neighbors around or any kind of distractions. We could do whatever we wanted. It was fun. It was fun getting to blow stuff up (laughs). Especially for me, because I didn't have any experience with those kinds of things yet. We had the farmhouse and barn built specifically for the film, so it could be exploded (laughs) and destroyed. That was not a miniature, that was the actual house that exploded."

In terms of casting, the process was mostly straightforward with producers Barry Opper and Rupert Harvey blending some known faces with some newcomers. "Basically we had standard readings and we picked those people that we felt could play the roles," recalls Barry Opper. "Billy Zane was not a name that anybody knew, neither was Nadine van der Velde or Scott Grimes. Terry Mann came on because of our contact with Richie Vetter. Don, my brother, had just been in *Android*, so he was approaching some kind of cult status, but he wasn't like a sought-after actor at that point. Lin Shaye was Bob's sister, but we really liked her prior roles. With Billy Green Bush, Rupert and I were pretty convinced he was the right choice for Jay Brown. M. Emmet Walsh was out of the Coen Brothers movie *Blood Simple*. He was probably the biggest star. He was, as a film person, probably the biggest star, even more than Terry was. Terry was a Broadway actor, but not known in films at all."

For the role of Ug, an intergalactic bounty hunter that assumes the appearance of rocker Johnny Steele, the producers had to find a singer who could also act. "Terry Mann was that person who obviously came to us having been a principal in *Cats*, except he was going to play a Billy Idol-type rocker for us," Barry Opper says. "One of the bounty hunters was gonna have that look and be able to sing "Power of the Night" as that character. So that's how that idea was brought to life. Terry was our choice to play that part because he had the acting chops. He was terrific to work with."

DID YOU KNOW?

Child actor Scott Grimes was not particularly proficient with his character's slingshot. Critter fabricator Dwight Roberts encountered him one afternoon struggling to hit a soda can off a fence in preparation for a scene. Well-versed in slinging stones since his childhood, Roberts showed Grimes a better technique and nailed the can on his first shot, thoroughly impressing the young actor.

Billy Green Bush and Dee Wallace partake in a publicity photo shoot on set which replicated the famous 1930 painting American Gothic by Grant Wood. (Source: the Chiodo brothers)

Director Stephen Herek told *Monster Land*, "When we wrote it, we had certain people in mind for it. When films are under a strict budget, we'll shoot for the sky and see what we end up with. We had some big names in mind, but they were so expensive that we couldn't really afford them. We could get Dee Wallace, and she's a big name, but we ended up paying money to get Dee Wallace."

Kansas-born actress Dee Wallace, who emerged as a tour de force in the industry and became known as the "mother of horror" for her roles in films like *The Hills Have Eyes*, *The Howling*, *Cujo*, and Steven Spielberg's blockbuster hit *E.T. the Extra-Terrestrial*, was the best possible choice to play the Brown family matriarch. "I believe I was just offered the part," explains Dee. "It was after *E.T.* and I was the choice of the month (laughs). I thought the script was well-written, and with some very strong actors. No reservations." Dee Wallace, credited in *Critters* for the first time as Dee Wallace Stone, fondly recalls working alongside Billy Green Bush, noting his kindness and generosity as both a person and actor. "I dearly loved working with Billy, and the kids were easy and very talented. The biggest challenge was the night shooting. There were many," explains Dee. "Many of the bigger puppets weren't completed when we shot... And we would laugh [afterwards] when we had a scene with the smaller ones, and we would all be in our emotional states, and then we would hear, '*Okay, roll 'em in!*' The Chiodo brothers were fun." Nevertheless, Dee remembers the shoot being filled with laughs and an abundance of support, both among fellow actors and the crew alike. "He [Stephen Herek] was always very clear in what his vision was, communicated it well, and welcomed ideas from us. My kind of director."

DID YOU KNOW?

Brian Muir and Mark Pritchard, co-hosts of the cable access show *Two Guys Who Watch Movies*, make brief cameos in *Critters* when Helen Brown changes the channel on her television. Amusingly, Clay Greenbush, the son of Jay Brown actor Billy Green Bush, also makes a cameo, appearing at the bowling alley and remarking "Holy shit" after Ug heaves a bowling ball into a set of bowling pins, turning them to dust. Producer Rupert Harvey also briefly appears during an insert shot at the chapel after Ug and Lee blow it to bits.

Rounding out a few of the supporting but nonetheless iconic roles in *Critters* were Lin Shaye as Sal (Sally), a dispatcher for the Sheriff's office, and Jeremy Lawrence as the preacher. "I got involved with *Critters* because my big brother, Bob Shaye, who was the creator of New Line Cinema, requested that they put me, his sister, in the film," Lin Shaye remarks with nostalgia, laughing. "I don't remember auditioning for the role or anything like that. Stephen Herek, the director of *Critters*, was just one of the nicest directors I had worked with. He was very humble, smart, a real student of film making. We created the look of that character, my character Sal, right there in the trailer. Stephen asked me, '*What does she look like, how does she sound, what is she all about?*' and we came up with this idea of this 1930's type character, a redhead with really exaggerated red lips. The bottom line is, she's really just this hick from this small town in Kansas (laughs). Here she is, with curlers in her hair in this stupid ass police station in the middle of nowhere, with aspirations to be somewhere else, like in a big city and dressed up, with everyone noticing her. Instead, she's in a small radio room calling in disturbances at the Bowl-A-Rama Lanes (laughs). You have to wonder how many people are out there like this in these types of small towns, with big dreams and wanting to be someone else but they're stuck in the webs of small town America."

Jeremy Lawrence, a New York stage actor, first moved to Los Angeles in 1978 with aspirations of working on stage and screen and arrived during "pilot season" when many speculative television pilots were underway. After landing a small role on the hit television series *Happy Days*, Lawrence was eager to keep working. Although he had an established working relationship with Lin Shaye from the New York theater scene, Jeremy auditioned for the role of the preacher at the behest of an acquaintance named Elisabeth Leustig, the casting director for *Critters*. "*Critters* was the first major film that I ever did," humbly reminisces Lawrence. "I'm mostly a stage actor, so at the time, it was a really big deal for me. I remember doing a lot of auditions for it. I was always put on tape, I didn't meet anyone higher up the production chain than the casting director. My audition was reading the monologue of the preacher doing his preaching, which I deliver in the film. That's what my audition consisted of. Eventually I was cast and I was thrilled."

Billy Green Bush, sometimes rendered Greenbush, father of the now retired acting twins Lindsay and Sidney Greenbush best known for playing the role of Carrie in the TV series *Little House on the Prairie* and actor Clay Greenbush, took on the role of Jay Brown, which marked his first role in a horror film. Green Bush, a known character actor, had memorable roles in various American dramas and westerns such as *Five Easy Pieces*, *The Culpepper Cattle Co.*, *Tom Horn*, and a recurring role on the award-winning TV series *Hill Street Blues*. But Green Bush nearly turned down the offer for *Critters*. "I read the script and wasn't so much concerned about the gore and violence as I was that *Critters* read like a movie for kids," Green Bush told *Fangoria*. "I couldn't think of any adults who would go see this film. My anxiety level really went up. But I changed my mind and I'm glad I did. I don't know who will ultimately wind up seeing this picture, but whoever does will have a good time."

Looking back on the experience in October 2023, Green Bush notes, "I'm in a different place in my life at 88 years old. But *Critters*, it was nice doing it and I always considered it a fond memory... and I was sorry that I didn't get in *Critters 2* or *3*. It was always good to have a job, to be working, because my career was not like a lot of actors that were called all the time and just asked if they were doing it. I always had to win the job before I could get it. So then it was one of those times in my career where I was just delighted to get offered the job. And so I saw all the technicalities they had and in the end of it when they did a miniature example of the house that we lived in because they were going to destroy it. And so I had to go through all that, I enjoyed that. Working with Dee, Scott [Grimes], Nadine, and of course her boyfriend [Billy Zane] – they were great. The puppets were a fun challenge. You had to give them life yourself, you know, because it was hard to do it. I hadn't been in that kind of an acting situation before, but I just had to adjust to whatever the movie presented to me to deal with and I had to do it the best I could at the time and sometimes it wasn't always the best choice but then that's all I could come up with at the time because they got to do it now."

DID YOU KNOW?

Elisabeth Leustig, the talented casting director for *Critters* and later known for her work on the Academy Award-winning *Dances with Wolves*, tragically died at the age of 50 after being struck by a vehicle on the set of *The Saint* in Moscow, Russia. Ultimately, *The Saint* was released by Paramount Pictures with a dedication in her honor.

WELCOME TO HOLLYWOOD
An Interview with Jeremy Lawrence
("Preacher," *Critters*)

Going back to the beginning, how did you get your start as an actor?

I moved to Los Angeles in January 1978. I went out for what they used to call 'pilot season.' The L.A. scene back then was much different. It was a completely different world for me than New York. It was quite an experience and an adventure for me. My first job in L.A. was on *Happy Days*. It was a big *Happy Days* episode, in which Richie's child was born. I played the doctor that delivered Richie's child. Richie's character was off the show and somewhere in Alaska.

Fonzie, played by Henry [Winkler], was the coach. They first cast me as the doctor and the character was acting crazy. Henry and I just had a ball with it. Toward the end of the week, this was the old four-camera sitcom era, and the production team took me aside and said, '*We need you to play the doctor straight. The public just won't allow for Richie's baby to be brought into the world by a crazy doctor*' (laughs). So, this was my start in Hollywood, and I thought I was well on my way. Well, I wasn't (laughs).

How did you get involved with playing the preacher in *Critters*?

Critters was the first major film that I ever did. I'm mostly a stage actor. At the time, it was a really big deal for me. I remember doing a lot of auditions for it. I was always put on tape, I didn't meet anyone higher up the production chain than the casting director. My audition was reading the monologue of the preacher doing his preaching, which I deliver in the film. That's what my audition consisted of. Eventually I was cast and I was thrilled. I don't even think I had an agent at the time, but I did know the casting director. A wonderful woman named Elisabeth Leustig. Sadly, she was killed in an automobile accident. She was the one who brought me in for the project. So, afterwards I was waiting for production to begin, and waiting and waiting. Every once in a while I would get a call asking if I had a body double. I didn't even know what that was, I was so new. I told them no and they said, '*Well, you need one.*' And I asked if this means I'll be shooting soon and they said '*Yes.*' Not long after, I get a call and they tell me I'll be shooting the next day at four o'clock. I thought, '*Okay, great.*' A more experienced actor would have figured out that, what they meant was I'd be shooting at 4 a.m., these were night shoots. But I didn't understand that. I thought it was 4 p.m. and figured I'd wrap up by midnight or so. The location was way out, far out, outside of Los Angeles. So, I drove out there and showed up at 4 p.m. and got into my minister outfit and waited around and waited around. It was a big scene, so there was lots to prepare. Nobody ever gave me any notes about how to play the preacher, so I played him with a mid-America, slightly southern accent, with my hair combed over my forehead. Nobody seemed to have any problem with that. Of course, there were lots of close-ups of people in the audience. Like a normal shoot, everything was fine.

It's great that your character is both the preacher and later morphs into a bounty hunter. What was that experience like getting to play both characters?

Then they said, '*Okay, now it's time for you to get into the bounty hunter outfit.*' We were shooting in a chapel. The front of the chapel had a false front built on it. Two stunt drivers had driven a car into the front of the chapel and knocked the false front down and over the car. Those two stunt drivers were released after that sequence was shot. So, they put me into this bounty hunter outfit, and I'm very amused (laughs). I was wearing a huge belt with this bolt on it – and the ballistics guy comes over to me with this huge space gun. He asks, '*Have you ever shot a gun before,*' and I say '*No.*' And he *rolls* his eyes at me and says, '*Oh* great.' (laughs). So the next sequence was me shooting up the chapel with the giant alien gun. We had already shot the part where I was ducking behind the pulpit, scared. So they told me '*Now it's time for you to shoot up the chapel, but whatever you do, don't blink.*' They put some low profile earplugs into my ears because the gun was very loud when it went off. And I'm a very nervous person and the slightest kind of noise makes me jump. I'm thinking, '*How am I going to keep my eyes open?*' What they don't tell me is they're going to throw debris at me after I shoot the cannon (laughs). I'm a small guy. I'm not necessarily the type of guy that you'd cast in such roles or in such films. The time comes, and I shoot the gun and they throw debris at me and I don't blink. I'm very proud of myself. There's a few more shots we took of me shooting the gun walking around the chapel with Terrence [Mann] who of course played the lead bounty hunter. Terrence didn't change, he didn't shape-shift after deciding to be the rockstar, he was happy with that. But these bounty hunters can change into whoever they want to be. So the idea was that my bounty hunter saw me and decided he wanted to be me, the preacher. So he turned into me, but I also continued to be the preacher as well.

So I'm shooting up the chapel and it's now approaching 4 a.m. and I've been there since 4 p.m. the previous day. I don't know whether I've been introduced to Stephen Herek, the director. I think who I was dealing with was the first assistant director. I never got any feedback at all from Steve or from anybody about my performance. I'm just following instructions and it's a whole new world to me. I'm trying my best to give a great performance and as actors do I'm thinking about what's the truth of the situation and I'm a bounty hunter, I'm a preacher who's scared to death, and here I am shooting up this little chapel. Nobody was complaining or telling me I'm horrible, '*We hate you, go home.*' (laughs). I'm feeling kind of good, I'm feeling my oats and I got to shoot this big gun and it's 4 a.m. or maybe a little later and they explain to me: '*Now Jeremy, you and Terrence are done shooting up the chapel, so you're going to turn around and walk out of the chapel and get into the car and you get in the driver seat. You think you know how to drive it. You're very cocky. But you don't know how to drive it. You look backwards, like you're going to drive in reverse, but what you really do is put it into drive and drive forward. Then you're going to drive out from under the debris and whatever you do, don't stop.*' At this point, Terrence and I are in this car and under the debris. I think at this point, any normal SAG actor would call SAG and explain the situation and say '*I don't think I should be doing this, this is a stunt person's job.*' But I'm feeling my oats and I want to do it. They also advise me to stay away from the car's windows in case some debris falls in. I've been living in Los Angeles and have been driving so I'm thinking I can do this.

Terrence and I get into the car and he leans over and says, '*Now Jeremy, I'm trusting you on this.*' (laughs) Now I'm feeling a little nervous. We rehearse just getting into the car, not driving it or anything, because all the debris is on top of the car. It's going to be a one take kinda thing. We have to get it right the first time. We shoot the sequence of us coming out of the chapel and getting into the car. Now, we are expected to drive out from under the debris and out onto a road. It's between 4 and 6 a.m. and there's no traffic. I asked when do I stop driving and they said '*When we yell cut.*' I said, '*Okay.*' So it happens. We start rolling, we get into the car, I turn around in the seat, put it into drive and I *gun* the car. The car goes forward and hits the steps of the chapel. So I kept gunning the car and it's growling, '*Rrrr, rrrr, rrrr*,' stuck on the steps, but I kept accelerating and we hopped over the steps and flew past the chapel and out onto the road. They yell '*Cut.*' I did it. Terrence looks over at me with his eyes big and wide and says, '*Thank you Jeremy*' (laughs). After that, I'm released to go home. It's past 6 a.m. and I haven't had any sleep the night before and I kept falling asleep on the ride back home. I was terrified for my life. And that was my first day on *Critters*. It was a helluva first day, I'll never forget it.

Do you remember how long you were on set for?

I was excited. This was such a big deal for me. I had a second day on *Critters*. I can't remember how many days I had on *Critters* but I was on set for at least two days. The second day we're shooting at this bowling alley. It's a real bowling alley and Terrence has the big shots in this scene, destroying the bowling alley and Terrence kept on pushing me out of frame (laughs).

I was, at the time, doing a show called *Rap Master Ronnie*. It was a social satire written by Garry Trudeau. We were doing this show in Los Angeles. It was called Studio One. They had this big disco floor but they also had this venue for private parties and we did the show there. It turned out to be a huge success. We had taken a week off because one of the leads was a stand-up comedian and he had written in his contract that he had obligations to play some gigs over this one particular week so they shut the show down during this one-week period. So this fits in perfectly with the week I was shooting *Critters*, so I never say anything about it. At the end of the day at the bowling alley… maybe there was another day before the bowling alley where I did some stunt driving. I remember they wanted some shots of the car driving up over a curb. I'm not sure if they ever kept it in the final cut. And Terrence says, '*Jeremy, you don't have to drive fast because they'll speed it up.*' In my mind, I'm now a stunt driver (laughs). The whole joke of the gag was this bounty hunter didn't really know how to drive but he's so arrogant he's just driving around like a maniac. I believe this sequence also included some car shots of us arriving at the bowling alley.

I remember doing this one sequence and Terrence admonishing me for being too aggressive. Toward the end of that day, I thought it was it for me as it was the last day of my shoot as stipulated by my contract. But because I was naive and didn't have an agent and I didn't have anybody explaining anything to me, but what a SAG contract means is, it's the end of your contract or until such time that principal photography is finished. Which means they can continue to call you until it's completed. We were supposed to start *Rap Master Ronnie* back up. At the end of the bowling alley day they say, '*We're going to need you tomorrow.*' And I explained that I had a performance the following day for *Rap Master Ronnie* and they said, '*No, you don't.*'

They had this special effects device connected to Terrence and I that would ripple when we would shape-shift into the different characters. I never understood this, but whatever it was, it was this huge thing that would wrap around your torso and had this big pack attached to it. When they wanted the effect they would turn it on and it rippled you. I truly never understood what it was. They told me this, about needing me for more shoots the following day, and I thought, '*I'm going to need to make some phone calls.*' This of course is before cell phones but there's a phone booth inside the bowling alley. I have to go to the phone booth but I have this big thing attached to my torso. Like a king, I have these tech people walking behind me holding up these wires and carrying this stuff to the phone booth where I'm calling the stage manager and the producer and explaining to them that I need to miss a performance and that I don't have an understudy because it wasn't an equity show. It was an American Guild of Variety Arts (AGVA) show because they wanted to produce it as cheaply as possible. So what type of contract was I going to violate? An AGVA contract or a SAG contract? Am I going to jeopardize a feature film or am I going to jeopardize a show that they should have an understudy for? I asked if they had an audience and they said they had a small audience projected and I told them '*I'm sorry but I can't make it.*' That's all there was to it. The hilarious thing was after the calls I had to go back on set and shoot some more sequences at the bowling alley and then the team had to carry me back to the phone again and make another call (laughs). They were then trying to see what they could do with the body double and get him on set. It was just chaos. Again, this was a night shoot. I was responsible for canceling a show, which was horrible, but it wasn't sold out, but it was the first show back and I felt very bad about it. It was a bad thing to do. I was young and didn't understand. But I had to go back out and perform.

At the time, did you have access to the whole script and have an understanding about the full scope of what *Critters* was as a horror-comedy film?

I don't ever remember seeing the whole script of the film. I believe all I was given were sides that explained that my character, the preacher, turns into this alien-bounty hunter. But of course I have no idea what that all meant, not seeing the whole script. I do remember the crew were constantly making recommendations not to shoot certain sequences because they were too complicated. I got the impression that this was Stephen's first movie and he seemed a bit hesitant on things.

The second unit at the time was up at the house shooting the critters terrorizing the farmhouse, though I'm sure Stephen was going up to do some of the principal shooting up there when it involved the main actors. Months later I saw *Critters* in a theater while I was back in Buffalo, New York doing a show and I remember when it was over walking up the aisle and some kid starts pointing at me in shock, and said '*Are you…*' (laughs) And I smiled and I said, '*Yes…*' I was in Buffalo because I was having my first play produced, I'm also a playwright. I had no idea what the other parts of *Critters* were about. I was in shock and terror when I saw these critters, I fright easily (laughs), and I just found the critters to be horrible little monsters. When I saw it, it was all a great surprise to me because it was a story that I knew nothing about. I had no idea. Even if I had read the entire script, I think I still would've found it scary. I haven't watched it since. I'm not very good about watching myself. I remember being worried about getting the right accent for him. But I knew the hair was going to be really important for this character. Since I never received any feedback, this character was all me. The look and feel of this character was all me. I never heard from New Line ever again. I was never invited to a cast and crew screening or anything.

What are your reflections on *Critters* all these years later?

Somebody once said to me that I truly captured the balance of *Critters* between the type of horror film and strange funny film that made it a cult hit. To this day it's one of my few credits that gets the most reaction. '*Oh my God, you were in* Critters!' (laughs) It's still on my résumé. You go to IMDb and watch the trailer for *Critters* and there I am. Lin Shaye and I had been dear friends when we were growing up. When she was cast, I think I had already finished my shoots on *Critters*. Terrence later auditioned for a show for me and he asked me to please cast him and I don't know why I didn't, I made a terrible mistake. I cast someone else, another star, with whom I had creative differences with. I haven't seen Terrence since that audition. Terrence got to do more roles in the *Critters* franchise but I never did. *Critters* will always remain a fond memory for me. I didn't see *Critters 2* or *Critters 3*, but I felt – in spite of my emotional repellency to the critters, I could tell that *Critters* had achieved this balance of horror and hilarity and I understand now why it's become a cult classic. It deserves to be. It's a fond memory in my career.

ON LOCATION IN VALENCIA

Principal photography began on July 24, 1985 for what would be a six-week shoot on location in Valencia, California where the daytime temperatures often soared to above 100 degrees Fahrenheit. The primary location used in Valencia was the Brown family's farmhouse and barn, both of which were specifically built for the film, a nearby field where the spaceship landing and dead cattle scenes were filmed, as well as a local chapel, bowling alley, and the LAPD police museum that doubled as the Sheriff's office. Though the excitement in the air was palpable among the cast and crew, the shoot did not start off on the greatest note.

"We're at the farmhouse and there was a hill down to the farmhouse from the barn. I believe the first shots that we shot, this is the first day of shooting, and we were shooting in the barn," remembers Barry Opper. "I was walking up from the house while the camera person and his assistant were walking down from the barn with the camera. On the way down the hill, the assistant who was holding what I learned was the magazine was open. He was holding it shut on the way down the hill. He tripped and the magazine opened and this film came rolling down the hill – all the film in the reel came rolling down the hill – and of course spoiling the entire first whatever it was, about 20 minutes of film that we had shot. So we had to go back up and shoot the whole morning all over again, or the whole first 20 minutes all over again. I remember the film rolling down to my feet. I remember looking up at the assistant and I said, '*It's your luck that it rolled to the producer's feet*.' Well you know, I was told afterwards that any more experienced producer would have fired the guy. But I don't think even after five years of producing, or ten years of producing, I would have fired the guy. I mean he was mortified."

DID YOU KNOW?

After wrapping *Critters* in Valencia, the Chiodo brothers packed the various critter puppets into the back of Dwight Roberts's pickup truck. The radio-controlled rolling puppets, which were contained within trash bags, blew out of the truck on the I-5 freeway just past the I-14, forcing Dwight and others to pull over and collect the precious props before they were destroyed in traffic. Though all of the radio-controlled puppets were saved, three lightweight stunt puppets blew into the fast lane and were obliterated by passing motorists.

Although the crew enjoyed strong creative synergy, which led to incredible innovations, especially given the amount of special effects and practical applications, the pressure to deliver outsized production value also led to an air of frustration among the crew members.

"You're working all the time when you're in production, especially on shows like *Critters*, where your budget is so stretched, trying not to let the sound of your own wheels drive you crazy," remembers Rupert Harvey. "It was very much a day-to-day production challenge. How do we do this? How do we get that? How can we move this? This actor, without naming any names, Barry and I were convinced that we'd somehow or another got an actor that just wasn't gonna cut it, that it was gonna be a disaster, and thought long and hard about making a change, and didn't, and I'm very glad that we didn't, because at the end of the day, we found that some actors, although they don't seem to be delivering on set, something about the process of filmmaking likes them. And at the end of the day, by the time everything's come together, it's all working fine. So that issue, financial issues, scheduling, just the critters themselves, the physical difficulties of making these little rat-like bowling balls work, were the biggest challenges we faced."

To maximize coverage, the producers hired another Corman-trained editor named Mark Helfrich as second unit director to focus on shooting scenes featuring stunt puppets as well as the barn scene in which Steve (Billy Zane) is devoured by Krites. Helfrich came onboard on 29 July, four days into principal photography. His experience in editorial, like that of Herek, positioned him well for understanding coverage needs and how the material would be best cut together by Helfrich's friend, the film's editor Larry Bock. Helfrich's enthusiasm for his second unit directorial debut led to some of the most zealous shot sequences in the film, though most were to be excised in order to maintain a PG-13 rating. Friction between the second unit crew and the Chiodos began almost immediately during the first shoot, in which only one of two fully functional hero puppets was nearly destroyed in the first scene to be shot.

"When we killed Billy Zane's character, we *really* slaughtered him," Helfrich enthusiastically recalls. "There was all sorts of blood and gore. Unfortunately it really got cut down for the final cut of the film. Billy was having fun – we were all having fun really. It was a really bloody mess in that barn. I remember the smells of that shoot. That was real hay in the barn. The stage blood we used was very sticky. If it got on a critter, the Chiodos considered that critter ruined. Unfortunately, we were getting this thick, corn syrup stage blood all over everything. They were not too happy about that. However, it was all serving the movie. That's what I thought."

The slaughtering of "Steve" (Billy Zane) by the carnivorous Krites during the barn loft attack scene included copious amounts of coverage despite it being destined for the cutting room floor. (Source: Bradford Plows)

"The very first thing we shot was in the barn when Billy Zane was getting killed," explains Stephen Chiodo. "So we had a cadaver, like a prosthetic of his chest cavity that was eaten out. And Mark wanted us to bury the head of the critter, chomping and chomping and chomping, in this pool of Karo corn syrup blood. This is our hero puppet, with all the mechanics and all the foam. And we said, '*This is going to ruin the puppet.*' We said, '*This is going to be cut out of the film. You're not going to see this, it's too visceral. It's not going to be in the film.*' And he was adamant about it, so there we were. We followed his direction. We smashed it. I was smashing it in the face and grunting. It just ruined the puppet. The Karo syrup soaked into the foam, hardened overnight. No matter how much you wet it, you couldn't get it out. And then it limited all the flexibility. That was day one with the hero puppet. Yeah, so if there was any friction, it was because of that and I just wish he had listened to us a little bit more and I don't know, you don't start out with blowing up a puppet on the first day of shooting. But that was it. I mean, it was like him not understanding our needs and us being kind of dictated by his needs. And it wasn't really better, it wasn't best for the production."

Shooting second unit also led to quarrels over the limited equipment shared with first unit and even disrupted the already tenuous barn sequence. "We would set up and then all of a sudden, the first unit would need a couple of C-stands and lights," laments Stephen Chiodo. "They take our lights away and we have to sit there and wait for them to kind of free them up so we can continue shooting. It was a lot of frustration like that and as the puppeteer, buried underneath the set with all of the hay and stuff and reaching up there – you'd have your hand up – so let's say the setup and in the focus and all the lighting and then by the time they got to the shot, you were pretty exhausted. Then you had to do all the work that was going to be seen on screen so there's that kind of frustration and producing your one night we're working."

In one instance, the Chiodo brothers and their team were shooting with first unit inside the Browns's home with many of the crew members and puppeteers operating underneath the floorboards in dark, hot, cramped spaces, only to be left behind during a lunch break. "So we're doing a shot. I think it was probably the living room or somewhere," recalls Edward Chiodo. "And so we're underneath the floor actually out on the dirt underneath the house. We have our monitors, and we're doing our rehearsals and stuff and all of a sudden gets really quiet. And they

The Chiodo brothers and Dwight Roberts rehearse an intricate setup involving a critter that walks across the planks of the barn loft. Note the monitors under the tabletop for the crew to watch the movement of the puppet above. (Source: the Chiodo brothers)

broke for lunch. They didn't tell us. They left us under the house. Someone from our team had to crawl underneath and say, '*Hey, they broke, you know.*' '*Thanks for telling us.*' Yeah, working underneath the sets is not very glorious. No matter how many monitors you have there, it's kind of lonely and isolated."

Dwindling resources and long days also led to some conflicts among crew members who were being tapped for extra duties, especially when it came to special effects and props. "One day we got on set and they said, '*Where's the cow,*' and I said, '*What cow,*' and they go, '*You know, the cow where the critters feed for the first time.*' I said, '*That's a prop,*'" explains a frustrated John Naulin. "I go, '*So why aren't you asking the head of special effects makeup?*' Because I was the head of *supervised* special effects makeup for the whole show. And they're going, '*Well, we don't have one.*' And so we had two days and no budget to make a full-size cow. But we did it. We made it out of PVC pipe, chicken wire, latex, and fake fur. We did get a real skull. So we got a skull with the horns on it. But everything else was done by build-up construction. It was done with latex and paper towels. They also fogged the whole valley that night with liquid nitrogen and they went way over the top, putting out way too much liquid nitrogen. It was like short-sleeve, shorts weather, and that night it dropped to like 40 degrees. Because liquid nitrogen is like 257 degrees below zero, so it's like, '*Oh dear God.*' And everybody's going, '*Why is it so cold?*' I said, '*Because you basically have lined the bottom of the whole damn place with dry ice.*' I said, '*You can just take it, flag a little bit of it.*' You know, they had these big 50 gallon tanks and this stuff expands 200 times by volume, something like that. It had its own weather front.

"I'll just be honest with you. When we placed the cow prop, we put the blood in, they got a couple of the puppeteers to come out because we actually had a critter that was right down in the meat of it, chomping away at it. And he turns and makes a shot at the camera. And so we had one of the Chiodos's puppet guys down underneath this thing and we had to kind of dig a hole behind the prop in the desert and all that. I think this is my funniest critter story. And it was so freaking cold, that the moment we didn't have to be there, we left. All right, the shoot went very, very late. We shot almost all night that night and I had other gags I had to do. I mean this was something that was added and was thrown into it, so we went and did another gag. I walked away from it. I mean – we made it, we set it up, couldn't somebody in the props department have at least picked it up? I mean, that was kind of our assumption that, you know, this is not a makeup effect, it's a freaking prop.

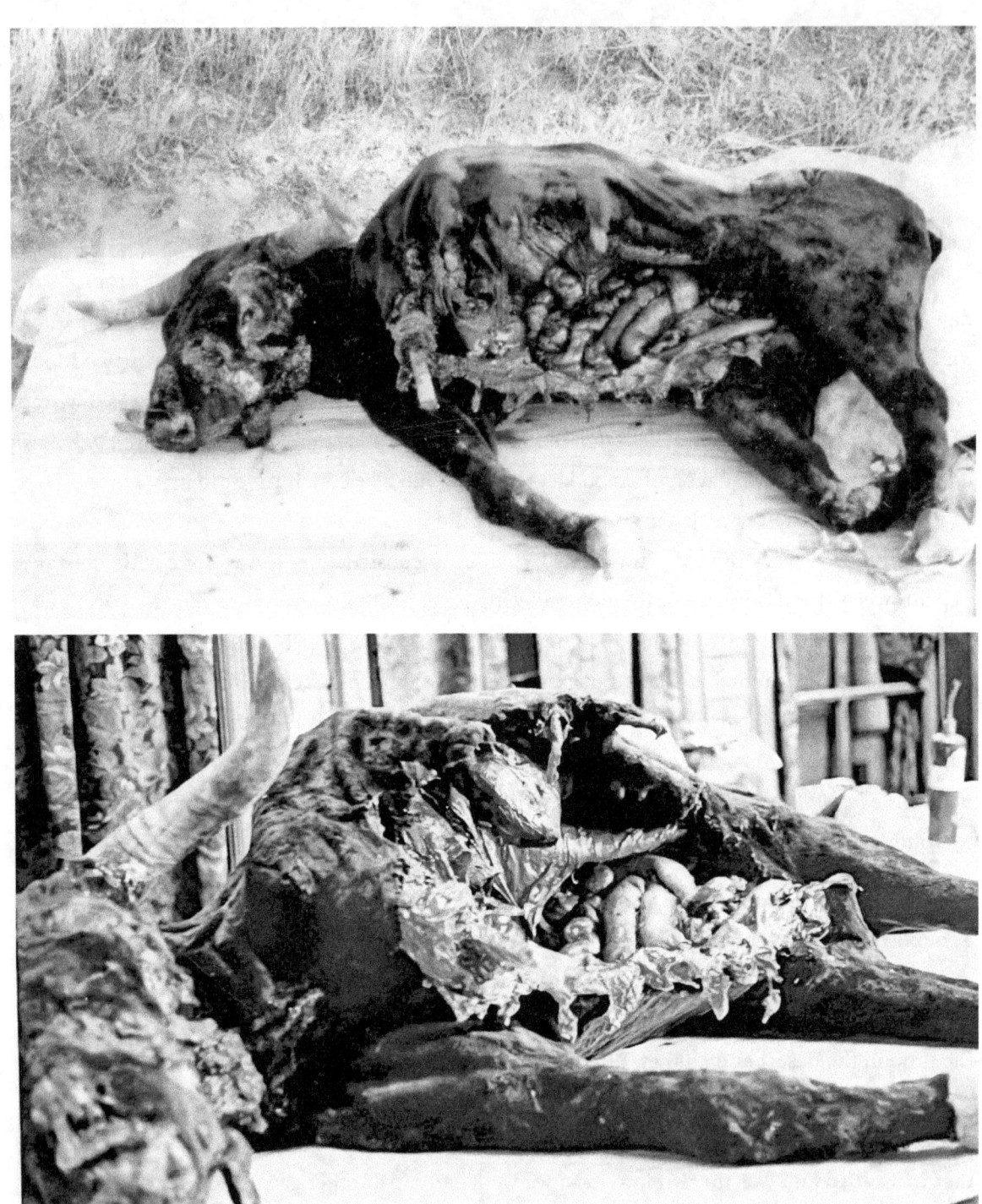

Despite his misgivings, John Naulin and his team constructed this memorable prop cow out of rudimentary products. The crew ultimately left the prop in the valley, only for it to be discovered by hikers months later.

(Source: Bradford Plows and John Naulin)

"So, we never picked it up because it was too cold and we never went back out there to pick it up or clean it up. Believe it or not, a while later I'm driving down the road and I'm completely done with *Critters*. I'm in pre-production on *From Beyond* with Stuart [Gordon]. I'm getting ready to go to Italy with him and all that stuff. I'm listening to talk radio and this person calls in and they say that there has been a cattle mutilation in the desert (laughs). They were out hiking and that they witnessed it and that they had called the police. And there were journalists going out for the papers and the whole bit, taking pictures, and it was *our* cow. Because nobody bothered to pick it up. And nobody noticed when we left there, I guess a few days later, but, you know, because it was over the hill from the base camp a little bit, that's where the critters's ship was also located, probably like 25 feet away. And so all of this emergency equipment and all these people go out to find out what killed this cow, only to find out that it's made out of fake fur and wool and latex and tissue paper (laughs). And I certainly wasn't going to get charged for littering or whatever."

Bradford Plows, a CalArts student and intern with the Chiodo brothers's team, lived nearby the set. "I went over to the set one winter day after they had wrapped *Critters*, because *Critters* was shot in the summer, and the spaceship was still standing over there," remembers Plows. "They just left it. It was above the ground, just like they built it out of plywood, and it was still there."

The volume of practical effects, the limited equipment shared among first and second unit, and the fragility of the puppets all led to grueling hours for most of the crew. "You know, when you're on set, it's just, you're going to go, go, go," explains Dwight Roberts. "If something were to break, like one of the critters, you would replace it with one of the working critters because you always have a standby. And then you would go down to the trailer, get caught up and get some fixed up. Usually you'd stay overnight and if there's any repairs to do, you'd do it after. So your 12 hour days turned into like 14 or 15 hour days."

"They did a lot of turnaround on that film and that's one of the things that made it so hard to do because you're turning your schedule around from day to night; generally most films schedule that to happen kind of all at once," recalls John Naulin. "But they did it a couple times on *Critters*, two or three times actually. So they would start off at 7 a.m. to 7 p.m. and it wouldn't stop at 7 p.m., so it would go to 9 p.m. So the next night, you're 9 a.m. to 9 p.m. and then it doesn't stop at 9 p.m. so you go to 11 p.m. and the next night you're 11 a.m. to 11 p.m. and you're working till 2 a.m. in the morning and pretty soon you're working all night. And that really screws with your circadian rhythm to the point where your body just doesn't know where it is. You know, because every day you're in a different time zone; it's like the ultimate in jet lag. It's the worst."

The crew constructed the spaceship commandeered by the Krites out of plywood and other construction materials.
Like the prop cow, the entire spaceship was left on location following the end of production.
(Source: Bradford Plows)

Shooting for first-time director Herek also posed similar challenges. "Everything's been a challenge because it's all so new," Herek explained to *Monster Land* in February 1986. "The thing that scared me the most was working with actors. I'd done a lot of acting in college, but I didn't do that much directing of actors. That was the scariest part – actually trying to convey my ideas to the people who were acting. A lot of that was insecurity, I think. I found out that actors are people too."

Despite the circumstances and personal misgivings among some crew members, there were also plenty of successes. "*Critters* was really positive for us," asserts Edward Chiodo. "It was really great because that was the year before *Killer Klowns* happened. It was a great production to be in because we learned so much, not only about practical effects and keying a show, but movie production in general. So it was really great as a field training for what we're going to do a year later on *Killer Klowns*. I thought Gregg Fonseca, the production designer and then Philip Foreman, the art director, I think they did a phenomenal job. And then Philip, we became really good friends with Philip, and he became art director on *Killer Klowns*."

Executive producer Bob Shaye (left) and director Stephen Herek (right)
during the making of *Critters*. (Source: Larry Bock)

THE BEST ACTOR I COULD POSSIBLY BE
An Interview with Billy Green Bush

("Jay Brown," *Critters*)

How did you get your start in the industry?

I was growing up when Marlon Brando and Jimmy Dean and Marilyn Monroe were all doing method acting. And I didn't know anything about method acting because I had been trained in college. I did a drama major at Long Beach State College and it was a young college at the time, it had just opened in 1953. I came out of the military in 1954 and I went right into college with the GI Bill. I was interested in a drama major because I always, even when I was six years old, wanted to be an actor. I was going through that in my life telling everybody I'm going to be an actor. So finally people used to say to me, '*When are you going to do that? You've been telling me that for 20 years.*' I thought, '*Well you're probably right, I should get on it,*' but I never lost that desire. I set out to train myself and to go to Hollywood and have a job so I could support myself while I was trying to be an actor.

After I moved to Hollywood, I also trained myself to be a cosmetologist. I dropped out of college because I thought, '*If I'm going to go to Hollywood, I better have something where I can take care of myself.*' So I trained myself to go to beauty school to be a cosmetologist because I thought that if I get the license to do this, I can work in the studios as a cosmetologist, doing the hair for movies and get to meet all the directors and all the cinematographers and get to learn what acting is all about from inside the studio. But then when I got there, I was all prepared for that, but then I found out that they didn't allow men in the union to be hairdressers in the studios.

It just negated all my plans that I thought I was planning for. There were only two men in the union. There was the head of MGM, Sydney Guilaroff, and the head of Universal Studios,

Larry Germain. But they were both in the union, the only two men, because they were there at the inception of the union. But then they didn't allow any other men to come into the union, because a lot of time in the movies, in the studios, when ladies are getting made up for the movies, sometimes they're getting body makeup too. So they don't want men in there doing their hair while they're naked getting their body makeup. This thwarted all my plans that I thought I was doing a good job planning my moves to go to Hollywood. But when I got there, I found out that I couldn't do it. So then I thought, '*Oh man, I can't do that.*' So I'm thinking, '*Well, if I can't do that, then what's the second best thing I should be doing?*' So I thought about it a lot, and I had two roommates living in the apartment that we rented when we moved to Hollywood because I was a cosmetologist. But my two friends, they wanted to go into that business because they were both entrepreneurs and they wanted to open up a chain of salons of cosmetology to do hair work for ladies because they knew that way back there were two professions that weren't hurt by the Depression years. One was the entertainment industry and the other was the beauty industry. They felt that if there's another economic downturn, it's not going to affect them if they were in the beauty business. At that point, we all decided we would try our hand at the cosmetology and hair side of the industry in Hollywood.

How did you transition from hairstyling to acting?

I trained myself for years and years to be an actor, to go to Hollywood, because I knew that I always thought that it's the industry that makes a star out of you. After all, you're such a good actor, they make you a star. So my commitment was to be the best actor I could possibly be. I never cared about being a star. I just wanted to work and get hired because of my previous work. '*Hire that guy because he was good in that movie.*' I never wanted to be a star because that was one thing I never desired. Because a star, if you're one of those, then wherever you go, everybody's Googling it, you know, following you and wanting your autograph and bothering you and watching you so they can see what that star does. But I never wanted to put myself in that kind of category. So I never pursued that, because I thought that it was always the industry and the fans that make a star out of you. I never felt I could do it myself.

I know what acting is all about because I trained myself to be a method actor, which greatly enhanced me when I came to Hollywood because I was always having to audition for actors, you know, to win a part. And sometimes I couldn't create it in a hurry, because they'd just give me a script and have me read the lines. Reading a script and acting have nothing to do with each other for me. Because me, you have to learn what you're doing and what you're saying and that takes a long time to figure it out so you can simply do it with yourself and nobody else but you doing it.

Going back to that summer of 1985 up in Valencia on location, what was it like on set?

It was hot, but I'm used to that, the heat. I'm not complaining about it. I remember it was out there in Valencia, somewhere around Magic Mountain. It was good for me because I trained myself to be the best actor I could be. I remember that working with Dee was such an experience because she was easy to work with and the director [Stephen Herek] was easy to work with because he was kind of inexperienced in a lot of ways and so he listened to me when I told him what I was trying to accomplish. That was a good thing. And Dee was good to work with, a sweet lady. It was easy to work with her as my wife because I appreciated her as the lady that she was.

How did you feel working with the puppets and the practical effects, was that challenging?

You had to give them life yourself because it was hard to do it. I hadn't been in that kind of an acting situation before, but I just had to adjust to whatever the movie presented to me to deal with and I had to do it the best I could at the time and sometimes it wasn't always the best choice. But then again, that's all I could come up with at the time, but I wasn't dissatisfied with it.

You were quoted as saying during the initial shoot that you were a little worried about the script being a blend of horror and comedy, you weren't sure what audience it would reach. Did you feel that after the movie came out and its reception, it kind of hit the mark?

Well, I thought the script was kind of original, like space marmots coming to Earth, you know, because they got imprisoned on their planet and they escaped and came to Earth, eating all the earthly cows and whatever they could do and attacking somebody's livestock. And the fact that they could shoot these poison needles at you, it was all interesting and my son was in that movie too, Clay, I guess you know that.

Billy Green Bush receives a special makeup effects touch up on location in Valencia in early August 1985.
(Source: Bradford Plows)

He was in the bowling alley scene?

Yeah well, what they did is, they asked me if I would like to work an extra day or an extra week or I can't remember exactly what they were asking me but then I told him that I would if you gave my son a part in the movie so he could get his Screen Actors Guild card. So I worked the last part of it for nothing just to get my son to have a job so he could go to the Screen Actors Guild and join. You have to have a job so a producer can tell you you're working. So the Screen Actors Guild, you know, he's working, then you gotta have a Screen Actors Guild card before you can go to work. It was like a catch-22 kind of situation. But then I didn't know how to get my son a job, so when they asked me to work for nothing, to do the last part of it, then I just said, '*Well, I'll do that for you if you'll do this for me. Give my son a part in the movie so he can get a SAG card.*' Well, I thought that was fantastic. I didn't mind doing it for nothing because it was, I forget why they had to go an extra week or something, but it was to do the miniature dismantling of the house.

And you were there that night when they blew up the barn and the big house, right?

I can't remember if I was there, but I was there to demolish the miniature house. Just to get a look at it because they had it all on cables so that when they, in a distance, you couldn't see the cables by the camera, but when they pulled all these cables, they all went into like fingers into the house that just crunched it, you know, and brought it into a dismantled state. But it was an interesting movie to do, and as an actor, I was always glad to work because it was always hard for me to find work. After all, I wasn't like an established star because I never cared anything about being a star. I always just wanted to train myself to do the best acting job I could do.

UNFILMED PRE-CREDIT SEQUENCE

Part of the lore around the production of *Critters* is the various script changes and alterations that occurred during pre-production as well as those – such as Bob Shaye's ask for a giant Krite – *during* production. One striking late script change involved a 90-second un-shot pre-credit sequence that opens on a scorched alien planet at night. Ug and Lee, the alien bounty hunters, hunt down two alien prisoner escapees on a stormy night and obliterate the convicts with cannon-fire. The short segment, almost certainly written by Brian Muir, was included in the script as late as 21 July 1985.

Special effects artist John Naulin, tasked with creating the alien escapees for the pre-credit sequence, worked with John Criswell and John Goodwin to design and build the alien masks. "The first AD came to me and said, '*We're adding a new pre-title sequence. It's the bounty hunters chasing these other aliens across a ravaged planetscape and killing them.*' I'm like, '*Well dude, that's more than a change, that's like a new movie,*' and he gave me the two and a half pages to be shot. This meant that I literally had to make whole head casts, make new pieces, make prosthetics, and do all of this stuff while we were still working on location out of the little makeup trailer. So John Criswell and I are doing sculptures and molds and I'm sending them out. John Goodwin was doing the foam work for me at that point because when you're working with either foam latex or any kind of sandwiched foam, you know, with urethanes or anything like that – encapsulation is what it's called – it takes hours. Foam latex, in order to mix it, cure it, and mold it takes over five hours. Five to seven hours. And the Zanti mold was huge. So the pieces at that point, I had taken all the molds over to John Goodwin, a 706 Union artist and a friend, still a dear friend of mine. After we made them, I showed up with the pieces and I said, '*Okay, we're here to shoot the pre-credit segment, where's the location for this chase sequence?*' And they went, '*What chase sequence?*' Now the day I arrived with these pieces, the first AD was gone, he had already left to go to another show in Arizona; he had left like the previous week. And I said, '*You know he ordered this stuff*', and they went, '*What are you talking about?*' Now I've never had this happen to me. I said, '*But here's the invoice for that.*' They go, '*We're not paying that.*' I got stiffed $1,500 for two full head aliens. And that's cheap. I mean, that's like my cost, no profit factored in. But I got completely stiffed for that. It's like the only time in 130 plus projects that anybody ever did anything like that to us. And it was like two days later that they wanted me to work more time and I said, '*I can't. I've already worked an extra week on this project, I've already done extra stuff that you're refusing to pay me for. I mean, how many favors do you think you can call in?*'"

The unrealized alien chase sequence would have included Naulin's two-foam piece alien masks, which were built around a mold applied to a petite female Russian gymnast who was less than five feet tall. "I had to take a full head and shoulders cast of her," says Naulin. "Then I did the sculpture on that and then the negative molds, and then you inject the foam in between and then you clean it all up and then you airbrush it. By the time I got the molds ready to go, that's when I went back and said, '*Okay, when are we shooting this?*'" Although the masks were never used and the sequence never shot, an extremely similar sequence was used as the introduction of *Critters 2*, which featured Ug, Lee, and Charlie McFadden hunting down a Hexapod alien on a dark and forested planet.

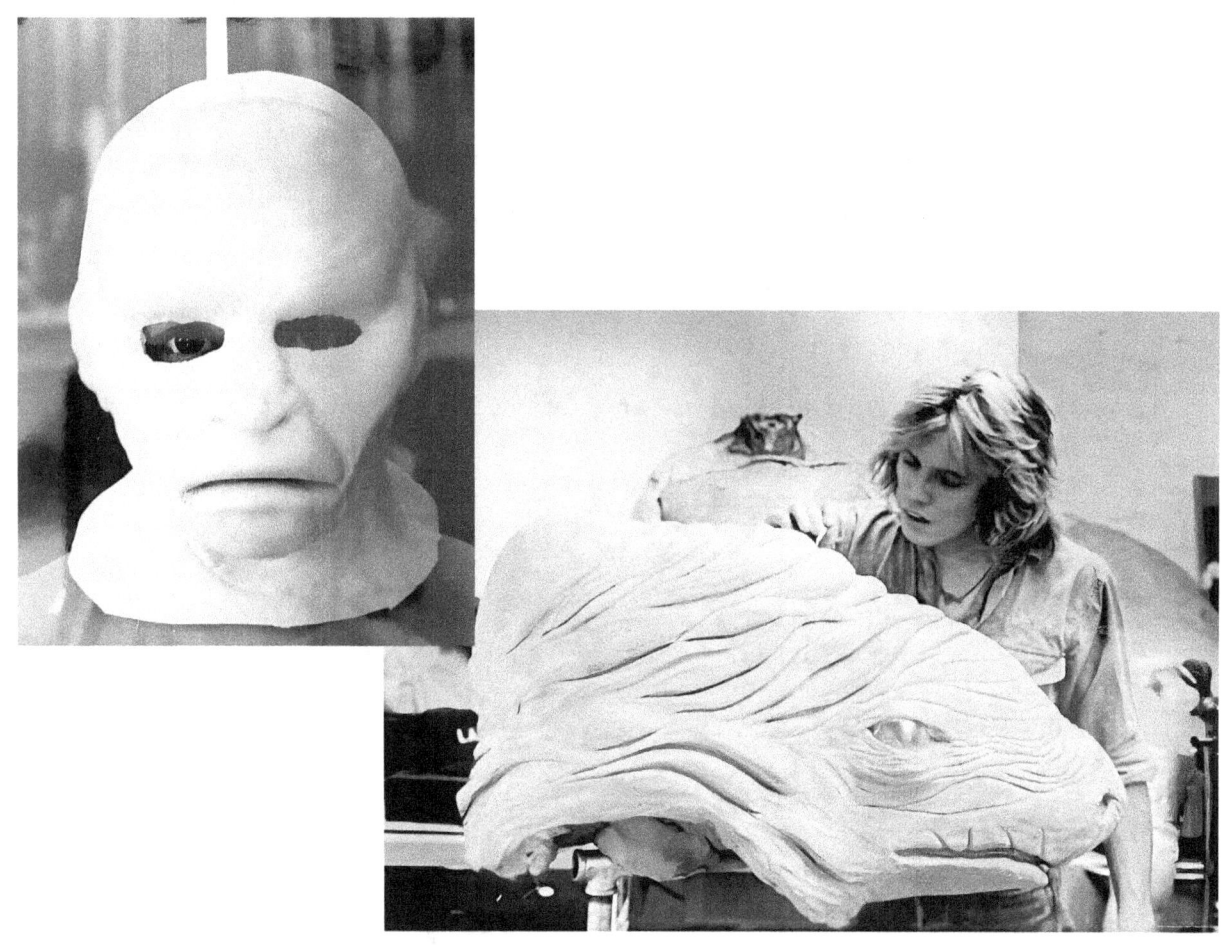

John Naulin created a Cro-Magnon type alien convict (left) for the unfilmed pre-title sequence along with John Criswell who also helped sculpt the asteroid prison guard alien (right) that did end up in the film's opening. (Source: John Naulin)

CLOSE in two pairs of feet running through terrain that has been burned by fire.

It is raining heavily. Their feet SLOSH.

Their legs are chained together, making it harder for them to run.

The two ALIENS Are dressed in plain prison garb. They are child-size, with long, stringy hair, cro-magnon brows, sharp teeth and long fingers.

They are BREATHING HEAVILY. They look back behind them in fear.

CLOSE on UG and Lee's boots. Walking calmly after the Aliens.

The Aliens try to run faster. They stumble.

The Hunters continue to walk. PAN UP to Lee's waist as he reveals his gun. He brings it up into action. The barrel extends. Moonlight glints off it.

LIGHTNING begins to flash.

The Aliens have regained their footing, and are starting to run again.

They look back in terror.

Lee fires his gun.

One of the Aliens is nailed in the back, falling forward. The other one trips up over him.

Ug and Lee continue to walk.

The living alien feels his friend's body. The hole in his back is huge. It is still smoking. Definitely dead.

The alien looks back. He can see Ug and Lee, shapes in the distance, getting closer.

He gets up and tries to run, but his chains are still connected to the dead one.

Through the rain, he sees Ug and Lee getting nearer.

He tries to drag the dead one behind him, but it is no use. Too slow.

Ug and Lee are getting closer.

E.C.U. on communication device on Ug's belt beginning to bleep and flash. A gloved hand presses a button and turns it off.

The alien frantically tries to pull the chains apart, to no avail.

He searches the ground for a tool, can only find a stick.

He tries to pry the chains off. The stick BREAKS.

He lifts the chain to his mouth, and uses his sharp teeth to try and bite through them. He suceeds in SNAPPING one of the links.

Ug and Lee's boots stand in front of him.

He looks up in horror, seeing the Bounty hunters as silhouettes against the night sky.

Lightning FLASHES behind them.

The alien begins to back away.

UG raises his gun up. It extends TOWARDS CAMERA.

The Alien is PLEADING for his life.

The barrel EXPLODES with a shot, filling the screen.

1 EXT. SPACE   1

Stars slowly move past camera as CREDITS emblazon the screen. As the credits ROLL we are still traveling through space, moving closer in on a floating structure seen in the distance.

FROM *ROCK 'n' ROLL HIGH SCHOOL* TO *CRITTERS*
An Interview with **Mark Helfrich**
(Second Unit Director, *Critters*)

How did you break into the film industry and become associated with *Critters*?

I moved to Hollywood after studying at the University of Wisconsin-Madison. I moved to Hollywood to see if one, I could make it, and two, if I would like it. Luckily, after three months here in Hollywood, I got the job on *Rock 'n' Roll High School*. All the friends I made on that film are still my best friends to this day. Allan Arkush is a really good friend, as is Larry [Bock] and Kent Beyda, the other assistant editor. And that's how I got onto *Critters*. I had worked with Larry and he had recommended me to the director, Steve Herek, who hadn't really directed before. I had quite a bit of experience by this time, relatively (laughs), and I always wanted to direct, and he hired me to do second unit.

What kind of experience did you have on *Critters* as a first time second unit director?

I remember *Critters* being a great time. It was the only movie I had been a second unit director the entire time. I've directed a lot of second unit scenes when I was editing a picture, but I did not edit *Critters*, my good friend Larry Bock did. I knew Larry because the first job I had when I moved to Hollywood was a production assistant and an assistant editor position on *Rock 'n' Roll High School*, which Larry Bock cut. That was my first film, and what a fantastic way to get into the business. It's a classic. I'm so happy about that.

I did most of the Chiodo brothers's special effects sequences, not much with the principal actors. I shot the barn sequence with Billy Zane, though. If it was something with the principal actors or a more important sequence, it was Steve that was doing it with the Chiodo brothers. But if it was a simple shot of a critter rolling or some critters outside the house or something, that was for the second unit to do. It sounds easier than it was. Just to bowling-ball one of the critters from point a to point b was not always easy (laughs). Most of these were night shoots too.

Do you recall reading the script for the first time?

First time I saw the script, I was angling to be selected as second unit director. I remember it being a low-budget horror movie script, which seemed like a lot of fun. I had just edited *Return of the Living Dead* and *Critters* was definitely in that genre and I thought this would be a lot of fun, to actually make one. I also edited *Rambo II*, so my editing career was getting off the ground but I really wanted some directing experience so that's why I took *Critters*.

What do you think are some of the biggest challenges you faced on *Critters*?

Without a doubt, the biggest challenge we faced on second unit was working with the critters. Just to get the critters to do what they were supposed to do was a challenge. Many of them were hand puppets, some of them were mechanical, and others were just furry balls that we rolled like bowling balls. To get them to walk was not easy. The Chiodo brothers did a great job of putting together artificial floors that had a slit in them so they could puppeteer them from below to make it look like the critters were walking. It was challenging to make the critters look like they were moving realistically, not just a puppet, which they were. You wanted the critters to ideally look as organic as possible. I don't know how successful we were, but we tried to give Larry the editor as much leeway as we could give him. If that was 40 frames that made the critters look most real, at least we had that to work with. It was very challenging. I wanted the critters to do things that of course they weren't designed to do [laughs]. The Chiodos would explain '*No, we can't get them to do that,*' so there was some tension there. I was just gung-ho to do anything, even if that meant destroying a critter, if it was for the betterment of the shot, then I was ready to do that. The Chiodos were more protective of their creations.

I know the Chiodos thought I was pushing their critters too hard. It was just so difficult to get the critters to do what you wanted them to do. Even the shot where the critter swallows the firecracker – that action just took forever to get right. Any specific action that a critter had to perform was not easy.

I remember shooting some critter sequences when critters were on the stairs and rolling down the hallway toward the toilet. But I did most of the exteriors and the barn scene, and the cop car crashing into the ditch and the critter attacks the deputy [Ethan Phillips]. The car crash I shot was done the old fashioned way. We had a stunt driver crash a real car into a real ditch. The fog you see at night was real fog. These days you'd shoot blue screen or green screen and just add stuff like that in. There's nothing like shooting on film. Even editing on film, which is a lost art.

I presume you really had to be innovative on this project, given the schedule and working with the puppets and all the gags?

I was very young, and anxious and energetic when shooting *Critters*. The idea of shooting quills was an idea that we came up with in pre-production, but I would say everybody had good ideas. And then either Brian or Steve would write them into the script. The one person who doesn't seem to still talk about *Critters* is Steve, and I don't know why. Steve came out of the editorial department, he was an experienced editor. After *Critters* he went on to continue directing, and did films like *Bill & Ted's Excellent Adventure* and *Mr. Holland's Opus*.

Did you get a chance to meet or work with Brian Muir?

I got to know Brian Muir real well. We became really good friends and remained friends for the rest of his life. We worked on projects and he wrote a couple scripts for me and stuff like that. He was a writer, that's what he did. He had this cable access TV program back in the 80s called *Two Guys Who Watch Movies*, kind of like a Siskel and Ebert movie review show. It was the early days of cable TV where anyone could get a show (laughs). It was great, it was a hilarious show.

Do you remember seeing the final cut for the first time?

I remember seeing an early cut before it was done with the visual effects, like the beginning. Larry showed me it. I thought it was a lot of fun, I still do. I think it's a really good film especially considering how young we were and how many of us were new to our roles in filmmaking. I think it's directed well and acted well and I think it delivers. Even if some of the effects look cheesy, it doesn't matter. There's tension. Even with the critters with their red eyeballs, it's cheesy, but it works because of the acting and everyone takes it seriously.

What's your feelings about *Critters* all these years later?

It's surprising, but here I am, speaking to you about *Critters* all these years later, and you're not the first. Quite a few times I've been interviewed about *Critters*, it's nuts. I think everyone who worked on it is proud of it. It was so low-budget but we were all doing things with such passion, it was a labor of love. It was such a real, unique, and a real Hollywood experience for me. You had this remarkable crew doing their damnedest. Everyone was serious about making the best film for the budget they had to work with, which wasn't much, from what I recall.

     Critters is one of those films that really took on an after-life that I don't think anyone at that time could have predicted. It was a wonderful experience just trying to make a movie with the amount of money we had. But to make something that people would be talking about years later? I don't think anyone was thinking that *Critters* would be a movie of that caliber. But thank goodness. I'm glad when films take on a second life or a forever life, and people write books about it and make documentaries about it.

     Because *Gremlins* was such a huge hit, there's not doubt people thought that *Critters* could probably make some money. I think that's what New Line was thinking and counting on. That's why Brian and Steve wrote the film. Brian had the idea way before *Gremlins* was even conceived, but because the size of the creatures in *Critters* and *Gremlins* are the same, both films will always be compared – the fuzziness and size of the creatures. But remember, *Gremlins* was made for a lot more money than *Critters* was (laughs).

POWER OF THE NIGHT

An unexpectedly resilient aspect of *Critters* as an anchor in 1980s cinematic pop-culture is the faux music video and epochal song "Power of the Night." The track is performed by imaginary rockstar Johnny Steele, portrayed by actor Terrence Mann, and later becomes a physical manifestation employed by the faceless bounty hunter Ug who decides to assume Johnny Steele's appearance. The song's energetic and electrifying vibe perfectly captures the film's blend of horror and adventure and features memorable guitar riffs and powerful vocals. "Power of the Night" has become synonymous with the legacy of *Critters*.

In earlier versions of the script, the now iconic Johnny Steele was left unnamed, merely described as a "punk rocker with a strong image." When the rocker first appears during the montage of earthly images during Ug and Lee's REM scan of earth culture for transformation possibilities, the music video in which he appears was written to take place on an alien landscape, dark and barren, during a rainstorm offset by flashes of colored lighting. Even as late as the script revisions dated June 26 and July 21, 1985, the rocker was still not named Johnny Steele. Instead, his name is listed as "Johnny Moadly" and his song "Power of the Night" was never identified by name.

"Richie Vetter had worked in theater with me and I brought Richie onto the project to be music supervisor and Richie was the one that got Terry [Mann] to be in the movies," notes Barry Opper. "And Richie is the reason Dodie Pettit was there. So it's Richie Vetter who's the magic connection here. My brother and I were in a theater, in two theaters, one called the Company Theatre and one called the Family Dog in San Francisco, which was one of the most well-known rock and roll houses in San Francisco in the 60s. And Richie was the guitar player living in the back of the Family Dog and he saw our theater perform and he moved to Los Angeles to be with our theater group as a guitar player. And then when Don and I went on to make movies, we brought Richie on to *Critters* as the music supervisor and he was the one that brought both Terry and Dodie into the project."

Dodie and Terrence Mann, both esteemed features in the Broadway show *Cats*, were well-positioned to tackle the musical arrangements required for *Critters*, in conjunction with Richie Vetter, who owned a recording studio at the time. "I have to tell you, we did this movie, and it came to us when we were at our studio because we were recording me and my then-partner, Richie, he was one of the owners of the studio and a lot of projects came through," says Dodie Pettit. "When this project came in, I was like, '*Let's grab it, let's see what we can do.*' When we were done, we didn't think anything of it because we moved on to the next project and were focused on how we were going to make some money. Who were we going to get who could get us our big break, you know, we were looking for record acts. They had Terry being the rock star, that was planned from the get-go. That's one of the reasons they wanted to hire him, because they knew he could handle that. I joined *Cats* in 1984. And so Terry was in the show, and we all became friends and we would hang out after the show.

"Terry came over to the studio quite a few times. Because Terry was a damn good piano player and singer *à la* Billy Joel-style. And so we're always looking for people to produce and we were talking to Terry about it and said, '*Hey, come over and sing some of your songs and maybe we should produce them for you and see if we can get you a deal.*' Because we were always trying to break people. We had a little side business going there of young songwriters. I was one of them, but there were others. And Terry came over quite a few times. Richie and I recorded that song, "The Rum Tum Tugger," fresh and new, for a promotion video in 1985. We did not take a soundtrack off of the *Cats* Broadway soundtrack, okay? Because they wanted it, they even rented, I think, the Broadhurst Theatre for the whole week or two that they shot it. And they set up a little set on the stage, a cat's set in that Broadhurst Theatre. And we would go there every day starting at, I don't know, nine in the morning, and we would shoot all day long. And then we had to go to the Winter Garden Theater and perform *Cats* at night. Let me tell you, that was hard… We spent a lot of time with Terry during that process because we recorded the song, "The Rum Tum Tugger," from scratch at Blank Tapes with Richie. I arranged a lot of the stuff and played the synthesizer that goes on in the beginning of the video. The first one minute or something, they wanted us to kind of make it a little more poppy and stuff. They wanted synthesizers and they want it spruced up, you know. Okay, so we did that. Terry came in and he re-sang the whole thing and the girls all sang the background. So we got to know Terry quite a bit.

"We knew that he was a songwriter, so we spent some time trying to write songs or listening to his songs. So when Barry Opper comes, I mean, it was just a no-brainer that Terry could do this role in *Critters*. Terry had the work ethic of a Broadway person that you could depend upon 100 percent to show up and do everything. He could play a rock star, but he didn't have any of the hang-ups. So they knew that they would, you know, could depend upon him. Because look, he's showing up to 400 shows a year on *Cats*. He's going to show up for a movie producer. And so we felt confident. I'm sure I can't speak for Richie, but I'm sure he just jumped at the opportunity to say, '*Hey, yeah, we'll write your song too. Yeah, we can do that.*' Because Terry wrote good songs and I was just a songwriter, and Richie just jumped at the opportunity. We didn't have one in mind, but we'd sit down and frigging do it, you know? It worked out okay. The only thing that I remember, everything was pretty smooth going, but the only thing that I kind of remember is that Terry was insistent about getting it just right. He kept coming back after we thought the song was done. And he'd go, '*You know, I'm not really happy with this quite yet. There's something we gotta keep working on here. It's this or that lyric or something, you know.*' So we'd have to go back in and sit down again until Terry was happy."

Although "Power of the Night" is the most memorable track in *Critters*, Pettit and Vetter penned a second song that also appeared in the film. "There was also another song called "Leathers" that I wrote with Richie that was in the film," explains Pettit. "It's just a little bit of background music in one scene. We were trying to break in as a duo singing team, me and Dana Calitri, we sang that song together. And that's in one of the scenes as background music. Not much of it, but enough of it. But it's a very sassy kind of rock song that me and Dana sang. And we recorded that at about the same time. We were actually recording that for another project to try and get that signed, but I guess we talked them into taking it for source music."

Nearly four decades later after the release of *Critters*, Pettit keeps a framed reminder of this flash in the pan experience, one of many in an illustrious career on Broadway and in the music industry. "I still have in a frame the front page of the *Daily News*," Petit notes. "We were friggin' dumbfounded. Dumbfounded! I still have it, the article, and it's in a frame on the wall (laughs), it reads: *Daily News*, New York Pictures newspaper, Friday, April 11, 1986. Above the *Daily News*, it says, '*Big Deal Fosse Show Hits Broadway,*' right? And then on the right-hand side, it says, '*That's no fuzzball, it's a man-eating alien,* Critters *opens today.*' Right above the title of *Daily News*. I must have cut out the movie section because there's a whole page of *Critters*, a giant ad. I must have put them together. But really, I mean, it's hilarious that it was in the news because we weren't paying attention (laughs)."

BLOWING THE HOUSE TO SMITHEREENS

Happy accidents usually make great stories, but in cinema, they usually result in legendary scenes or profound moments showcasing visual effects. For *Critters*, the controlled demolition of the Browns's farmhouse ranks as a legendary happy accident that undoubtedly propelled the film's otherwise minuscule production value. Special effects supervisor Chuck Stewart and Frank Ceglia brought in renowned special effects talent Joseph (Joe) Lombardi, known for his work on iconic films such as *The Godfather* and *Apocalypse Now*. Not able to officially afford a Hollywood icon like Lombardi, the crew brought him in under the auspices as an uncredited consultant and together rigged the set-built house with explosive Primacord, barrels of gasoline, conventional black powder explosives, and high powered flares.

"I was hired by Special Effects Unlimited for *Critters* because I had a one card pyrotechnic license, which means I can pull permits, purchase explosives, and detonate," explains Frank Ceglia, the special effects supervisor responsible for all of the pyrotechnic effects on *Critters*. "On *Critters*, there were all kinds of pyro effects. We blew up one of the critters, we blew a hole in the wall with one of the critters, we blew up the toilet and of course, we blew up the farmhouse at the end. That was big. Joe Lombardi, the grand puba of all special effects guys, came in to help me with that. He actually owned Special Effects Unlimited. He came out and showed me the best way to blow up the farmhouse, which for all intents and purposes, was a real house, except it didn't have electricity or plumbing. It otherwise was built like a real house. It took us a few days to rig the house up with all the explosives and to put together all the pyrotechnics. The way we approached setting up the pyrotechnics for the farmhouse was we went in and scored everything. In other words, we cut everything. We cut into the joists and the framing and drilled holes into the walls and ran the explosives, which resemble a sash cord, throughout the house. When you detonate it, it just blows everything apart. We chased it with some gasoline and some black powder bombs to give it the color and fireball effect. The house really went up. You can see 4' X 8' pieces of plywood just soaring through the air, I think those were the decking used for the roof. The sequence was shot by multiple cameras and we were totally confident that the explosion was going to go off as expected."

"One of my dominant memories of *Critters* was when it was time to blow up the house," remembers cinematographer Tim Suhrstedt. "Somehow they ended up getting Joe Lombardi, and he had done many, many movies, including *Apocalypse Now*. And I remember hearing that, they

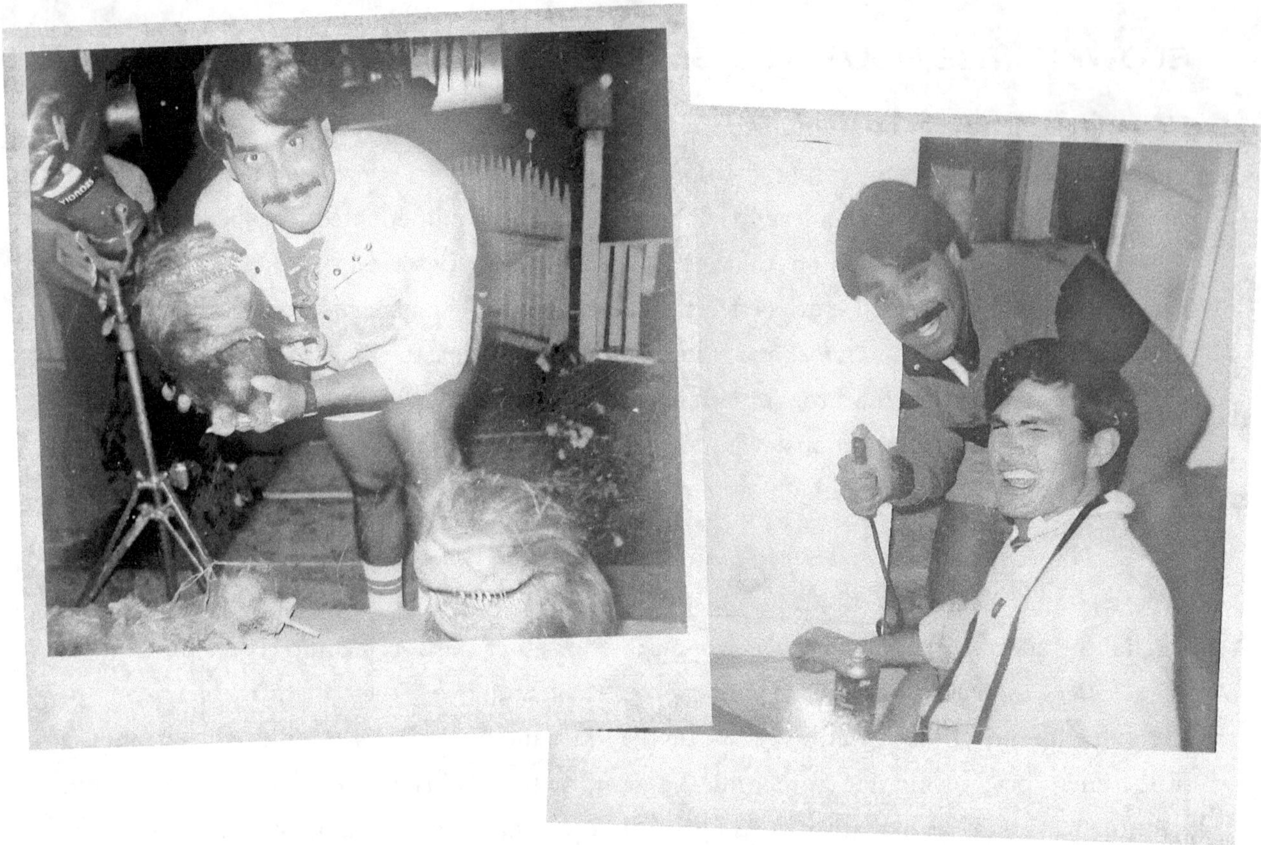

Left: Frank Ceglia was in charge of pyrotechnics on the set of *Critters* as seen in this rare photo.
Right: Frank and Casey Cavanaugh rig a wall for detonation inside the Browns's farmhouse. (Source: Frank Ceglia)

DID YOU KNOW?

Joe Lombardi, a legend among Hollywood's pyrotechnic experts, provided uncredited consultation to *Critters* and assisted in creating the extravagant explosion that destroyed the Brown family's farmhouse and barn. Lombardi, who started his career in 1946 as a set construction foreman for Lucille Ball, later named his famous company Special Effects Unlimited after Ball noted Lombardi's "limitless potential" while working on *I Love Lucy*.

said, '*Look, Lombardi isn't working, so he's willing to do this for a small fee.*' I mean nothing like he would normally get paid. So Joe came in there and I remember that they said, I think we had four cameras running, which at the time was extremely unusual to be able to get four cameras on a setup. And I remember Lombardi saying, '*Okay, this wall is going to blow out this way and go this far, so put this camera here.*' I remember when it happened, it was a huge explosion, and exactly how he described it. I remember it was just kind of fantastic to see these old pros blow this house to smithereens. They knew what they were doing to the point where they could say, '*Put this camera here, don't get too close here, put this camera over here,*' and we got all these great angles on this thing. It was interesting, because a lot of times when you were doing, well most of the time, when you were doing these low-budget movies, I've certainly had the experience with Roger Corman before, you'd get a low-budget special effects person and it would be a disaster. It would either look terrible or you might feel you were in danger or it was out of control. But man, these guys were pros. And I remember walking away going, '*Wow, that was fun.*' I mean, we had to be all done shooting before we blew the house, but it was a pretty successful blow up, I have to say. I mean even to this very day it looks so impressive."

To finesse the effect, Herek and crew set up the complex arrangement during the day and waited until 5 a.m. for high winds to subside before detonating the house. "They blew up that house and they used way too much primer cord," remembers Dwight Roberts. "I mean, even after all these years, that explosion just looks way more than the budget allotted. There's few explosions that even come close to that thing. I brought my daughter and a bunch of her school friends out to see the explosion and we were way too close. Even though they had us pretty far away, it wasn't far enough because when that house started raining down – oh my gosh, we were looking for cover. They didn't have very much to clean up after that."

"Joe Lombardi came out of retirement as one of the owners of Special Effects Unlimited to do the house explosion and one of the reasons it was so spectacular is because he had a couple of like 2 million candle power flares that he had made for the last James Bond movie that he worked on and they didn't need them because they didn't end up having to do subsequent takes," John Naulin says. "So he still had those and that's what the basic flash was. I mean that film couldn't have afforded that gag any other way. I mean they had a lot of luck. In fact, that a lot of the right people were just in the right place at the right time and knew what they were doing enough to make things work. The whole house was built slightly to scale and there was no back on it, but the whole front of it was there and you could actually go in and I mean there were functional interiors and stuff like that. For all intents and purposes they kind of built a house, but they also built it in such a way that it would kind of come apart. So they wrapped it with over a mile of explosive det cord. And it was a heavy duty det cord. And then they put these flares and a bunch of other stuff and they sprayed some chemicals around that would burn, you know, a rubber cement mixture that would burn. So that once the effect went off, I mean, I swear to God, it almost looked like the ship launched. From my POV, I was in the first bunker out front, because I was helping him that night. I wasn't using my pyro card or my insurance or any of that stuff, but they were short handed, so I stayed up all night with them. And we did that about 30 minutes before the sun came up. Again, it got to the point where it's like, '*Guys, we've got to do this shot.*' We can't wait through the rest of the day because everything's already hot and set. Because it would all have to be unhooked if we didn't detonate it that night. And once that's done, it's going to take hours and cost a lot more money to re-hook everything. Plus all these chemicals have already been sprayed; it's just it's got to be shot. '*You've got to stop doing what you're doing and come over here with a couple of cameras and shoot this.*' You know, but that's the way the whole shoot was."

The Browns's farmhouse days before it was rigged with explosives and flammable liquids and blown sky-high.
(Source: Bradford Plows)

THE QUEEN OF HAIR FABRICATION
An Interview with Deborah Galvez

(Fabricator, *Critters 1-4*)

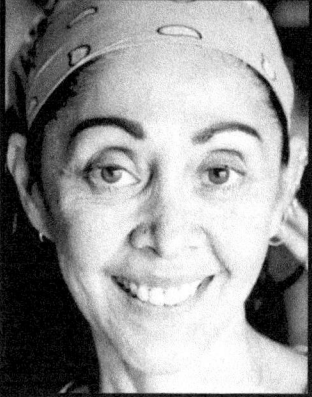

I can't thank you enough for carving out some time to talk *Critters*...

It's interesting that you're interested in *Critters* because at the time it was like, you know, nobody cared at all. So there's a big following and there's a lot of fans, you know. It's such a remarkable life to that film and this whole franchise. Yeah, yeah I was brand new. That was my first show.

Oh, was it really?

Yeah, I was super young and super green and that was my first show, you know. Yeah, and I kind of learned as I went along. I went to makeup school, but they don't really teach you, you know, the stuff that we do in school. I mean, you get the basics, but a lot of it I had to learn on my own, you know, at show.

Going back to that time, do you remember kind of how you got involved with the project?

Well, it was 1985, I believe, when the first *Critters* was being shot. The way I got my start is I was a very good friend of Charlie's [Chiodo] wife Jeannette Franco and we had a girls's night out and we ended up in a club in Hollywood and she met Charlie Chiodo that night and she said, '*Oh I'll just probably go out with him a few times*' and now they've been married with five kids all these years later. So through Jeannette, that's how I kind of got my in. I was going to school because I knew I wanted to be in the film industry in some aspect, whether it be makeup or costumes or hair. I knew I wanted to be in film. I already decided that. But my in was knowing Jeannette and having that girls's night out. She met Charlie and through Charlie I met the Chiodo brothers and they actually gave me my start. They hired me on and I was green, you know, I didn't know what the heck I was doing but I learned a lot.

So when they hired you for that project you were not familiar with the project at that time such as the creatures or anything, until you got onto the set and the workshop? What kind of stuff did they have you doing on the first one?

I was just kind of hands-on, kind of all around, like I was running foam and I was seaming and, you know, like basic stuff and then they needed somebody to do hair and I was actually really good at it. I've always been good with hair and makeup. I used to make my own costumes. I was always good at that, so I ended up doing the hair and we went through a few decisions before we ended up having the design of the hair and, at that time, I didn't know about NFT – the National Fiber Technology – it's a synthetic fur. Now they've come a long way; they have like, you know, mohair and yak hair and goat hair. They come a very long way and it's on a stretch backing. But back then, I didn't know what the heck that was and I can't really remember who came up with the moose pelts, but that's what we used and it worked because it was real fur but it didn't have the longevity the synthetic fur has. I think by the time we did the second, third, and fourth *Critters*, we were using the NFT fur, the synthetic fur, which is a lot easier to work with. I actually still have an original critter, but the moose pelt, I mean, it's in really sad shape. Throughout the years it's just deteriorated because it was a foam latex puppet.

Oh I see, and does the moose pelt kind of shrink or the fur fall out?

Yeah that's exactly what happened. I mean we were filming out in Valencia and during the day and it'd be around 100 degrees and I think just the environment – the hair started coming out in clumps. It got very brittle, so that was a problem. We had scrap moose piles and I kept having to repair the first critters because the hair was so brittle it just fell out in clumps. So I was constantly repairing those puppets with the moose pelts because the hair did not last. It just got very dry and brittle and so it fell out. So it was a constant repair with that.

How difficult was it to work with the moose pelts?

It's hard because it was on a hard leather. It's not flexible, you know, it's not flexible at all. Nowadays, I mean even back then, you had to have a flexible puppet that moved because it had to be animated. We left it on the leather backing on the pelts so it wasn't flexible at all.

What, you know, with the environmental factors, what else would you say were some of the biggest challenges that you faced with the creatures on that film?

I mean, that was the one that stuck out. I mean, the Chiodo brothers made it very fun to work on set. It was hard work, long hours, and I didn't know what I was in for. I was new. I didn't know what normal was. So I didn't know if there were problems until it came up. I knew early on that there's a thing called stunt puppets and hero puppets. I remember that being a challenge communicating the sensitivities around when to use a hero puppet that had all the mechanics and motors in it and when to use a stunt puppet because producers sometimes don't understand that side of production; don't understand the build and what goes into it and the repair and how long long it takes. They think you just whip it out in an hour and that's not the case. It takes days, weeks, months to do something, you know, right and I remember that was challenging and frustrating for me so I learned early on that that side of production does not. And to this day, they don't. And the first *Critters* also had that issue, I think they added this to the script during production, like the giant critter. They thought it would be easy to create this thing on short notice. Well, it wasn't.

Did you have any reservations about going back to *Critters 2*?

No, I mean, I was new, so I needed to get established, so I was all about getting all the work I could. And that one, I can't remember off the top of my head, I think the second one had a fairly significant budget, you know, comparatively speaking, to the first one.

And you guys had the whole critter ball design going on *Critters 2*...

Yeah, I was part of that too. That was a big 10'x10', or maybe even bigger, I'm not sure, but yeah, that was interesting on set. And that was a pretty fascinating rig to come up with on the moving vehicle and stuff.

Does anything stand out to you from *Critters 2* on the design side?

I think we started using the NFT fur. We didn't use the moose pelt, so the NFT fur was more flexible, and the puppets were more flexible, and, you know, they were a better design. It probably didn't look as menacing, but it was better for the puppet as far as movement.

Working with the NFT fur, you could repair and build them a little bit quicker?

Yeah. It was longer-lasting and less repairs and you know by then I already had it down as far as the hairstyle. It's just with a different medium of hair.

What was it like creating and working on that giant critter ball?

It was funny. I mean, it was just a bunch of balls being glued to this metal frame. I forget who built it, but we had a gluing party of just gluing these half faces full of balls and putting hair on them, you know. If I recall, some of them moved. They chattered, some of them did. But yeah, that was fun on set. You see a big ball rolling down the road.

Now a lot of the people who had worked on the second one were making comments about just how unnaturally cold the temperatures were.

Yeah, it was so hot during the day and then at night it would be so cold. We filmed at night but when we got there, because you have to be there early, it was hot. I remember it being really hot during the day and then really cold at night.

And at that point how had the, you know, in terms of development of the critters, but by that point was it pretty much down to a science in building them quickly and getting them ready?

Yeah, we already knew the design and the hairstyle, you know. The fabrication got better so the puppets could roll into a ball better. The one guy came in, Norman Tempe, I used to work for Henson's, and he made this really cool fabricated body and it just, he could tuck it and make it roll. There was more movement, I remember that. Then they have the baby critters too, in the later films, and those were made out of rabbit pelt, so the fur looks more soft and like a baby.

And at that point, it was with the synthetic hair, which made it a little quicker as well?

Yeah. The previous one was the only one with the moose pelt. All the rest were like the synthetic NFT hair with the stretch backing, so it was more flexible. And the eyes had a special reflective coating. The Scotchlite, so when the light, there was a special camera rig when it hit the puppet, it made the eyes red. Yeah, I think there was a special rig, special camera, special light, but it was the Scotchlite reflecting, and so when the camera hit it, the eyes looked like it was glowing.

You know, looking back on the *Critters* franchise, how do you feel about it after all these years compared to when you worked on them initially when they were first coming out?

It really surprised me that people really love them because at the time, it was just a movie. I met one kid, and I told him I worked on *Critters*, and he was like, 'Oh,' in awe of me. And then when I told him I had a puppet, he was like, 'Oh!' And I think I brought it in to show him, and he wanted to buy it from me. I was like, 'No, it's not for sale.' That's my first film. I've had collectors reach out to me to try to buy it. I mean, I heard they sell for big bucks, you know? I had some lady in Vegas, that wanted to buy this original critter from me. I go, 'It's in really poor shape.' She didn't care. She had money. She wanted to buy it. I go, 'No, that's my first film.' And Charlie wanted to repair it. And I brought it to the shop. And he goes, 'Oh, it's really disintegrated. I don't even know if it's repairable.' They would probably have to run a new skin because I mean it's foam latex. It's almost 40 years old and it's really disintegrating. I think the pelts are in good shape but that's about it.

I mean, that was a long time ago. But I'm glad that people love it because at the time it was just a low-budget film. It's nice to know that *Killer Klowns* and *Critters* have become cult classics, so that's cool. It's so great. I'm happy to be a part of it and, like I said, I'm very grateful to the Chiodo brothers; they gave me my start. If it wasn't for me going out on a girls's night, I never would have been a part of it because they gave me my start. A lot of kids come up from school and they start as a runner or an intern and I was lucky, they just hired me. It was kind of like on-the-job training. I was brand new and young, I didn't know anything. It's different from going to school and stuff because they don't teach you half of what you do in the shops. Especially not how to handle moose pelts. It looked great, it just didn't have longevity.

POST-PRODUCTION

Despite the contending production challenges on *Critters*, whether it was the complex practical makeup effects, animatronic puppets, or the enormity of the farmhouse explosion, entering post-production ranks among the smoothest aspects of the film's creation. Director Stephen Herek's own editorial experience coupled with the magic hands of fellow Corman editor and USC Film School alumnus Larry Bock and his team of assistant and apprentice editors led to a polished cut in relatively short order. Originally, Herek had asked another editor from the Corman camp named Bob Kaiser to cut the film.

"Bob [Kaiser] felt weird about it because Steve had been his assistant, so Bob said '*No*,'" notes Larry Bock. "Steve then asked me if I wanted to cut it and I agreed to. Steve made a joke and said, '*I don't know what was wrong with you, but you never hired me* [as an assistant editor].' (laughs) Steve still hired me."

Bock's personal notes during the first week of production revealed that the first screening of dailies occurred on 25 July, remarking the footage looked "good, but red." Producer Bob Shaye viewed a reprint of the dailies the next day for scene 19 – a sequence in the film's opening where Helen and Jay Brown discuss April's new boy interest, Steve. Of course, given the era of the production, *Critters* was shot on 35mm filmstock, which in turn was edited by physically cutting and splicing the best takes using an archaic editing device that first debuted in 1924.

"We cut *Critters* on a Moviola. I don't know how we ever did it. Cutting on film is such a bitch," explains Larry Bock. "Probably cost us our hearing working on them. The machines made so much noise. The only good thing was, you could cut the picture and its one soundtrack, you didn't have to worry about all the mixes and other things. You didn't do mixes and additional soundtracks until it was all locked down."

Perhaps unsurprisingly, Herek took a hands-on role in the editing room and even cut some of the high impact third act scenes with Bock and his team. "Coming from an editorial background, Herek cut some portions of *Critters* himself," explains Bock. "He cut the big ending, a chunk of the ending at least. He did a great job too. What he liked to do was, when a scene was cut, he would experiment playing the scene with different types of temp music. This would inspire him to try different things or rearrange the sequence. He was really good at that. It was really kind of exciting, being with him as he went up the ladder. I loved working with him."

Famed Hollywood editor Larry Bock and his trusty Moviola while cutting the cult classic *Alligator* in 1980.
(Source: Larry Bock; Photo Credit Stephen Jerrome)

Accompanying Bock in the editing department was assistant editor Hilarie Roope, a UCLA film student, and apprentice editor Rebekah Rudd, who would later become the Executive Vice President for Post Production at MGM Studios. New to editing, Roope enjoyed the mentoring provided by Bock, who let her experience cutting her first scene: the film's charming opening scene that establishes the Brown family's morning ritual around the breakfast table. Roope's scene, perhaps pedestrian by today's standards, remains tantamount to the film's success, according to a statement by producer Rupert Harvey who spoke to *Den of Geek* in 2021. "That was one of the things that appealed to me about the script," he noted in the interview. "If you set that up properly and the audience is in there with you. They gain an understanding of the family dynamic right away and they are engaged. It helps you then feel for each one of them subsequently. The rules are the same, and they have been since the first Greek dramas; storytelling is still about humans and the human condition. Just making stuff about what the monsters are doing has no appeal."

So how did Roope, a relatively brand new editor, cut such a crucial yet seemingly forgettable scene? "Larry was an amazing mentor and very generous with his time and energy and with shepherding me as an assistant," fondly remembers Roope. "He was fantastic. He let me cut a couple scenes and I was so excited. So again, remember, here we are, we're on Sunset Boulevard off of Doheny [Drive]. It was a little funky back in those days, up the street from the Whisky a Go Go. I was super stoked, super excited, and Larry was letting me get hands-on working with the Moviola. And again, reminding you, film. We were *physically* cutting film.

"So, I put together this scene, I had it on the Moviola to show Steve, who was coming in at the end of the day after wrapping. And so he comes in, and of course I'm very nervous. And I don't know if you've ever been around a Moviola or experienced the mechanics of a Moviola, but it's a very detailed integrated machine, even just to thread it properly. There's this technique where you have to hold the bottom of the film below the little pitch-box because it tends to jitter, right? So you kind of hold it right before the gate where the teeth are so that it slows it down a bit and so that it's not so fluttery. Anyway, you kind of hold it lightly because obviously it's cranking and it's got to be at real speed and you're kind of pushing these foot pedals at the same time. I mean, you turn it on, you're pushing these pedals, and then you're holding the thing. So you definitely have to be very coordinated using your feet, your hands, your eyes simultaneously.

"And, again, I'm super nervous. So I'm not at my best self. And there's Steve, super close to me. I'm all nervous and fluttery. I mean, he was super cute back then, too, but he was married. Don't get me wrong. But he was super cute and young, and I was just like, all nervous. And my finger went into the gauge and severed through the film-like mechanic of the teeth. Like, basically, my finger went into the frame, got stuck, then we couldn't open it – so my finger is *stuck* in the teeth that are adhered to these sprockets, and Steve and Larry are on either side of me. I look over and Larry is turning pure white. I think Steve was also about to pass out. I mean, they turn off the machine, but we can't get the gate open. Literally, my finger was wedged in it so deeply, we couldn't get it open. And then finally, somebody got a screwdriver. I think Steve, because I think Larry was just out of it. He was just like, I don't know if he was passed out or about to throw up or something, but I think Steve grabbed a screwdriver but I didn't see the whole thing. I mean, remind you, this took like a while, like it wasn't an instant. And I'm just standing there. I'm not really in pain. I'm sort of in shock, but I'm not freaking out because it's almost like time stopped and there's no pain because the blood, everything was just stopped. It was *stopped*.

"So, Steve was able to get the gate open for the film. My finger popped out and of course, it was still intact, thank God. But to this day, I have a scar on the inside of my middle finger on my right hand. They rushed me to Cedars-Sinai Hospital, which fortunately was a stone's throw away.

I remember Steve drove me, because again, I think Larry was like, either gagging or passed out or ready to pass out. I remember having like a ginormous band-aid on my middle finger and trying to do even normal things was difficult for a bit. (laughs)"

Though Herek and Bock were more familiar with Corman's editorial style, which usually entailed Corman being physically present in the editing room and making suggestions in real time, both had to adjust to Bob Shaye's style of sending notes after watching a reel. While most adjustments were minor, Shaye had been initially opposed to incorporating subtitles for the scenes in which the Krites communicated verbally. The earliest script drafts did include sequences in which the Krites communicate, and ultimately the shooting script did include minor dialogue scenes among the Krites through the use of subtitles, an inclusion that Bob Shaye remained opposed to until the very first test screening. According to Brian Muir in *They Bite!: The Making Of Critters* documentary, it was Stephen Herek who inserted a single, roughly constructed sequence with subtitles in preparation for the first test screening, as both Muir and Herek were convinced it would play well to audiences. In the scene, Dee Wallace's Helen Brown obliterates a Krite in the front yard with a powerful blast from her double-barrel shotgun. A nearby surviving Krite utters a guttural growl that translates to "Oh fuck!" in subtitles. Muir remarked the test screening's audience howled for nearly two full minutes, convincing Shaye to incorporate additional subtitle sequences into the final cut of the film.

Another minor, though not less significant issue in post-production, involved the curation of the film's PG-13 rating. Several initial cuts provided to the Motion Picture Association of America (MPAA) resulted in an R-rating, a non-starter for Shaye who had always remained committed to achieving the newer but family-friendlier PG-13 rating. Excessive gore, like the overzealously shot sequence involving Billy Zane having his chest cavity devoured by hungry

DID YOU KNOW?

Voice actor Corey Burton designed the Krite's language partly based on his his rudimentary understanding of French and Japanese and their respective annunciative differences. Burton also applied a distinct sound for each size of the Krites, using a higher pitched, conversation tone for the small Krites; a guttural, raspy tone for the medium-sized Krites; and a deeper, guttural snarl tone for the giant-sized Krite.

Krites as well as his digits being chomped off in a single bite, were ultimately excised from the final cut. The segment in which Zane's fingers are devoured had to be meticulously trimmed, at one point involving a scant six frames of celluloid, resulting in an abrupt jump cut but avoiding the onscreen depiction of his fingers actually being severed.

Although the film would be cut in a relatively straightforward fashion, Bob Shaye feared the film's original ending as overly downbeat, which concludes with the Brown family gathering around the smoldering wreckage of their home, together, but with the bleak prospect of rebuilding.

"I remember the biggest argument with Bob I had, and he won because it was his money, was about blowing up the house at the end," contended Rupert Harvey. "And I think Steve [Herek] was very non-committal about it, but I kind of went to the mattresses over it. But I didn't want the whole house to come back together at the end. I didn't want the happy ending that Bob did."

Again, it was during the conclusion of a test screening that Shaye related to producers that he was dissatisfied and requested that additional footage be shot to improve the mood of the film's ending. The idea was that the transponder provided to Brad would allow for the miraculous reconstruction of the Brown family farmhouse and barn, now a smoldering pile of ruins. A foreground miniature effect designed by Gene Warren Jr. and his team of experts created the illusion of the house being reconstructed, and cut with several insert shots of the family observing this miracle, rounded out the film's new, Shaye-approved upbeat ending.

Though editorial tweaks made during the initial test screenings included the revamped ending as well as subtle additions such as the inclusion of subtitles for the Krites, it became apparent to some that *Critters* possessed special cinematic ingredients that would propel the film toward its destiny as a cult classic.

"I don't know how many tests we did, two or three probably, before the picture was finally locked down and all of the tweaking is over and done with," remembers Rupert Harvey. "The moment when the critters first appeared, they came rolling across the farmyard, the family rushing into the house. Billy's [Zane] in the barn getting his stomach ripped out. They come rushing across and the family just make it into the house in time and slam the door. And you have two critters at the front door outside the house. And there's an exchange between them with a subtitle underneath, and mom is standing there with a shotgun, blows one of them away, and the subtitle says, '*Oh fuck!*' And at that moment, unexpectedly, I mean, we thought it was amusing, but it totally brought the house down. The house absolutely erupted. Absolutely, I've never, when

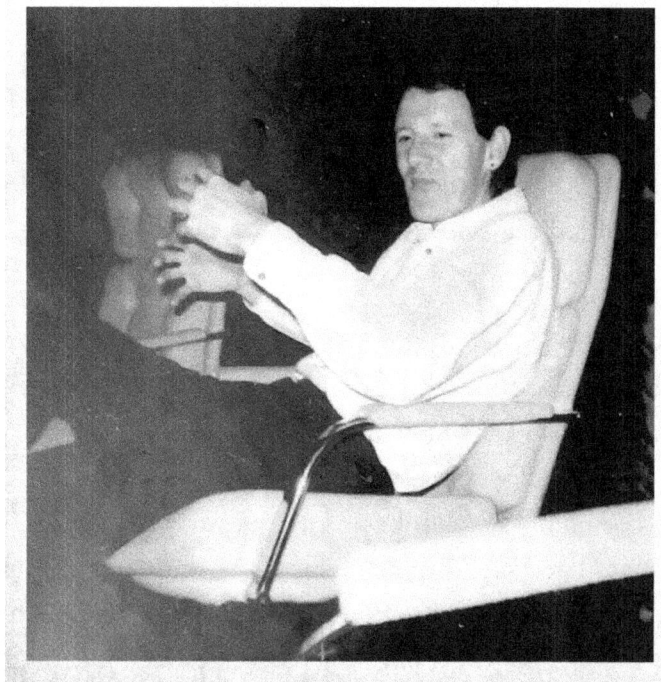

PHANTOM PRODUCER RUPERT HARVEY

Producer Rupert Harvey discusses an early cut of *Critters*
with the editorial team. (Source: Larry Bock)

I, way back in the day, I was involved in exhibition. I worked in cinema in the UK. So I've seen lots of movies and gauged lots of audience reactions, but I'd never seen anything like that. It totally blew the house apart. And we had a problem in dealing with it because it disrupted the next scene, because the audience was still rolling in the aisles (laughs). And I figured, okay, that moment, that was the moment I thought, '*Okay, we got this.*'"

New Line exhibited the film at the annual Film West film market convention at the MGM Grand Hotel in Las Vegas and featured Kevin Thompson in the film's large critter suit, accompanied by special effects fabricator Dwight Roberts.

"I was well aware this was going to be a hit and that was all because of me," chuckles Kevin Thompson, half-joking. "It really was because of me. I walked, when I was selling the film, and it was a good film, but a lot of good films don't get traction. Bob Shaye took me to what was called Film West, I think at the time, where they launched the films and everybody's got their little tepee out and their little table of wares and trying to sell it. And we want, his idea was, '*Well, let's take*

Kevin and put him in the outfit and walk around the whole convention floor.' But here's the leader of this huge theater chain, Mann Theatres, he walks by me and says, *'I want that film. I want* that *film!'* And so that's why I'm saying I sold that film. Now, do I get credit for it? That was a good film. So maybe it would have gotten traction. Maybe it would have been something like *Everything Everywhere All at Once*, an independent film that goes and makes $150 million. That's, you know, it's done for $25 million. But I remember that well, the theater chain owner yelling *'I want that film, I need that film!'* (laughs)"

"I went one year, then I couldn't go the next year because I was working on something and then my wife ended up taking the costume with Kevin," remembers Dwight Roberts. "When I took it, I had the whole thing, I had a crate made, you know, everything so it would be handled correctly. I got to the airport and they're like, *'That's too big.'* I thought, you gotta be kidding me. I thought we had checked on the size, but I guess not. So my wife had to drive down. We threw everything in plastic bags, the whole costume, and just sent it through luggage like that. We were in the MGM Grand Hotel and were just walking around the lobby handing out brochures for this up-and-coming event that they were having – it was like a distribution thing for films where movie theater people would come in and say, *'Oh yeah we want that one or that one.'* I'm not sure how that part of the industry works, but Kevin was a lot of fun to be with because he just loved to entertain people and he took full advantage of being in that costume. You know we had borrowed one of the bellhops's carts. It had this rack on top that you can hold on to and so Kevin would hop up on that. We'd roll him around so we'd be coming out of the room going down the hall and some poor house cleaning lady would be standing out there with her cart and as he went by he would just go off into character, and she would freak out (laughs). He got the biggest kick out of doing that kind of stuff. Even without the costume he was doing these pratfalls right in the middle of the lobby. He would just slip up and land on the ground like, *'Oh God!'* And everybody would be coming around and just laughing; he loved doing that kind of stuff."

Dwight Roberts (right) and Kevin Thompson (inside critter suit) pose with a model while taking a break showcasing *Critters* at the MGM Grand Hotel in 1987. (Source: Dwight Roberts)

RELEASE AND RECEPTION

Prior to the film's release on 25 April 1986, Brian Muir and Mark Pritchard briefly highlighted the upcoming release on the 20th episode of their cable access television program *Two Guys That Watch Movies*. In the short clip, Mark sets the scene with a brief synopsis and describes it as a "science fiction-type picture" before asking Muir for some of the film's punchy taglines. Muir responds, "When they come to Earth, it's strictly eat and run... They eat, you run," followed by both Muir and Pritchard howling with laughter. After previewing a short clip of the scene in which Bradley Brown (Scott Grimes) encounters both bounty hunters for the first time on the deserted stretch of Route 22, Pritchard teases Muir about the film's PG-13 rating and laments it just wasn't bloody enough for his taste. Muir reassures Pritchard that he had tried to keep the production to an R-rating, thinking some core audience demographics would have been turned off by the PG-13 rating. Muir quipped, "But do they listen to the writer of the film?"

"Anyway, Dee Wallace and M. Emmet Walsh are the only stars of particular note, although the kid is really good. I was really impressed with the kid," opines Pritchard. "And the critters, although they look like porcupines rolling around, are fairly entertaining. And, let's see, the director, as a way of note, was on the show, what, last summer? And we had the editor on just the last show. So, that will also probably make you rush right out and see that sucker. But did you want to add anything to that?"

"No, how can I? I wrote it," jokes Muir. And as quickly as the *Critters* segment began, Muir humbly shifts from *Critters* to the next segment without missing a beat.

Critters premiered in New York on 11 April, 1986 followed by a national release later that month on 25 April. To the surprise of many of the cast and crew, *Critters* met near instant critical praise and became a burgeoning commercial success for Shaye and New Line Cinema. Film critics Siskel and Ebert famously gave *Critters* "two thumbs up" and Ebert later praised the film's humor and sense of style in a published review, noting the film's ambitious mashup of several genre favorites, specifically *Gremlins*, *E.T. the Extra-Terrestrial*, *The Terminator*, and *Starman*. Famed "King of the Drive-in" Joe Bob Briggs hailed *Critters* as "numero uno on the Best of '86 Drive-in Stud List," bestowing the film a four-star rating and praising the "title-role performance by the man-eating porcupine tumbleweeds with enormous teeth."

Critters earned a staggering $13,167,232 at the box office despite only screening at 633 theaters nationwide, a remarkable feat for a low-budget independent horror-comedy with a PG-13 rating. In addition, *Critters* would go on to ride the lucrative wave of the home-video rental market, improving its financial standing and galvanizing its reputation as a campy, fan-favorite.

DID YOU KNOW?

New Line's *Teenage Mutant Ninja Turtles* (1990) depicts a solemn Raphael blowing off steam at a dingy movie theater where he offers a nonplussed reaction to watching *Critters*, as labeled on the theater's marquee. In various graphic novel adaptations of the 1990 movie, Raphael can be seen alternatively watching *E.T.* as well as a fictional film that's a veiled reference to *Batman*.

"It was the first show we keyed and to have it being seen, a lot of times you do a project and it doesn't get distribution, but it was seen, it was pretty major for us, so it was a big, big boost for our company," explains Stephen Chiodo. "I remember even Roger Ebert really kind of dug it."

In one of his last recorded interviews, Muir expressed surprise and appreciation that nearly 20 years after *Critters*, people were still enjoying the film and new generations were discovering it. Muir judged that *Critters* still held up, remarking he felt "pretty proud of it."

Top and bottom left: The Krites smile for their close-up during a set visit from news media.
Bottom right: Charlie Chiodo escorts Kevin Thompson to set in Valencia. (Source: *Entertainment This Week*.)

DID YOU EVER FEEL THAT
CRITTERS
WAS DESTINED TO BECOME
A CULT CLASSIC?

"No, no I didn't. We just approached it like it was just a job. You just don't know what's going to happen. How they'll be edited or how the audiences will receive them. I think people really love *Critters*, and if another one was made with the Chiodo Brothers, I think people would really want to go see it. They're campy, but people like these types of films."

– Frank Ceglia, special effects coordinator, *Critters*

"I had no idea. But *Critters* really did pick up a wonderful audience and fanbase. People still love it."

– Lin Shaye, "Sal" in *Critters*

"Hell no. It was kind of just like a regular project. I mean, every movie I've ever worked on has been like, '*Oh well, that was another piece of shit.*' It was a fun film. I did enjoy seeing it in the theater, but it was just kind of like, you know, I always expect movies that I work on are just gonna go straight to video."

– Chris Biggs, special makeup effects, *Critters*

"No, I had no idea. It kind of felt just like a regular low-budget monster movie. Back then the big thrill was getting your picture in *Fangoria*, or one of those movie monster magazines. That was a claim to fame. We did that. That was a lot of fun."

– Dwight Roberts, mechanics and fabrication: Critters Crew, *Critters*

"Not at all. *Critters* to me was just a B-film. I thought it was just a low-budget film that nobody cared about. But then again, I've been in this business almost 40 years and I still meet younger people and they're like, '*Oh my God you worked on* Critters!' I'm like a celebrity to them. (laughs) It's funny because it's the same with *Killer Klowns from Outer Space* – that wasn't a big hit, but now these young people just love it. They are classics now. They just continue to gain in popularity as the years go on."

– **Deborah Galvez, fabricator and hair expert: Critters Crew,** *Critters*

"I didn't have a good sense of how well *Critters* would play because I'm not a horror aficionado whatsoever, so I wasn't used to seeing those kinds of films and creature effects. I couldn't tell whether *Critters* was cutting edge or not."

– **Larry Bock, editor,** *Critters*

"To my memory, there was no real '*ah-ha*' moment. Unlike *Android,* for which Rupert and I could experience the house coming down at screenings for packed houses at, for instance, The Seattle Film Festival and the London Film Festival, *Critters* screenings hosted by New Line were tamer affairs. I frankly didn't really realize the 'cult' part of it until, years later, my brother Don was asked to attend *Critters* revival screenings and he texted me pictures of *Critters* tattoos in the weirdest places on various bodies attending the screenings."

– **Barry Opper, producer,** *Critters*

"Well, I might be in the minority, but I felt that we really had something during our test screenings. Seeing the audience react and tear the house down is when I thought, '*Yes, we've got something here.*' I turned out to be right."

– **Rupert Harvey, producer,** *Critters*

"No, but I think people tend to forget that these were just movies in this era. This was just before the home video market, which later became the DVD home market craze that got a lot more movies made. Back then, a movie was a movie that was going to end up in the theater and you needed to get distribution. I was happy to be part of it. We all did the best job we could and had as much fun as we could while doing it."

– **Tim Suhrstedt, cinematographer,** *Critters*

CHAPTER TWO

CRITTERS 2

HUNGRY FOR MORE

New Line Cinema, still hot from the success of the budding franchise *A Nightmare on Elm Street* and the commercially viable *Critters*, opted for a *Critters* sequel in 1987. Gone were director Stephen Herek and writer Brian Muir, replaced by Mick Garris, a promising screenwriter and young director, and screenwriter David Twohy, who's first draft of the sequel became the blueprint for *Critters 2*. Armed with a larger budget and considerably longer shooting schedule, *Critters 2* features more elaborate gags, more Krites, and a larger cast. Scott Grimes returned to play a slightly older Bradley Brown and both Don Opper and Terrence Mann returned to play their respective characters of Charlie and Ug. Interestingly, the film ultimately was a commercial flop for New Line Cinema and would create a lingering sense of hesitancy for the third and fourth installments to eventually be made. However, the quirky film has garnered its own cult following given the film's grandiose use of special effect gags and humorous edge.

"When we made a deal with New Line for *Critters*, to sweeten the deal, they made it a two picture deal… The second picture didn't become *Critters 2* until the first *Critters* opened fairly successfully for New Line. So we didn't know at the time that we signed the deal that we were going to make a *Critters 2*," recalls Barry Opper. "We were kind of young and eager and this idea of making a sequel, I don't remember that it was all that exciting. That Steve Herek was a nervous first-time director on the first one but we were just pleased that we made a movie a success and we're pleased that someone came back to us and said '*Okay, this is what we've got.*' In a way, I think we might have been a little let down because we had hoped that one of the other projects we had in development would have been the second movie. But they wanted *Critters 2*, so we shifted gears and decided to make a *Critters 2*… Except for the ending of the first *Critters*, Rupert and I essentially called the shots on the first *Critters* movie. *Except* for the ending of *Critters*, which was not the intended ending we shot, the ending that we actually ended up using for the first *Critters* was one that Bob Shaye had insisted on. So that was the only studio intervention on the entire first *Critters*. *Critters 2* was a totally new experience to us because now we had a studio with us from the very beginning. We were assigned a New Line executive, a guy named Jeff Schechtman."

Initially, New Line approached director Stephen Herek for the opportunity to helm the sequel, an offer he declined. "I was proud of it [*Critters*] and pleased I'd pulled it off, yet I never saw it as anything more than a fun little movie," Herek told *Starburst* magazine. "I was offered the sequel by New Line, but they only wanted to spend the same amount of money. I had a whole different idea of where this story should go, too, but New Line couldn't agree. I wasn't sure I wanted to repeat myself anyway."

Little is known about Herek's idea for a sequel, but actor Scott Grimes alluded to at least a partial plot element, telling *Fangoria*, "…I heard the story was going to take place 40 years in the future. I didn't figure I could play a 53-year-old man, so I sort of forgot about it until they called and said I only had to be 16."

Replacing Herek was the up and coming writer-director, Mick Garris. Born in Santa Monica, California in 1953, Mick Garris and his family moved around before settling in the Phoenix area where he spent most of his formative years. Garris later returned to California and studied TV production at Grossmont College where he developed an interest in writing while pursuing his passion for music. Garris's love for rock n' roll inspired him to form a progressive rock band called Horsefeathers in 1970, which eventually became one of San Diego's leading acts. Seeking greater opportunities and bigger venues, Garris and Horsefeathers relocated to Los Angeles in 1976, but like many bands before them, failed to gain the traction and attention they desired and the band dissolved in 1977. Garris turned his attention back to writing and experimented with screenwriting while freelancing for *Fangoria*, *Starlog*, and *Cinefantastique*. Stints at the Star Wars Corporation and a private public relations firm promoting films like *Halloween II* and *The Fog* led Garris to a position at Universal Studios where he made documentaries about genre films such as *The Thing* and *Videodrome*. Still writing screenplays, Garris became an industry go-to for script doctoring and first drafts before eventually landing a golden opportunity working with Hollywood's then-hottest filmmaker, Steven Spielberg. Garris became a leading contributor for Spielberg's *Amazing Stories* series, writing or co-writing 10 of the show's first 22 episodes. Spielberg briefly entertained financing an original Garris screenplay titled *Uncle Willie*, a blended comedy-drama set in Southern California in the 1950s, but the project was canceled along with numerous other projects as the rate of potential productions had overwhelmed the Spielberg camp. Caught in development hell with stalled projects like *Black Sheep*, a comedy script for Eddie Murphy, and a horror script called *Bloodstone* that featured an evil genie, Garris continued to pursue his passions despite the frustrations and eventually landed a gig writing, directing, and producing a *Disney Sunday Movie* segment called "*Fuzzbucket*." Garris's reputation as a script doctor, his connections to Spielberg and other well-connected industry icons, and a flair for the whimsical while also exuding family-oriented sensibilities, placed Garris on the shortlist for New Line Cinema as it marched toward pre-production for *Critters 2*.

EARLY SCRIPT AND PRE-PRODUCTION

Before the arrival of Mick Garris on *Critters 2*, New Line had a burgeoning screenwriter named David Twohy take a stab at the film's first draft, though Twohy would eventually depart from the project after creative differences emerged between him and Bob Shaye.

"For *Critters 2*, we had a partner, a very active partner, and it was a different process for us. I say this as to explain why David Twohy's script, which was darker than Mick Garris's script, was not done and probably why David has, if he does, I don't know, I haven't talked to him in years, kind of ill feelings, ill memories of the process," explains Barry Opper. "Mick, who was the choice of

DID YOU KNOW?

Mick Garris and Brian Muir had similar starts in the film industry. Like Muir, who co-hosted the *Two Guys Who Watch Movies* cable access program, Garris hosted a show called *Fantasy Film Festival*, which focused on fantasy and sci-fi and included interview appearances with filmmakers such as John Landis, Joe Dante, and even Steven Spielberg. Additionally, both Garris and Muir had been separately asked to write early script versions for *Gremlins 2*, though nothing ultimately materialized from those early offers.

New Line, I mean, New Line then began going through the agent world, which hadn't really been in our lives. Our creative choices were made from people we'd worked with, other artists, other creative people. We hadn't had any agents bringing us talent before. And one of those was Mick Garris, who was considered about to be pretty hot. Ultimately we went with Mick, which changed *Critters* in a way, a sensibility that certainly was pretty distant from David Twohy's sensibility. And so a lot of the more goofy ideas for the critters came from Mick. And if you can look at the two movies, you can see the differences in sensibility because although we weren't making in our minds something like *Nightmare on Elm Street,* which was much harder edged than what we were making with *Critters.* So *Critters 2* became a little goofier... And it became, in a lot of ways, Mick's baby and New Line's baby, much more than our baby, I would say. Although, we were hands-on producers. And as Rupert said, maybe me more so than Rupert, but the new partner was New Line, which really hadn't been our partner on the first one, except on the ending of the first one."

David Twohy, best known for his work on sci-fi films like *The Chronicles of Riddick* series, famously avoids discussing his role in penning the original draft for *Critters 2*, telling *Starlog* magazine: "*Critters 2* is something I'm still not terribly pleased it's on my résumé. But there it is. I've done better work." According to the then-CEO of New Line Cinema Bob Shaye, Twohy bowed out of *Critters 2* after declining to rework and polish the script during a meeting with Shaye. The pair did not end up speaking to each other for nearly 20 years afterwards. Nevertheless, Twohy's initial story for *Critters 2* largely remained intact and usable for Mick Garris, who inherited the script and reworked some of the character treatments, injected his own flavor of humor, and over-the-top cartoonish critter gags. Garris would even provide his own voice-over work for the Krites and even contributed sound effects.

Just prior to *Critters 2*, Garris had finished many scripts and rewrites on many different projects, including three drafts of *The Fly 2*, but it was the cancellation of his directorial outing on *Uncle Willie* that ultimately led Garris to *Critters 2*. "I guess I was acting like a snob," Garris told *Fangoria*. "All my work up to that point had been with major studios, and I wasn't sure if doing a low-budget, independent horror film would be the best career move." Garris came around, redrafting Twohy's script, which he felt largely anchored itself to a conventional Western premise, and signed on to direct. However, never a fan of Westerns, Garris took a crash course in reviewing the classics from John Ford, Howard Hawks, and John Wayne, all of which influenced the scene in which Sheriff Harv rallies the townsfolk to collectively fight the Krites and save Grover's Bend.

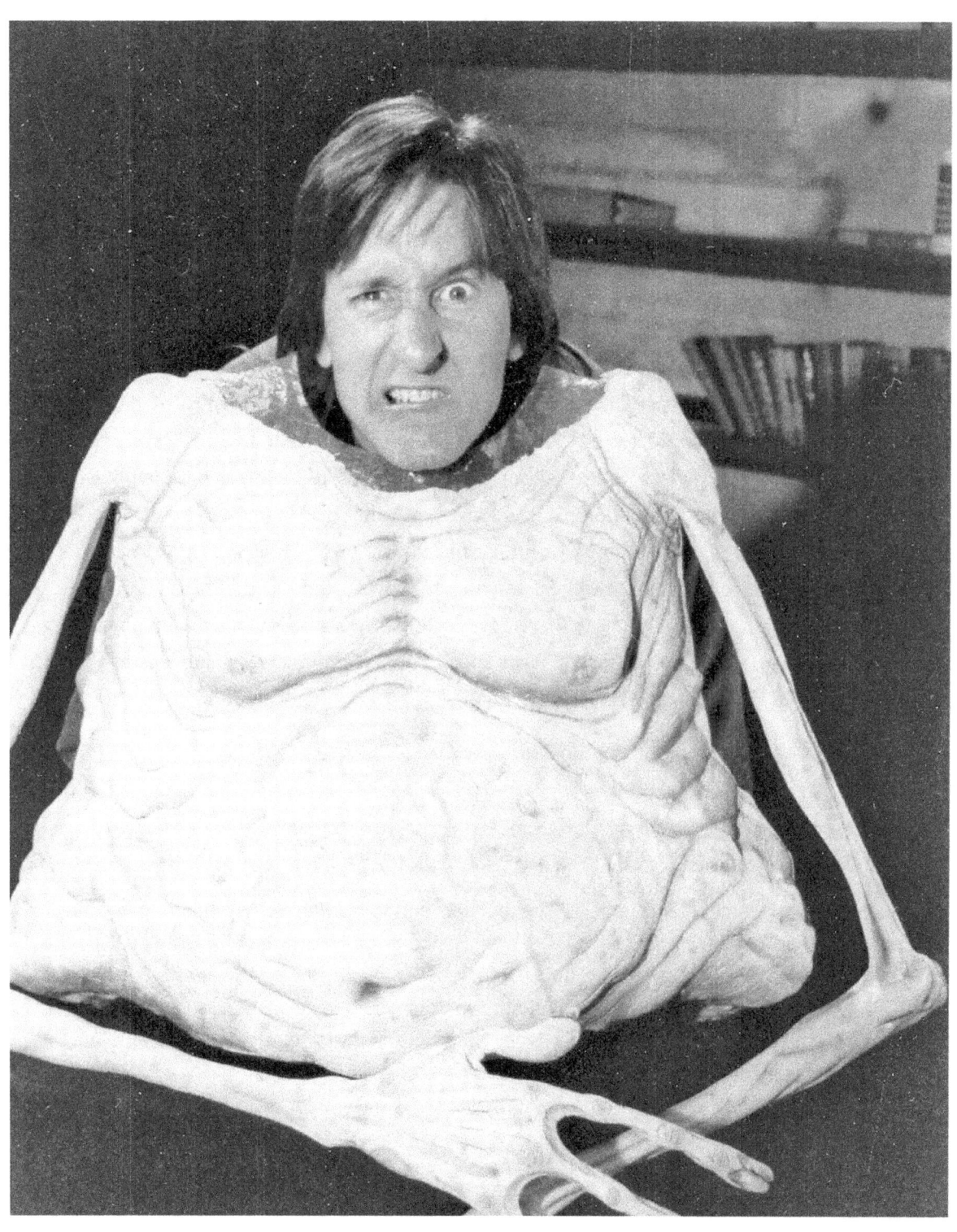

Mick Garris and the revamped Warden Zanti prosthetic on the set of *Critters 2*. (Source: Chris Biggs)

New Line permitted Garris to inject his own sensibilities into Twohy's foundational script, which included an homage to Warner Bros.'s styled cartoon comedic violence and an invasion of the Norman Rockwell portrait of Americana. In fact, many of the gags involving the critters were directly inspired with the likes of Wile E. Coyote and the Road Runner cartoon, including a splatted, flattened critter carcass, bulging eyes complete with a "boing-yoing-yoing" sound effect (voiced by Mick Garris), as well as a cannon blast to the head that sheers off the scalp of a critter.

Though Twohy is credited as a co-screenwriter, it was Twohy's story that would largely remain unchanged in Garris's rewrite. The story takes place two years after the events of the first film and opens up with a scene in which bounty hunters Ug and Lee, accompanied by Charlie McFadden, hunt down a sinister alien cryptid on a distant planet. The trio is informed by Warden Zanti that Krites have been detected on Earth and they must be destroyed. Zanti withholds payment to the bounty hunters until they can prove that all Krite lifeforms on Earth have been terminated. Back in Grover's Bend, a batch of Krite eggs that have survived from the previous invasion, hatch, releasing a new group of hungry and mischievous Krites. (This also marks the first screen appearance of baby Krites.) Meanwhile, the town is preparing for the annual Easter celebration, attracting a large number of visitors. A dimwitted duo snatch the incubating eggs from the now abandoned Brown family farm and end up selling some of the eggs to the local church to be used as Easter egg decorations.

DID YOU KNOW?

A light-hearted anti-meat theme is present throughout *Critters 2*, highlighted by the eccentric and lovable Nana (Herta Ware), who encourages her grandson Bradley (Scott Grimes) to accept vegetarianism and curses the Krites for their red meat obsession. Fittingly, the gluttonous Krites are later lured to their death inside the town's hamburger factory. Though not vegetarian at the time, writer/director Mick Garris later became and a vegetarian in the early 2000s following a near-fatal heart blockage.

HOME OF THE

HUNGRY
HEIFER

FOR THE FINEST IN FAST FOOOOOD!

POLAR ICE BURGER

Unexpected icons from *Critters 2* include the Hungry Heifer fast food joint
and Polar Ice Burger meat-packing plant. (Artwork by George Todoroff.)

Bradley Brown, the protagonist from the first film, returns to Grover's Bend which coincides with the reappearance of the ferocious alien invaders. Despite initial skepticism that something's awry, the town eventually realizes that the Krites are back and pose a significant threat. As chaos ensues, Brad, together with his newfound love interest Megan Morgan and other locals, including the town's former sheriff, team up to battle the Krites. They try to contain the creatures and prevent them from multiplying or escaping the town. Pairing up with the trio of bounty hunters, Brad, Megan and the townsfolk of Grover's Bend band together, utilizing improvised weapons and wits to defend their homes and loved ones. This time, hundreds of Krites face off against the entire town, eventually merging into an enormous and seemingly unstoppable critter ball. The final showdown between the townsfolk and the critters takes place in a meat-packing factory, leading to an action-packed and explosive conclusion.

CASTING

Mick Garris felt it was critical to bring back the characters and the actors who played them in the first installment, since they were among the main reasons why a sequel was being made in the first place. Producer Barry Opper agreed.

"There were certain givens we knew; we were going to bring my brother back, we knew that Terry Mann would be back, and we wanted to bring back Emmet Walsh, but he wouldn't do the second one," states Barry Opper. "So we got Barry Corbin to play Harv, hoping the audience would forgive us for that. We essentially knew who we were going to bring back, and we knew that Brad was too old to be the boy he was in the first one. So we knew we had to deal with a Brad that's a few years older. At any rate, we couldn't get M. Emmet [Walsh] so we got Barry Corbin, who we felt was a legitimate replacement for him. He was somewhat known as an actor. But we repeated with Terry [Mann], my brother [Don Opper], and Scott Grimes, but Tommy Hodges was an unknown. Douglas Rowe who played Quigley, Liane Curtis who played Megan, they were mostly unknown. Herta Ware, I had known from the stage, she was Will Geer's wife. He's a remarkable actor. And there were several goofy choices that were Mick's choice on *Critters 2*. Eddie Deezen I didn't even know of, but Mick did. But a lot of these were people I brought in, some of the supporting actors I just brought. But overall, the main characters were cast by Mick in conjunction with us, except for the ones that returned from the first *Critters*."

Mann, returning for his second stint as the bounty hunter "Ug," did so knowing there was a limited range on what he had to work with character-wise. "Ug is basically the same guy," Mann told *Fangoria*. "There's a definite limit on what an actor can do with this kind of role. This is an effects movie. Even though Mick and I have discussed the part, we know there's only so much that can be done. But hey, this is a fun movie to do and the people are great to work with! Every role doesn't have to be something that's going to get you an Oscar nominate."

Lin Shaye also returned, reprising her role as Sal, though this time around she works for the town's newspaper. "The second *Critters* I don't remember as well, the first one was really it for me, but I was very excited to hear that they were bringing Sal back," notes Lin Shaye. "I do recall my wardrobe though, between the hat, my Easter bonnet, which I kept for the longest time but I eventually gave it away and I'm so sad I did that, it probably could've helped finance my old age (laughs). I also wore this great flowered dress. There's this wonderful scene of me watching the critters roll down the hill. I watched it recently. It just tickles me to see me playing Sal."

For the newcomers, auditions were held and roles were conventionally competed for. "There was a whole audition process. I was such a cocky fucker," laughs Liane Curtis. "I went in and I met Robin Lippin [casting director] and she put me on tape. And then I went in to meet the producers and then it got down to the wire and they couldn't decide. And then this other chick and I had to go in like on the same day and one would go in and read, but the thing that made the difference was, I knew how to drive a stick shift and she didn't. Literally (laughs)."

The biggest outward difference between *Critters* and *Critters 2* is the depiction of shape-shifting bounty hunter Lee as a gorgeous blonde *Playboy* Playmate played by Roxanne Kernohan. "I don't think Rupert or I would have gone with a Playboy Bunny-type as a bounty hunter," laments Barry Opper. "And so he did, that was Mick's idea. It was tough."

Scott Grimes reprised his role as the likable Bradley Brown, "the boy who cried critter," in *Critters 2*.
(Source: Bradford Plows)

Besides acting bonafides and natural beauty, Roxanne caught the eye of Mick and the executive producers because she had actually completed a photography shoot for *Playboy* Magazine, an attribute that played a key part in the film. Kernohan had never become an official *Playboy* Playmate, but her photos taken by the *Playboy* photographer were provided and included in the faux *Playboy* issue that Charlie flips through shortly after landing back on Earth, prompting Lee's transformation into the stunningly beautiful Kernohan.

Garris is not quick to take credit for the *Playboy* Playmate incarnation. "I want whoever came up with it to get proper credit," Garris explains in his official biography. "It might have been me, it might have been David Twohy, it might have been Bob Shaye. What Bob did come up with was the [visual] punch line that makes it work best, that once the transformation was done, she still has the staple across her navel. And so we made a prop giant staple that matched where the staple was in her magazine layout. Lee feels it, looks down, pulls it out, and tosses it away." Garris is fond of the incarnation's commentary on gender issues, noting the assumed-to-be-male character Lee feeling most comfortable in the body of a *Playboy* Playmate was not something widely done in mainstream movies in the 1980s. The female portrayal of Lee also compliments the familiar face of Ug, played again by Terrence Mann.

"Terrence [Mann] was definitely the cool one," remembers Liane Curtis. "He brought a very rock n' roll vibe, but he also brought a very ethereal aspect to his character, like it was very believable that he could be from outer space, right? His sidekick [Roxanne] was very nice. She was pretty shy for the most part, not super outgoing, but she wasn't *not* friendly. If you approached her, she was very friendly and ingratiating. Just a very kind, very kind lady."

DID YOU KNOW?

Bounty hunter Lee nearly transforms into Freddy Krueger in *Critters 2* after spotting a full-sized cardboard cutout of the slasher. New Line Cinema, the studio responsible for both *Critters* and *A Nightmare on Elm Street*, would frequently feature these properties in other projects. In *A Nightmare on Elm Street 3*, Penelope Sudrow's Jennifer Caulfield watches *Critters* on television before Freddy morphs out of the television set to kill her.

THE GODMOTHER OF HORROR
Reflections from Lin Shaye
("Sal," *Critters* and *Critters 2*)

On Bob Shaye…

My brother Bob, who I just absolutely adore with all my heart, has really been a major forerunner in our industry and deserves way more kudos than he's received, for all he's done for young actors, young directors, and writers. So many people got their first start from Bob. He's just one of the most generous spirits and also one of the smartest producers in the business in terms of good taste, what works in terms of story, what's commercial. He was really involved in all aspects of filmmaking especially when he had first created New Line Cinema, and *Critters* was one of New Line's first projects. *A Nightmare on Elm Street* was the first movie entirely produced by New Line Cinema, they were a distribution company at first and didn't do any producing. By the time *Critters* came around, it was still kind of a new venture for Bob. I was around, kind of kicking the can around, waiting for small roles hoping to get a line or two, and I was totally fine with that. If I got a role with one line even, I was just as excited as if it were a more important role. That was just my exuberance about acting, that's still the way I feel, it's so fun and interesting.

  Critters was my first real film adventure out here in California. I remember when my brother Bob had a screening of it and he really loved the character. Everyone, it turned out, really loved Sal. I had no vision of what it was going to be or how it was going to be received. I remember later on, I was watching it with Bob, and he was always kind of a tough older brother, and when I came on screen, he elbowed me in the ribs a few times, kind of like '*Look at that, would you look at that.*' I was so proud of myself and so happy that Bob was happy. I'm so grateful to Bob for giving me the chance and having me in *Critters* and for nudging me in the ribs to let me know he was happy with my performance. Bob was such an innovator in the industry and New Line Cinema did so much for so many filmmakers and actors, Wes Craven and Johnny Depp for instance.

On M. Emmet Walsh…

So, we developed the look of this character and then Emmet Walsh led me through the gate to filmmaking. It was so much fun. Emmet Walsh as Harv, the sheriff, he's just priceless. He was so wonderful. It was really my first role of sorts, I haven't done much at that point, and Emmet would come over and was gracious enough to run through the lines with me. He really shepherded me through the scenes because I was nervous and a bit scared and I'm trying to do a great job for my big brother. I was so new to film, I really didn't understand it yet. I didn't understand pacing and really just taking your time because delivery for theater is quite different from film. There's different techniques for saying your lines in a close-up versus a master, there's just so much to learn. That's why I'll always be sweet on Emmet Wash for helping me through that first night, he knew how nervous I was. This was my first scene that was more than just one line.

On the Chiodo brothers…

The Chiodo brothers are extraordinary. They created these creatures with such detail and reverence. They had a workshop where they were building all different types of critters, with different molds and all sorts of things, and I remember going in there and seeing all different incarnations of critters; smiling ones, scary ones, big ones, half critters, and it was like walking into this fairyland of critters. It was exciting and beautiful. Their work is just exquisite. I was a happy camper.

On the early days…

I went to the University of Michigan, I was an Art History major, I didn't major in theater. I just really liked acting in plays. When I graduated college I just thought I'd end up working at the Metropolitan Museum of Art, which I did, and then it dawned on me, working in the basement, *'What am I doing down there?'* It was fascinating being able to work there though. Being able to walk through the Egyptian exhibit at eight o'clock in the morning with nobody there, I get chills just thinking about it. It's just loaded with the most amazing pieces. So I decided to go back to school and I did three years at Columbia in the theater arts program and got my fix of theater and I ended up doing theater in New York for several years.

PRODUCTION

Armed with a much larger budget and lengthier schedule, the cast and crew shot *Critters 2* on a set built on a law enforcement training site in Santa Clarita, California over the course of 38 days in late 1987. This time around, the Krites weren't restricted to the isolated, rural Brown family farm to terrorize their victims; instead, the Krites ran roughshod over the *entire* town of Grover's Bend and its townsfolk. But like *Critters*, the sequel would once again use the Chiodo brothers to design and puppeteer the Krites while Chris Biggs would design a whole new Warden Zanti (played by Mick's wife, Cynthia), handle the bounty hunter transformations, and create several additional non-Krite aliens for the film's opening sequence.

Chris Biggs designed a much larger "butthead" alien for the revamped look of Warden Zanti, this time played by Cynthia Garris. (Source: Chris Biggs)

REIMAGINING WARDEN ZANTI

An Interview with **Chris Biggs** (Part Two)

(Special Makeup Effects, *Critters* and *Critters 2*)

By the time *Critters 2* rolls around, you were formally brought in for that one, right?

Yeah, that was from day one. They called me up and said, '*Okay, we want you to do everything but the critters.*' I needed one mold for when we did the transformation of the critter into the bounty hunter. So they were very cool about that. We got the mold and did a press out of it, pointed it up, and then sculpted the things that we needed to have happening in it. Charlie and Steve and Ed were always just the best for working with. But that was a fun one. I love the opening bit, the freezer. That was just, '*Hey guys, sculpt whatever kind of an alien head you wanna do. Just go for it.*' So, you know, and some of the molds lasted forever. Some of the molds we barely got one full use out of because we were making them so quickly. I think we sculpted like 25 heads and then I went around to every makeup effects guy in town and said, '*Hey, you got any alien masks or heads or anything that's very alien looking?*' We actually have an alien from *Aliens* in there, it's in the very back. We didn't really show it because if you look carefully, you can kind of see a piece of it showing through a little bit. But, you know, they stole our idea and used it in *Predator 2*.

And did you get to design?

Oh yeah. We designed the Hexapod alien, which was the big monster bug thing, that was a big mechanical device. It was a big mechanical puppet. You see the big mechanical puppet in one shot. And then the next time you see it, it's the big floppy stunt version that lands on Charlie [Don Opper]. That was, that was a really cool design. That was one I got to draw and then I designed the new Zanti. That was fun too. When I started sculpting it, it was just after Halloween and Greg Cannom had done what in our industry we call a butthead alien. The bulbous head alien and he had done one that was like *Twilight Zone* or something and it was really huge. It was a big hit. It was probably two and a half feet across, maybe two feet tall. So I started sculpting and my sculpture had gotten to a point where I just roughed it in and it was about the same size as Greg's makeup.

And everyone just stops, and is like, '*You gotta beat Greg, you gotta go bigger, you gotta go a lot bigger*'. So I beat through it. It went okay. I made it just monstrous. And Mick Garris, the director, his wife wanted to be in the movie in the worst way, so he made sure it *was* the worst way. She would play Zanti. And her life cast was her standing with her arms at her side. We did her body cast that way because we weren't going to use her arms in any way she had before. They were going to be puppet arms. And then she had a really long, thin neck, which was great. So the prosthetic that's on her neck is probably like an eighth of an inch thick. It's just so thin and willowy. And then the head, of course, was this monster.

So we did this giant sculpture piece, which we broke down into three or four pieces. It was the head, which was a poly foam latex piece. And then we had a face piece that was glued on her and then onto the head piece. And we hid the dividing line in the wrinkles of the forehead and the sides of the head and all that stuff. And then there was a chin. It was like the upper lip, face, and then lower lip, chin. And I used these like two inch ball bearings for the eyes when I sculpted it. And Mick had come in and seen the ball bearings, and said, '*Silver eyes, wow, that's a great idea*.' So we polished them all up and she had to stand there and she couldn't move her body. We lightened it up in the first makeup test we did on her. It was like she couldn't lift her head up. So we had to hollow all the poly foam out of it and make it so it was just being held together by sheer will. So she could now move her head around because, otherwise it was just too heavy for her. But she couldn't move because she couldn't see and she could only breathe out of her mouth. She was in that for about 4 hours. The great thing was that we pre-painted everything so all we had to do is just glue it down and everything blended into each other. So there was really no working and making edges disappear. They all fell right into a wrinkle. It was really great. She got out of it and said, '*Yep, okay, uh, fuck you all very much*' (laughs). On top of that, she was claustrophobic. I didn't know any of that until we did our life cast. She comes out of it and then it's like a panic attack. And luckily Mick was there when we were doing the cast, he just held her hand the whole time. But that was what she said to me, '*Well I wanted to be in this in the worst way, and made sure it was.*' (laughs)

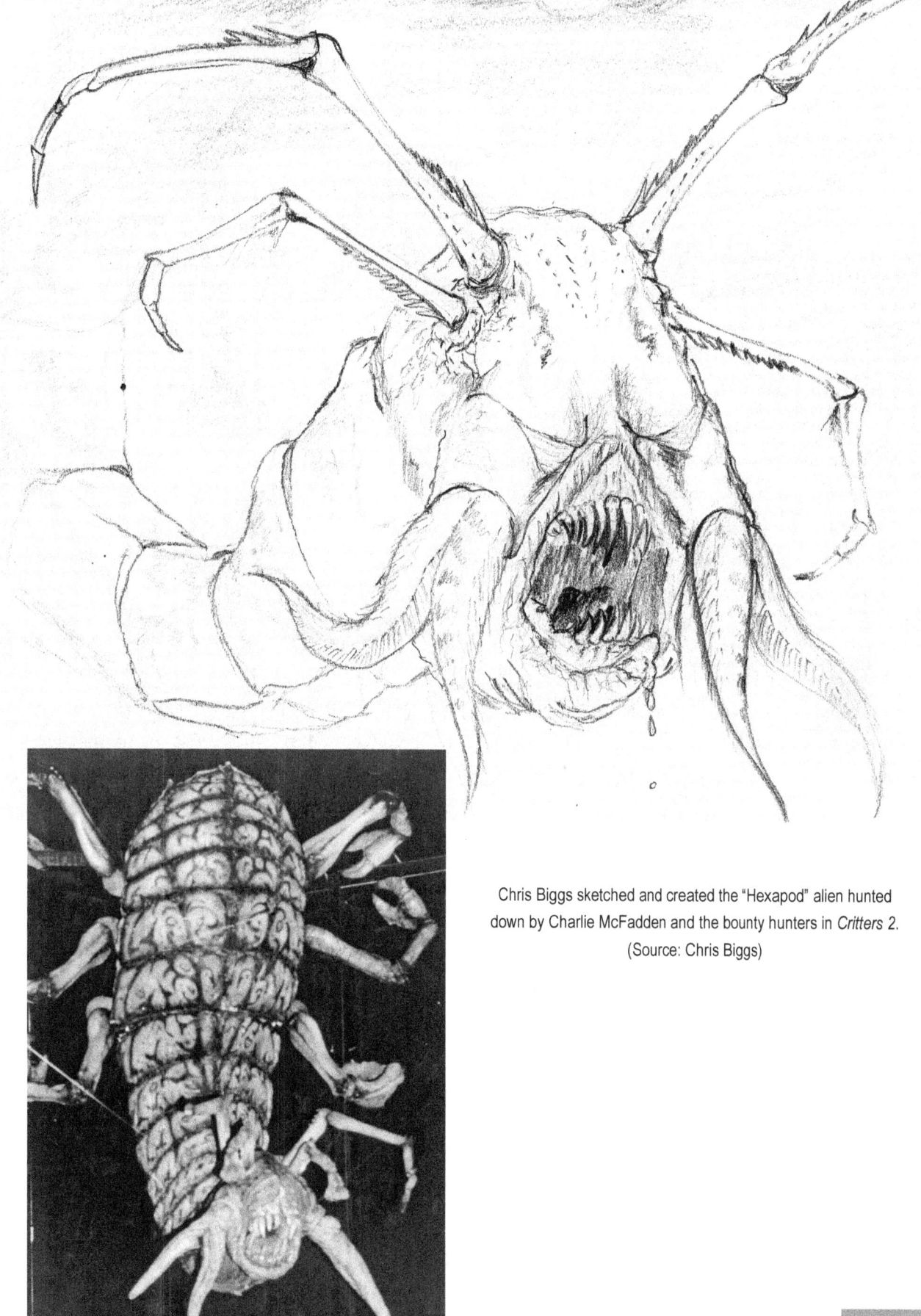

Chris Biggs sketched and created the "Hexapod" alien hunted down by Charlie McFadden and the bounty hunters in *Critters 2*. (Source: Chris Biggs)

I mean, clearly, like, the second one was a much different experience…

Oh yeah, we had a lot more fun with it. We knew what we were doing. Some of the wounds, the old farmer guy. I had his eyeball hanging out, you know, the top of his skull was ripped off. But my favorite one to this day, and I've got a friend of mine who didn't know me until maybe 10 years ago, and she had always been enamored with all the movies I'd worked on. You know, she was a fan, and it was kind of strange having her tell me that the one gag that I did in there that was such a throwaway was the one thing that terrified her the most in the movie, which was the big critter ball. It rolls over the guy and it leaves the bloody skeleton behind. When we shot that, the right foot was just off camera. So we just had the ball floating over the top of it on our rig. So when they pushed the ball off, I just grabbed the right foot and gave it a wiggle. And it moved the whole skeleton. It's like a twitch. And to this day, they're like, '*What kind of mechanism did you use?*' And I was like, '*Uh, wires?*' (laughs) I don't know, it was one of those scientific skeletons you buy for 150 bucks that are all plastic and we dressed it up with cotton latex and it was all jointed already, and we just laid it down on the ground.

The funny thing is we shot this in a studio with about a 25 foot square piece of sod. It was shot on stage. We were shooting so many pickups that day. This was an add-on. This was not one that was in the script originally. We need to see a victim of the critter ball. Because up to that point, you just see it rolling around. You don't see it doing anything. Basically a big weather balloon that they had glued little critter faces on and that had stayed inflated. I think it was like ten feet across. I mean it was huge.

And then they had the close-up one, which was puppet faces. They're all little mechanisms. And then they had the big roller ball that was on a rig so that they could literally pull it across, you know, so like they wanted to see the ball just spinning and stuff like that. They could just start spinning it. They could have it for close-ups of the camera and hitting it. That's the one we used because we were going to see the edges because it had holes coming out the sides, you know, going onto these rigs that were on wheels. But that's what we used for the skeleton gag. That one turned out the best. That's one of my favorite things, because everyone thinks it's like this really involved mechanism. And it's just like, I grab the foot and shook. You know, sometimes just the toothpick makes a difference. Mechanical makeup effects are always held together with duct tape and toothpicks (laughs).

What would you say were some of the biggest challenges that you faced on *Critters 2*? Or was it fairly smooth?

The Zanti head and the Hexapod bug were the two biggest gags. The transformation from the critter to the bounty hunter, and then when the bounty hunter loses his shit, that was an insert shot. What we did when the bounty hunter loses his shit – we started with the actor, and we had him standing up, and I used a 16mm projector, and we filmed a lot of the alien masks on heads we'd made. We filmed those early on and lined them all up. God, I'm glad we had the DP on that. Russ Carpenter, he's a fucking brilliant man. I've worked with him on like three different films, but the guys who did that was fucking brilliant. He lined it up with – when we shot it on stage – with the heads, and then we were on location up in Santa Clarita, and we lined the projector up, had an XY, like a cross at the first part of the projection. And so we got the head perfectly lined up with that, ran the projection while we were filming it from like two different angles. And it was just a series of heads flashing across. We started with the actor projecting on his face and then cut to this other head that was just kind of like his life cast with a balloon on top of it, it was like vacuumed on. And then we let the vacuum go and it sort of pushes out into the shape of the bounty hunter heads. And then the rest of it was just bladders pushing up and down inside the head and projection on the faces, going through images of creatures. It worked really well.

The other one was the female bounty hunter transformation, that was a fun one. She [Roxanne Kernohan] came in and we did a body cast of her and head cast and everything. She called me about a week later and she had the body cast all raked up and said, '*I'm not happy with the nipples.*' I was like, '*What? What do you mean? They're your nipples.*' She explained to us the nipples were all crinkled up and that they wouldn't look that way, they'd be more relaxed. She had us replace them on the body cast that we had. So the scene where she tears out of the clothes, you see the nipples, right? Funny thing was, that the day they shot that scene, it was so cold out that her nipples were not particularly relaxed anyway. I mean it was *cold*; the crew gift was thermal socks with *Critters 2* written on them. We were freezing our asses off up there. We were on top of a hill in Santa Clarita in November and when it wasn't raining it was colder than fuck. It actually snowed up there a couple of times. They built that entire town from scratch. It was all built on top of a hill. And the church and all the buildings and everything because they had to blow it all up. The thing was that because they were building these things, they were all fly walls. And so it's like the interiors were actually exterior, you know. None of them were on stages. All the buildings were real buildings. The church had a real interior that they shot in. The farmer, his barn was shot in a different location, because it wasn't in town. It was supposed to be outside of town. The entire town was built and they built it like a real town. In fact, we used one of the stores as our shop. So we had all our stuff right there prepped ready to go. They only bring what they're shooting for the day and we just had everything there.

And your experience working with Mick, sounded like it was a really great one.

Oh yeah, yeah, we're still friends. I mean, every time I see him, it's like, *'Oh my god, how are you doing?'* In fact, they had a screening of *Critters 2*. It was like one of the anniversaries or something like that, and he called me up and said, *'Dude, we're going to screen the thing.'* He says, *'They don't have you on the list of speakers, but I'll fix that.'* So, yeah, he got me into the movie, got to see the movie, but my wife had never seen it, so it was the first time she got to see it. She's always kind of like, *'Ehhh.'* She said, *'That's actually quite funny.'* I said, *'Yeah, that's the point.'* I was just sitting in the audience and he called me up and said, *'Come on down.'* And we all sat on the edge of the thing and passed microphones back and forth. It was a nice evening.

In conclusion, Chris, has anything else come to mind for either of the two projects?

One of my favorite make-ups of the whole film, which was just a little throwaway, is... the guy who played the father in the film, Sam Anderson, gets zapped in the neck with a critter dart. I had this great book of skin disease and I had another book that was great, of forensic pathology, but I had one that was just on insect bites. And I found this one, it was like a little blood clot with this big nasty clear boil around it, so I did that, and it was all gelatin and it's one of the most disturbing looking pieces ever. It was because it looked real. It was translucent but it looked like there was something growing inside of it. There's all these weird colors and it kind of goes off like octopus tentacles. It's still one of my favorites. It was just such a throwaway because I sculpted it in like one afternoon, you know, not even an afternoon, I think I sculpted it in about 25 minutes, threw a mold on it, and then I decided at that point that I was going to go with gelatin. And so I painted a little thin coat of clear in, and painted some of the gelatin with some colors, things like that, and then laid another layer of clear in, and then made a little grape-sized blood nodule with some of the blood, but purple and blue and stuff like that, and I laid that inside that, and then poured more clear, more little veins coming off of it, did the layers, and I only made the one piece because it only had to shoot once. I spent more time on it than I did on actually [applying it]. The application was like glue it, blend it, done. Because it was clear mostly and it was just like tinted. And so it looked just like skin that had been discolored. And because it was picking up his skin tones underneath it. Like foam latex, you're dealing with a white surface. It's opaque. It's white. You've got to spend hours painting it to make it look like it's not opaque. It's got some translucency to it. The new silicone stuff is brilliant for that. I still haven't seen things where they're using silicone with things inside of it. They're using skins for textures and things like that.

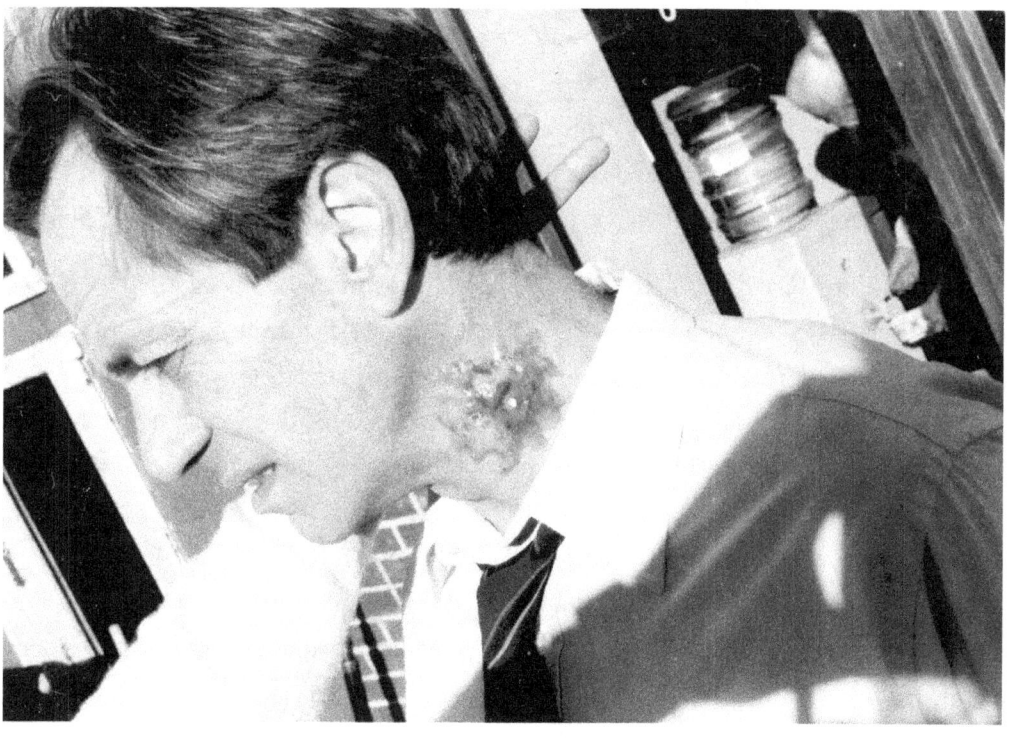

The festering wound on actor Sam Anderson's neck was a gag Chris Biggs found particularly delightful to work on. (Source: Chris Biggs)

Initially, the production sought to shoot on location in the Midwest using a real town, but harsh weather and logistics changed the plan and the production designer was tasked with dressing a dilapidated law enforcement facility not far from where the original *Critters* was shot.

"We argued on *Critters 2*. We just lost a lot of arguments with New Line," recalls Barry Opper. "We had built a whole town from scratch. We didn't go on a sound stage, we built the structures you saw there. We were thinking we could use it again for other projects or perhaps another *Critters*. I'm convinced they should've keep that set up. This as an old Roger Corman idea, that money you invest in one movie, you use again and again. So when New Line decided to destroy the town, which was our Grover's Bend, which we never really saw in *Critters*, except for the bowling alley and the police station, we were very disappointed. Rupert and I were thinking it would leave room to shoot further *Critters* movies on, if they ever decided to do more, but after *Critters 2* was not a financial success, I think they decided never to do another *Critters* again, at least at that time. So they let the town be destroyed. We were arguing, '*Look, even if you don't shoot any further* Critters *movies, that's a western town. You could use it for any number of films*.'"

Fresh off of *Killer Klowns from Outer Space* and working alongside the Chiodos, Philip Dean Foreman served as the production designer for *Critters 2* and was tasked with building the entire town setting for Grover's Bend. Foreman had previously served as the art director on *Critters* and his talents were limitless. The location used as Grover's Bend actually served as a training facility for the sheriff's department and other law enforcement agencies in Santa Clarita. The sprawling campus included several low standing concrete and brick structures and warehouses. These structures were meticulously dressed to resemble Main Street in Grover's Bend. The myriad of storefronts included a hardware store, hay and feed store, mercantile company, bank, bar and pool hall, the newspaper office, a fast-food burger joint, sheriff's office, pharmacy, welder's shop, gas station, TV repair shop, and a hillside church that was built entirely from scratch.

With Foreman onboard, he assembled a team of competent and like-minded artists who he knew could manage the rapid pace and devotion required to transform the styleless training grounds into the town square of Grover's Bend. Among those tapped for the challenge, Mick Strawn, another New Line Cinema talent and close friend of Foreman. The effort would be plagued by unseasonably cold temperatures and dangerously high winds, of which damaged many of the initial façades used in building the town. Nevertheless, the crew persevered over the course of 5 weeks and completed the designs, constructed the façades and signage, painted, and dressed the town center.

A church and main street in Grover's Bend was built around existing structures on a law enforcement training facility in Santa Clarita, California. (Source: Bradford Plows and James Belohovek)

GROVER'S BEND
TOWN MAP

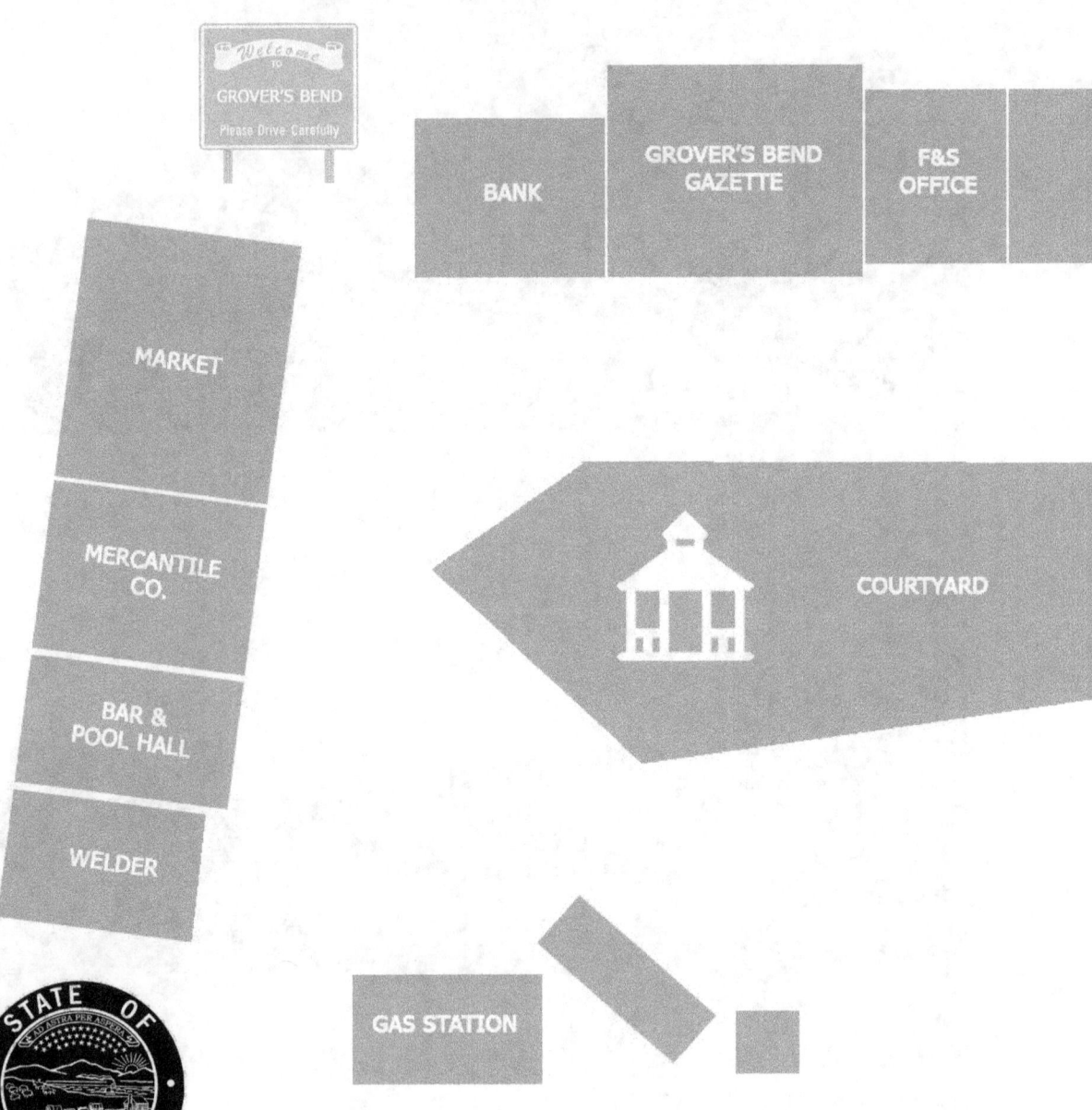

Welcome TO GROVER'S BEND
Please Drive Carefully

BANK

GROVER'S BEND GAZETTE

F&S OFFICE

MARKET

MERCANTILE CO.

BAR & POOL HALL

WELDER

COURTYARD

STATE OF KANSAS

GAS STATION

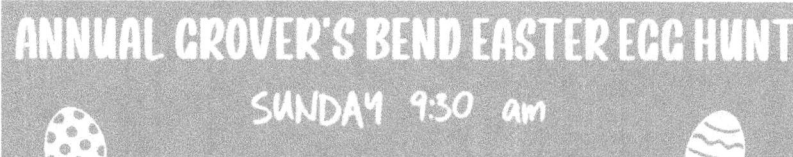

ANNUAL GROVER'S BEND EASTER EGG HUNT
SUNDAY 9:30 am

SIMMONS CO.

BARBER

PETERSON HARDWARE & PUMPS

TV REPAIR

CHURCH

FARM SUPPLY & FEED

PHARMACY

LAND COMPANY

SHERIFF

THE HUNGRY HEIFER

TRACTOR REPAIR

N
W E
S

BUILDING GROVER'S BEND
An Interview with **Mick Strawn**
(Town Construction Coordinator, *Critters 2*)

Going back to the prep for *Critters 2*, you noted that you know you had some connections at New Line and it was Philip Dean Foreman that called you up in somewhat of a crisis mode to assist with building the town of Grover's Bend?

Trust me when I say Philip [Dean Foreman] won't talk to anybody about this at all. He just doesn't believe in it for some reason. I mean, I talk to Philip from time to time, he's living in New Mexico. He bought himself a large crumbled down hotel in Albuquerque and he's been rebuilding it one room at a time. So that's what he's doing these days. I keep going to him, you know, '*Is there anything that would get you to come out and join me at shows and doing interviews?*' And he says '*No.*' I have become the unofficial spokesman for our work in a way. (laughs)

So for *Critters 2,* around that time, I worked a lot of projects over at New Line Cinema. I got called up by Philip and he was saying that basically they had a town that they were going to do, now this is back in the Midwest. I think it came out that we started in September or maybe a little later, I'm going to say, and because what happened was they had a town that they were going to do this in, right? Where they were going to burn things, they were going to have explosions and all the rest of that, and the town was basically empty. And it was in the Midwest somewhere. And all of a sudden they had the worst winter that they had had in like 40 years. And so the town was completely under the snow. The thing is you have to understand, if you live in L.A., your concept that the rest of the country occasionally has things like snow and shit like that, it just surprises the hell out of everybody in L.A.. They go, '*Oh my god, what disaster happened? Oh, weather, oh, I see, okay, I gotcha.*' I mean, people in L.A. just don't think about the weather ever. It's not required. My son, up until he finally went on a trip to go up into the mountains when he was like 16, and he was so surprised by real snow because he'd spent so much time on set with fake snow. That real snow is nothing to write home about. It really is. It sucks. So, they had a big snowstorm in the Midwest and had to find somewhere else. So, they came up with this location [in Santa Clarita] and Philip and I had to build an entire town. They had this – think of a classroom, right? Think of a school. And the thing is, everything in Bouquet Canyon was basically facing the other way from where we were and where we were going to build. So we built it in the parking lot using one row of low buildings that they had there already and we built some façades on top of them. As you come into town you see the Hungry Heifer right? We built that from scratch and the tower of buildings on the right – if you went to the street on the right, you have the printing press and all the buildings like the bank and all the rest of that. Those were the façades that were attached to buildings for the school. And the big main block of buildings was all up the side. And then as you came back all the way around, then you were looking at a field that looked out into the canyon country area, which was very sparsely populated back then. And then you had the church that we built from scratch. And then the buildings on the right, you know, the ones that were close to the side that the Hungry Heifer was on, we built all those buildings too.

Holy shit…

So we built all that in five weeks. Now here's the thing. I sat down and designed it. I pulled together everybody I had used at New Line. A lot of the people that I used at Renaissance and stuff, I just pulled together everybody and put them on it. Because they lost the town location in the Midwest and they need to start building in five weeks. So I said, '*Okay, I'll just get everybody together.*' And there were so many foibles of doing that so fast, but we just started in, right? We just started and we got it done. We had bad winds, so we had to go up and cut holes in everything and put pieces of screen in it so that the wind could blow through it. Luckily, we never had anything go down, but we had a lot of cables completely snapped and then had to replace them with bigger cables.

It was a challenge, including one day when we were up there building and the school that they had up there had been abandoned for a long period of time. And so, I guess whoever let us use that area and let us start building there hadn't bothered to cancel the FBI training seminar that they had on one given weekend. Literally canisters with tear gas come into my office. My office was one of the buildings that was there, right? And we had put a façade on it. And the other side of the school was literally being attacked by FBI people coming across it. So this bomb comes in and we're running out, and as we're running out, we're running out into these, you know, you can imagine what they look like, right? The face masks and the suits and the vests and all the shit was like, '*What the fuck are we doing here?*' Well, '*What the fuck are* you *doing here?*' (laughs)

Wow, that is wild…

The thing I learned about tear gas is that tear gas is kind of forever, man. I mean, that's some shit. And it destroyed my clothes. We essentially had to go naked and then wear a bunch of their clothes for the rest of the day. They're like tiny uniforms and shit. You know this white paper material. So we had a day where we were all wearing those white paper outfits. But you know, it all gets done, it always gets done. Somebody once asked me, he said, '*What is it like when you're under pressure from, as an art department, what happens when you're not done?*' I said, '*Well, I don't know. Someday I'll find out though.*'

Five weeks, a massive town to build, large amounts of crew members – did you feel like you had the right amount of resources, material, and people to do like what you had envisioned?

That is such an interesting way to put it. Because it was Philip and I together, we're literally drawing things as fast as we possibly could. It was like one of those things where if you put a wall down, there was always somebody right over your shoulder that was gonna go build that wall immediately. To erase a line, you can't just erase that line. The wall or the signage was already being built and prepped for painting as fast as we were laying down the designs. So to say that there was a great deal of thought put into it – like it was just one thing spilling over the other that you called every happy accident your own.

Then occasionally you blame things on the fact that you are doing it that fast, but I remember one time when we were finishing the church, we had put down grass. We had put down grass all across the front of that, and we hadn't put the front window in because we hadn't built the big front window of the church. I got up there with the guys, and I figured, '*Well, I can understand we can't get any equipment on the grass. Let's do this. We'll get one of the 80 foot condors and we'll get it to the side and we'll just swing the window in.*' That turned out to be kind of problematic because I was up there with the guys swinging in because it was towards the end when it was all hands on deck. So, no more climbing, we're just getting it done. I remember swinging that window in and the flex of the crane – it was one of the older condors that we had and the flex on the head of it at

80 feet sideways was intense. We came in, like swinging it in, and pressed stop, but we got it right where we wanted it. And the flex in the arm literally pushed me and the guy that was holding it through the window in place, right? I'm stabling it, stabling it, and doing that roll, right? I ain't got that shit! I was like, '*Quick! Look, I know they tried to kill us and all, but grab a screw gun and get that thing in place now! Before the trident comes flying!*' (laughs) When I see the film today, I have to tell you, there is one thing that really just bugs the hell out of me. We were doing it so fast that we didn't have any glass cut for anything. We just used plexiglass, any type we could get our hands on. And in the end, we used cheap plexiglass for the windows on the Hungry Heifer. And the outside, it was that six-sided building and it had glass all the way around it, but it had plexiglass. It was cheap plexiglass. You can see the big waves in it. Bugs the shit out of me. But you know there are these things that like only I would go right to and be like, '*Oh, brother.*'

In the script I have, which is listed as the third draft, back then it was still called Happy Cow…

Yeah, it came out as the Hungry Heifer in the end. I got to tell you, I can't remember because the thing is, we would build the sign for it, and as fast as we finished it, we'd have to redo it with another name. It literally changed names every 2 days. See, back then the process of getting a name approved by a lawyer took forever because you didn't have the internet. So, they would have to get clearance on things and there was a promotions departments that went in and made sure that you didn't call something a name that already existed. Because somebody that owned a particular name could come in and there'd be litigation. So literally every two days, we would be building a new sign for the Hungry Heifer. We just had all these signs like in some of the spaces that we had storage. Because you know that the whole interior of the whole middle building was just our storage, and it was loaded with these signs. It was just like one restaurant name right after the other all the way down. '*There's another one, and another one, and another one.*' (laughs)

DID YOU KNOW?

Cynthia Garris, wife of sequel director Mick Garris and a musician in her own right, not only donned the massive prosthetic appliance to play Warden Zanti in the film's opener, but she also wrote and performed the jingle heard playing throughout the Hungry Heifer restaurant and the final credits sequence.

Building this all in 5 weeks, it sounds like you guys were in fifth gear the entire time.

You know, when you do what I do for a living, you do things and then you're a specialist at that and then you never do exactly that thing again ever. For instance, I worked on *Runaway Train*. I'll tell you what I can do with an actual locomotive GP40; I can actually operate the braking system standing beside the railroad. I can run that fucking thing up and down exactly like it's a real train as long as I'm the one that's rigged the whole damn thing right, and I know that because I've done it before. I did it for *Runaway Train*. And you know how many people have hired me to rewire a GP40 since? Take a guess?

Two?

No! Of course not. Never! See what I'm saying? So what you were asking is, when somebody normally wants somebody to come in and build a façade of a 1950s town for a movie, what would it normally take? I would guess that 5 weeks is pretty goddamn fast.

In terms of working with Philip Dean Foreman, that sounded like it was a pretty positive experience.

Oh yeah, I love Philip. Philip and I worked on and off together for three or four years. Actually, I came in one time, I think in the middle of the 90s, and redesigned and acted as a contractor to redo his bathroom at his house in Venice.

***Critters 2* was one of Mick Garris's earlier directorial efforts. What was it like working with him?**

I had more interaction with Mick Garris on *Freddy's Nightmares* than I did on *Critters 2*, oddly enough. He's a really nice guy, but he's kind of a quieter guy. As a person, I'm a very flamboyant person and he is not; he's kind of a quieter person. I don't tend to remember the quiet people. But I battled with the Chiodo brothers quite a bit. I went nose to nose with the Chiodos. I had about 20 to 25 people in the middle of the town all working off of this one huge generator. They came up and started unplugging everyone's cables so they could plug their stuff in. We just didn't get off to a great start.

But the greatest thing was they came up and they had a version of the critter ball, probably the first version of it. It was made out of these metal tubes, kind of like a geodesic dome with these little aluminum spars that were kind of screwed into place. They had glued all of these critter faces to it and they were gonna roll it down the hill as a test. Me and my crew all lined up to watch because I wanted to see this circus. So, they put the critter ball up on the top of the hill, and this thing is like seven feet tall or bigger, and they lose control of it right away. They were testing it on this grass hill, you can actually see these grassy hills in the film. Well, the ball is rolling down that hill. They lose control of it. And basically, now they're all running behind it. And as they run behind it, the ball is starting to compress. It would bounce. And then the aluminum would just twist. So at the top of the hill it was seven feet. By the bottom of the hill it was the size of a basketball. Critters are flying off left and right. I am sure that today I can go to that hill and I could point at where that one was and there's probably still critters somewhere in that fucking field.

We had storms, we had everything that you could imagine but everything in there was built by us. I did come back at one point during filming. And I would, from time to time, you know, I would be a production designer, but that would only do about six months a year for me. Marty Bresin, who did the pyro for *Critters 2*, he just gives me a call and he says '*Hey listen, why don't you come in, this is your design and you know this layout really well.*' He asked me to come up and help him wire up these explosions and fires and stuff for like 2 days. So one day we pre-rigged everything and we had all these different explosions, I think it was the meat-packing factory. That big explosion there, at the end of it, we were filming that and Marty was such a goofball. You know, he's one of those guys that at no time in life did you ever shake his hand right because he would fucking have a buzzer ring on his finger (laughs). So, we wire all this up to explode, and we wire it all back to all our looms, our wiring looms all come back to the printing press room.

So we're sitting in the printing press room, and he's telling me a story. And the wiring isn't really done yet, the loom isn't even hooked up, he doesn't even have it hooked up to his battery box. And he picks up his radio and says, '*I'm ready, we're ready, we're completely ready. Okay, go ahead and roll cameras.*' And then he continued to tell me the story. And he's telling me the story, and in the meantime, I hear the radio go, '*Okay, roll on camera one. Roll on camera two, three, four. Action!*' And he's been telling me this story all along, right? He picks up the radio and he says, '*Uh, cut. We have a problem here. I'm going to have to check it again. Go ahead and cut. Cut. Let's reset.*' And so he goes, '*Oh, Mick, excuse me.*' And he'd go out and he'd do like this acting thing, acting, right? He'd pick up the loom and he'd look at it, go down about 10 feet, and pick up some more of it, and he'd look at it. And then he'd say into the radio, '*Okay, everybody, we're live, we have live exposures in here. You guys just stay clear.*' Then he'd go in the building and fuck around, I don't know what the hell he did, and then he'd come back like 5 minutes later and says, '*Okay I think we got it all worked out.*' He then starts telling me the rest of the story and nothing's wired, you know, nothing's hooked up. He's like, '*Go ahead, start rolling.*' And they're rolling, camera one, camera two, and he goes, '*Hey, Mick, hold on a sec, I've got this thing to fix here.*'

And he'd go out and he'd do his acting thing again, you know, go through and look for wire, and all the time he's like hyping it up. He says, '*Okay, everybody, so we don't know what's going on.*' He'd go back into that building, and come back minutes later, and then he'd say into the radio, '*Okay, we're ready to go.*' He comes back in, hooks it up, and then he blows it. And I'm sitting there, and I go, '*Well, what the fuck was that all about?*' And he goes, '*I just wanted to make sure they really,* really *wanted it. That's all.*' I didn't know what to say after that, you know? (laughs)

Oh my gosh, that's incredible. You know, you guys also faced, well, at least during filming, did the weird cold weather snap affect you guys?

Yeah. We were just fighting these horrible winds, and all the time we're trying to keep these big façades up that were made in five weeks. Seriously. Built in five weeks, down in 15 seconds is what I used to think all the time as I'm looking around, going '*Wow.*' Because I remember walking between two of the buildings, and we had 70 mile per hour winds. And a 2x4 just kicked itself up and just went in over right past me. I was like, '*Wow.*' Luckily that 2x4 didn't have my name on it. I know we fought it all the time that we were up there. It was pretty brutal. And here it is, we were supposed to be filming for springtime, it takes place at Easter time. And it just wasn't that late in the year. And what kind of weather do we get in L.A. anyway? I mean, let's face it, the L.A. basin isn't exactly known for 70 mile per hour winds.

Daytime temperatures were somewhat regular, but nighttime was totally frigid, right?

Yeah, yeah. But luckily I wasn't around at night. So they finally made a big axle for the critter ball and ran it around with two trucks on the sides that moved it. So they fixed that. We managed not to kill anybody. Nothing fell on anybody. And only half of my crew ever got hit by tear gas. So in the end, I'll have to say that it's still a win for us.

In terms of seeing the finished film for the first time, and then perhaps years later and stuff, have your impressions of it changed at all over the years or still really satisfied?

I like it a lot. I think that it stands out as being kind of the most family-friendly in a way. The rest of them seem a lot darker and *Critters 2* had its own, I want to say, quaint likability to it, as far as horror films go. I was production designer on *A Nightmare on Elm Street 3* and *4*, and I think Philip actually worked on the first *Critters*. The town we built for *Critters 2* kind of has both of our aesthetics together at the same time. I mean it really does. When you think of the way that *A Nightmare on Elm Street 3* and *4* looked and then you think of the way that the original *Critters* looked and you mash those looks together and I think you actually get *Critters 2*. Because it stands out a little bit different from the third *Critters* and it stands out very differently from the first one.

That's something that I had always thought about. And I think the end product just speaks volumes of the synergy on set and how so many great things kind of were pulled together and it all worked out despite those environmental factors, like the odd weather. And it still looks awesome all these years later…

I have to say that it looks shockingly good. It looks, it is a completely convincing film. Kudos to Russ Carpenter, who shot *Critters 2* and went on to do things like *Titanic* and the *Avatar* films, just one amazing thing after the other. I worked with Russ on *A Nightmare on Elm Street 4* actually, he did some second unit work. You know it's really strange because you sit down and over the years you realize that, '*Wow, I have these connections and I've worked with these people.*' It's just fascinating.

SCALING UP THE KRITES

The Chiodo brothers, who had just completed their production of *Killer Klowns from Outer Space*, returned to *Critters 2* with even bigger and better ideas for the Krites and various gags. This time around, the Chiodos and their team built over 50 puppets, including 22 background puppets, four special function puppets and four different close-up puppets, a massive 10-foot critter ball, a variety of stunt puppets and single-use puppets, as well as a special rig that involved up to 30 moving critter puppets. Just about everything involving the puppets was scaled up, from the overall size of each individual puppet, enlarging the eyes, to a more robust use of motorized rigs and animatronics to articulate the movement of the puppets instead of cable controls. However, gone from the production design were the moose pelts; this time the Krite puppets would be punched with more flexible synthetic fur to enhance the overall durability of the puppet. *Critters 2* also introduced baby Krites (rod puppets) as well as gags that allowed individual Krites to become distinct and recognizable, such as "Baldy," a Krite who loses his scalp in a close call with a cannon blast.

"The first thing we did was we made the puppets a little bit bigger," explains Stephen Chiodo. "They were so small, and I would get cramps in my hands trying to make it go, so we just made them maybe 25 percent bigger, just a little bit. So we could actually get more movement out of the characters. More room for mechanics. Actually we separated the head from the body. So we had this boning type structure for the body and then the head was separate from that. So the head would move against the body instead of having the head move with the body as a single unit."

"We redesigned the body structure," agrees Edward Chiodo. "Instead of foam latex skin supporting all the fur and everything, we designed more of a traditional puppet fabrication where it was a hooped construction of fabric that was far more flexible. We also went with National Fiber Tech, known as NFT, it's synthetic fur, you know, woven onto specific nets, so you can get different densities, different blends and stuff. So that's the look that was established in *Critters 2*. But synthetic fur is synthetic. Some of it looks really good. It's far more flexible, but yeah, it didn't have quite the same look as the moose pelts used in *Critters*."

Although the larger Krites would be assembled incorporating the newer synthetic furs, the baby Krites would use authentic rabbit pelts to establish a fluffier, pre-molting look. "I believe it was real rabbit fur," recalls Stephen Chiodo. "The baby critters didn't flex and move as much, especially as far as the head moving against the body went. It didn't really have that kind of mobility, so it didn't matter. So the actual rabbit pelt didn't infringe on the movement of those characters. It

A majestic Stephen Chiodo prepares to work with a bigger and better Krite hero puppet in *Critters 2*.
(Source: Bradford Plows)

gave them kind of a fluffier, gentle look." The Chiodos acquired the pelts from legitimate sources, including Bischoff's Taxidermy in Los Angeles, though both Stephen and Edward agreed that using real fur these days would most likely not be an option.

To make it all happen, the Chiodo brothers established a workshop inside the structure used to portray the Grover's Bend hardware store, allowing the team to rebuild, repair, clean up, and tinker with the many stunt puppets and rigs used for the production. (The Grover's Bend general store, by contrast, served as the production office.) The workshop also provided much needed relief from the unbearably cold temperatures and heavy winds.

Another creative addition to the franchise is the giant critter ball, an idea devised by Mick Garris during the initial script rewrite. The giant critter ball involved critters clinging together in groups of three or four to make a larger critter and eventually, a massive entwined mass of critters as a single unit. This culminates with the film's climax when the horde of critters – now hundreds strong – link together to make an enormous 10-foot diameter critter ball, a difficult and complex design that evolved through trial-and-error. The initial script called for a nearly 30-foot diameter critter ball, a design that would have been impossible to pull off. The Chiodos demonstrated the more practically sized 10-foot critter ball as a prototype, which the production quickly agreed to, but the logistics of the ball and its various iterations were no easy task.

"By the time *Critters 2* came along, we had a better shop, more tools, and hired more people. Actually, the guy that did the giant critter ball, his name was Jarn Heil. He was from the first company I worked for; he was the shop foreman that left," explained Dwight Roberts. Heil, who also worked with the Chiodo brothers on *Killer Klowns from Outer Space*, was hired to design and construct the articulating 10-foot critter ball. The most intricate of the designs

DID YOU KNOW?

For years, rumors persisted that the Chiodo brothers designed the Krite eggs in *Critters 2* after the Central American fruit known as cherimoya, or custard apple. Although textual similarities certainly exist between the fruit and the eggs, it remains pure coincidence. Charlie Chiodo designed the Krite eggs around a general conception of an alligator egg and added a scale pattern to the final product, which offered some dimensionality and uniqueness compared to the otherwise smooth surface of a true alligator egg.

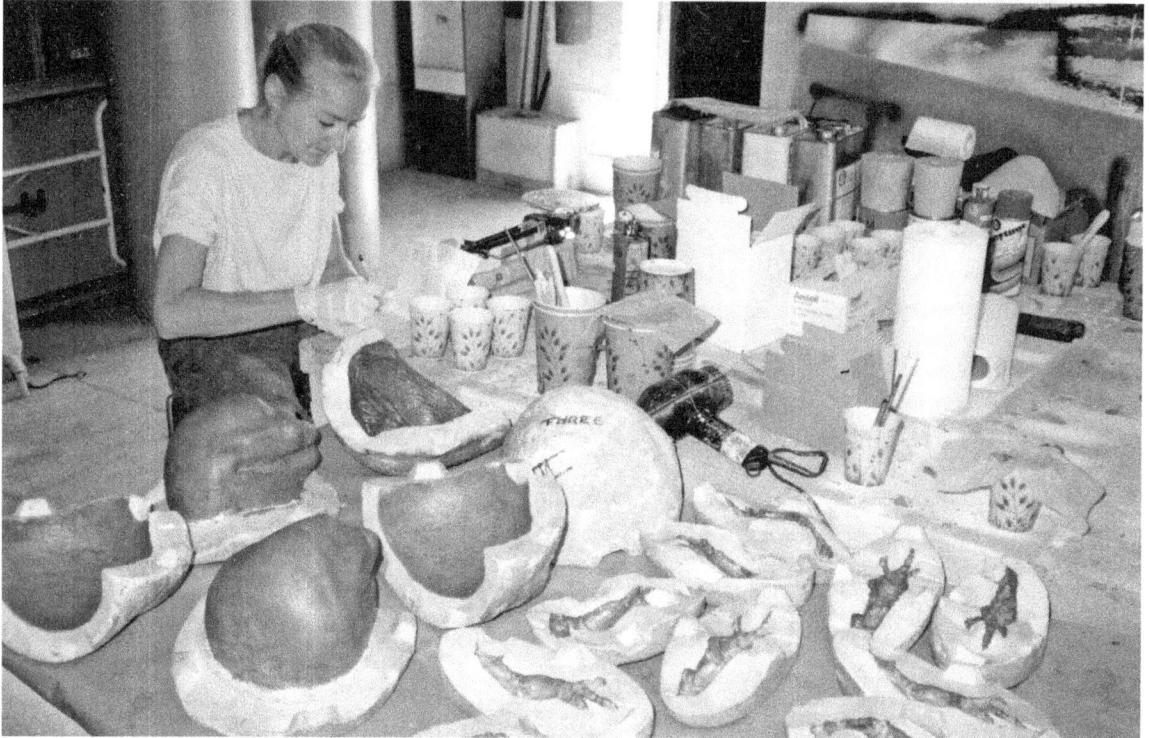

Girl Power: Deborah Galvez (top) and Ans Ellis (bottom) were instrumental in creating the look and texture of the Krites used in *Critters 2*. (Source: Bradford Plows)

involved a 10-foot wide aluminum frame with nearly 300 critter faces and bodies attached to it, with many of the critter faces having blinking eyes and snapping jaws. For the heavy ball to move, a rudimentary axle was run through the center of the ball, but early tests were not promising and the sheer weight of the design began to crush the fragile critter faces and damage the working eyes and jaw mechanisms."

"The giant critter ball was a brilliant idea. Again, making the monster bigger at the end, that's a great concept," Stephen Chiodo says. "And we went through a couple of variations on how that was going to be manipulated. We made a geodesic dome. We put two aluminum geodesic domes together and kind of built our critters around that. And then we built an inflatable critter ball that was a weather balloon with critters laminated on the outside. And we kind of pushed that around. Marty Bresin, the effects stunt coordinator, wanted to get a little dune buggy and kind of bump it. But we weren't getting the effect that we needed, not the reliability. So Marty built a yoke, a rig that went onto the camera crane. And we actually were able to shoot above it, around it, below it, as this thing was rolling on its own by the camera car. Which made a lot of great coverage. And we also had another technique. We had a rod that would go through the critter ball and maybe four or five feet out the other side. And then we would have puppeteers actually holding that rod, holding that bar, and pushing it. And they were off camera. So you wouldn't see the people back there. And that was a way that we kind of rolled up. But even that was limited as far as the coverage you can get out of it."

"Marty's solution with the rig was superior," admits Edward Chiodo. "Marty built an outrigger that went through the axle of our ball, so he was able to sling it out there. And again, Mick had wanted to do his *Ben-Hur* sequence. So with that rig Marty came up with, we were able to get that. It's funny, the first night we used it, because originally we were supposed to be able to push and roll it. And the first night we did that, we found out that it wasn't really stable enough to do that. And actually some of it broke. And the mechanism in the battery inside shorted out. There was this little fire inside the ball, and I had to go inside the ball to disconnect the battery. Otherwise, the thing would have caught fire and burned. I ended up in the hospital that night because the foam we used was, when it burns, it gives off like a cyanide vapor, a toxic gas. So they took me to the hospital to make sure I didn't have any smoke inhalation issues."

The critter ball, once completed, involved enormous amounts of various and very toxic chemicals, paint, and industrial strength glue to hold it all together. "The giant critter ball was put

The Chiodo brothers convinced producers to use a more practical 10' diameter giant critter ball, which consisted of dozens of Krite faces stitched together and wrapped around an aluminum frame. (Source: the Chiodo brothers)

together with contact cement," explains Ans Ellis, who helped sew and attach the critter faces to the ball. "The frame was very large, made out of metal. We used a lot of contact cement. It's a very strong glue used to make sneakers. Back in those days we used a non-water soluble kind, very toxic, poisonous. So they came in these five gallon buckets with no instructions and we began using it. We had to be very careful using it."

A second stunt critter ball was also made using a weather balloon wrapped in a canvas skin, which was then smothered with critter pelts. Since critter faces were not attached to this ball, the idea was this ball would only be used while in motion in medium to long shots. Crew members used ATVs to hit the ball off camera to initiate its momentum, but also used ramps and even manually pushed it around for several shots. A special panel of critter faces was also designed and was shot in close-up while rotating, which would be cut in between the medium and long shots of the critter ball in motion.

"We had a better second unit," chuckles Edward Chiodo. "They [first unit] weren't coming and stealing our lights (laughs). But we would set up the shot, and then Mick would come in and do a little; Mick was a little more hands-on. He would actually come in and direct a lot of the gags. But Allan [Holzman] shot most of the scenes at the Hungry Heifer." The critters's destruction of the Hungry Heifer and ensuing food fight was originally earmarked for a single day of shooting and featured specialty puppets and plenty of gags. Since real meat and condiments like ketchup and mustard were used but never cleaned up, the pickup shots needed several days later forced the puppeteers to endure the sickening aroma of spoiled beef and rancid ketchup. "We were working with chopped beef, hamburger meat, and mustard, and ketchup," a clearly grossed out Stephen Chiodo recalls. "And they were throwing it all around, squirting it on us. The puppets got so dirty and they *smelled*. When I was eating hamburger meat with the puppet, it got all in the face – stuck in every crevice. Even though we cleaned them up as best we could, there was always a residual bit of beef there. And they just smelled *awful*."

Similar events unfolded during sequences shot at the meat-packing plant, which also involved various puppets and real meat. "Then they decided they wanted to go back and do reshoots in the meat factory and it was a couple of days and we had to go back and the meat was starting to go rancid and stuff because nobody thought we were going to go back so they didn't clean up. It was horrible," laughs Edward Chiodo.

The Chiodo brothers and their crew experimented with several different rigs to move the giant critter ball, including this yoke that was operated by crew members. (Source: the Chiodo brothers)

THE "JEWISH JOHN WATERS"
An Interview with **Allan Holzman**
(Second Unit Director, *Critters 2*)

You have tremendous experience in editorial as well as directing sci-fi pictures for Roger Corman, is that how you ended up shooting second unit on *Critters 2*?

I was actually at New World recutting my film *Out of Control* while Steve Herek was editing trailers, developing *Critters*. I knew him before he directed. I just knew Steve because he was in the editing room. It was the editing room at New World that I actually built, but I was the first occupant and I designed it. That was used for *Battle Beyond the Stars*. I actually drove Roger [Corman] nuts because he wanted four separate rooms and I'm totally against any claustrophobic space for an editor. I built my whole career about refusing to edit without a window. It was very difficult managing that, but I did. Roger had windows, but he wanted four individual rooms so that when he came to the office in the morning or the editing room in the morning, none of the other editors would see what he was saying, et cetera. I couldn't say '*No.*' So, the weekend that the construction people were building the editing rooms above the construction area at the lumber yard, which was Roger's studio, I asked the construction people to take the walls out and just leave a center divider that only went to two-thirds, so the room basically would have a U-shape. There was some privacy, but lots of open space. Roger came in Monday morning and said, '*What happened? Where are my walls?*' And the construction people, defending me because they liked me, said, '*Oh, some guy came in and told us to take it down.*' (laughs). Roger knew exactly who it was. He didn't change it because it would've cost more money to fix it.

I knew Steve years later after that, when Roger had sold New World and they had gotten bigger and were making lots of A's, comedies, and stuff. I always used the trailers department, and

I knew Steve was using it the same way, as a way to keep busy earning money while still being able to pursue your directing goals. The commitment for a trailer was only 2 or 3 weeks at a time and so you were always free to have meetings and all that kind of stuff. That was a way to work your way through low-budget directing. Allan Arkush and Joe Dante kind of paved that path. They were cutting trailers when I was cutting *Candy Stripe Nurses* and *Crazy Mama* for Roger. And that's when Joe and Allan got their break to do *Hollywood Boulevard*, which combined all their crash scenes in their girl movies and starred Candice Wilson, who died quite young, but she was the main star in Roger's films. Joe Allen and John Davidson convinced Roger to give them 2 weeks of production where they had two separate units going. And that's when Roger had his place on Sunset Boulevard, and he had two floors and the top was a roof, and the roof is where everyone shot inserts, so you could just point the camera towards the dark sky at night.

By the time *Critters 2* rolled around, how did you find your way to getting onto that production?

I knew Don and Barry Opper from Corman's *Battle Beyond the Stars*. Actually, I had met them on my movie *Forbidden World* for Corman, which was originally called *Mutant*, because Don was the construction chief in that, and he had written *Android* too, during that time. They had called me in to direct a music video segment for *Slam Dance*. I directed *Grunt! The Wrestling Movie* prior to that and *Programmed to Kill,* which I directed actually just half of the movie but I had to take credit for the whole movie. I had to use 20 minutes from each of the prior two directors's failed attempts and then do that.

I was trying to get my next movie made. So Barry hired me to do the music video, and then *Critters 2* came up. And that was actually at the same time that I was offered to do the pilot for Glen Larson's project, *The Highwayman*. But I'd already committed to Barry for the second unit, and that was actually a dumb move on my part financially because I really didn't know what directing a pilot meant. On TV it was a lot more money than directing a segment. But I did *Critters 2* instead. And there was one funny story from that. John Waters's *Hairspray* was coming out, and they wanted to do a music video for that using a set they had access to. I just had to get the '*Okay*' from John Waters. And I'm from Baltimore, as is John. And when my movie for Roger opened there, I went and I described myself as the Jewish John Waters. And I told that to John, thinking that he would get a big laugh out of that, and he hung up on me. I thought, '*Well, there's no music video, now*.' There's only one John Waters. (laughs)

By the time that you had gotten attached to *Critters 2*, were you familiar with the first *Critters* and how it had performed and stuff?

Yeah, I liked the movie. Even though I did a monster movie, I really wasn't that much of a monster movie geek. I did a monster movie because that's what Roger gave me. So if he didn't do that, I wouldn't have been involved with monsters. But I have a technical mind, so I like working out problems. And taking full responsibility for whatever gag there is, etc. With *Mutant*, we had to do four different monsters in four weeks. Plus talking. And two great sex scenes.

In *Critters 2*, I worked with all the critters. So that was my job. Mick [Garris] did the talking scenes and I took the critters, I did the critter action. The big ball was really my biggest challenge. I really am into point of view and my father-in-law builds airplanes in his backyard. So I presented him with the problem of how to get a camera, which in those days were quite big, a 35mm camera, to do a 360 of the critters's big ball point of view. And he came up with a brilliant idea which we enacted, which was to use one of those big electrical cable spools. Basically, you put the camera on the inside of that spool and rolled it. The spool was like five feet high. You roll the camera and the camera rolls around in it. It worked brilliantly. It's great.

That is pretty brilliant. It's a pretty simple concept, but it worked, right?

Yeah, yeah. And Greg Gardner, our second unit DP, was an excellent technician as well. He was really quite brilliant with lighting and what we had to do with the gags. He was like the stunt coordinator for the critters. The first thing I had to shoot was the critters out in the parking lot, about 20 of them. And so they had built this three-foot-high grass box, basically, where they're lying underneath, each guy was operating a puppet with each hand. I'm there above ground talking to them below ground. I said, '*Okay, everybody turn right, turn to the right,*' and everyone went every which way. So then I said, '*Okay, turn towards the parking lot,*' and it worked out.

And you guys also did the big spinning rolling ball on like a truck mounted rig?

I didn't do that one. I did the bit going up to the farmer with a little group of people, but not the one with the truck. That cost too much money. We had a very small budget, we were low income on the second unit. You know, no one pays attention to you. So you can get out and not try to ask for too many things.

Among the new gags on *Critters 2*: baby Krites, of which second unit director Allan Holzman had the opportunity to work with.
(Source: the Chiodo brothers)

I know how difficult it must be working with puppets and creature effects. Did you face any big challenges working with the creature designs themselves?

Well, the challenge every day was to make it look believable. That was the challenge. So with lighting and movement, camera angles, you just tried your best. The good thing is that the intent most of the time is to be funny. So you could do exaggerations and such. The food fight was probably the best. You know, especially the one with the fried oil? The critter goes, '*Bitchin*', after the hair falls off. The overall intent was to be funny rather than scary. It was like, '*What critter gag are we doing today?*' It was fun.

And those had been prepared, like written out, or did you guys have some creative freedom to kind of experiment with some gags?

I studied the script every night. I would install the subtext, and I would install the rewrites, and you know, just find out where the critters were coming from (laughs). It was also really cold. We shot mostly at night. And it was bitter cold. It was extremely windy; very difficult conditions. It was a 50-minute drive too, not in a rush hour, from L.A. And of course you always got caught in that area when you crossed the river, the mountains. It was not a pleasant shooting schedule. But you know what was? The spirit of everyone; that was really strong. It was like a very light-hearted person. People knew they were on something that was... where the intent was good, you know, just trying to do the best they could. I think the most formal one on the crew was Russell Carpenter. He kind of had, you know, an A-plus level attitude, and he carried around a large notebook with all of his lighting so he would remember where to go so when we had to do a second unit on his sets we could recreate the lighting. He was extremely professional. Of course, he went from *Critters 2* to *Titanic,* which was rather a big jump. But you could just tell that he knew his stuff. Even at that stage, he took it to a much different level than what you would normally see. He was like, you know, auditioning for a big studio film, basically. He had to observe the set.

And you got along well with Mick?

Yeah, Mick's really easy to get along with. He's a very happy guy. He comes to directing through writing, so he's just sitting and thinking. Not so much running around and checking with this and checking with that. He had a big crew. It was an over-produced show, for what it was. Way over-produced. But the first one was successful, and they wanted to upscale everything.

Do any of the segments that you shot stand out to be some of your favorites from *Critters 2*?

Well, the point of view shot was a big ball, that's my favorite. And the food fight is good. But, you know, I was just really doing my job. I didn't really have a passion for it. I knew what I had to do. There were limits to what you could do. But everything was kind of mechanical until I'm in front of the camera.

Looking back on the life cycle that this film has had over the decades, are you surprised how well it's kind of stood up among different generations of fans?

Yeah, of course. I mean, I just, well, it's still there. I don't understand the fascination. But I guess it's fun, you know. When I look up *Critters 2*, the food scene seems to be the dominant thing that they advertise. I think that they advertise in terms of the pictures. You know, the featured villains are the critters and they don't show up for the first 30 minutes. But when people think of *Critters 2*, they think of the giant critter ball and the food fight scene.

Given how vast and interesting your career has been, you know, for you personally, where does *Critters 2* kind of fit into your calculus in terms of...

Every few years I get a call. That's about it. No, it was really perhaps the dumbest choice I could have made because I could have gotten a pilot for a TV show and that they wanted me to come in to bring my look to it. Really, it was probably the stupidest decision of my life. Be loyal, I believe. But I definitely should not have done it. I should have taken the pilot.

| END TRANSMISSION |

BUILDING THE MINIATURES

In conjunction with the Chiodo brothers's monumental work on scaling up the Krites, sequences involving dozens of the murderous furballs assembling and rolling through the prairie would be done using matte paintings and miniature effects. Similar to the creative work by Gene Warren Jr., who provided the astounding visual effects in *Critters* when the Browns's family home is reconstructed after being detonated to high heavens, Kevin Kutchaver of VCE Inc. and Peter Kuran's effects shop were hired to create the miniature work on *Critters 2*.

To achieve the effect of the critters rolling through the field and the spaceship landing, two miniature sets were created. James Belohovek, who worked on *Critters 2* with Stephen Sharp building the newly designed cannons carried by Ug and Lee, would also play an instrumental role working on the miniature sets.

"I had my old crew from *Beetlejuice* – Rick Kess and Tom Conti – help me out," says Belohovek. "Jim Aupperle was our camera man and he lit the two miniature set-ups. It was a really cheap production, so to save cost, I had to use the same miniature landscape for both shots, just dressed differently. The first shot was the spaceship landing. Both Rick Kess and Tom Conti built the set while I worked on the trees. Jim Aupperle wanted to smoke the set to give it an atmosphere, so Tom and Rick built four huge wooden frames and covered it with plastic painters tarps to let light into the set but would hold in the smoke. The production gave us the spaceship but it was the wrong one, it was the bad guy's ship from the first movie. Oh well, we had to use it. The idea was to have it land behind a hill with trees swaying and dust billowing."

To shoot the sequence, a miniature spaceship had to be rigged and moved into frame, which at first blush, sounds straightforward but additional challenges quickly emerged. "Well, the ship was made out of plastic and was much too heavy for the monofilament [fishing line] and we quickly had to make a cardboard replica," continues Belohovek. "That worked well. While Rick Kess worked on that, I made the track and motor to move and lower the ship. Tom Conti and Rick had made the set. I also experimented with swaying trees and came up with using ostrich feathers with miniature branches glued on the stems. Well, it worked alright for what it was. The dust was Fuller's earth. Once that shot was done, it was time to work on the field shot. I went out and bought different size brown fluff balls at a local art store and had Rick Kess see how he could roll them into the shot. He tried several techniques, using monofilament and tried to pull them into the shot. Didn't work. At this time, I had to have Rick take over. He came up with cutting PVC

A FIELD BLANKETED BY CRITTERS!

James Belohovek and his team created a detailed miniature version of the actual Santa Clarita valley where the horde of critters assemble and roll toward the hamburger meat plant. The miniature project perfectly reflected the composition as laid out in the storyboards. (Source: James Belohovek)

pipe in half and using several of them just out of camera range and to roll the balls into the shot. Jim Aupperle shot it at a higher frame rate to smooth out the moves the fluff balls made."

PRODUCTION CHALLENGES

From the start, it was apparent that a nearly 40-day schedule being shot on location at night, with underage actors, animals, and heavy visual effects would pose a myriad of challenges. What nobody could have predicted was the coldest winter to hit California in 100 years occurred during principal photography. High winds and abnormally frigid temperatures introduced even more problems for the cast and crew, from damaging set pieces to making night shoots pure torture. On more than one occasion, it snowed, leaving the fluorescent green painted grass smothered in white snow, not the most ideal aesthetic for a springtime in Kansas-setting.

"It ended up being really cold for that shoot of all things, it even snowed one night" remembers Dwight Roberts, a sentiment shared by others. "The cold weather and night shoots were some of our biggest challenges, but for the puppeteers, it was very difficult," remembers Ans Ellis. "To be in these crawlspaces all bent up and trying to animate the creatures, that was very difficult work. We had these trailers on the sets, like workshops. When it was really cold, it was nice to be able to work inside the trailers."

To alleviate giving away how cold it was during the takes, actress Liane Curtis took to chewing ice cubes to cut down on the amount of vapor coming out of her mouth and nose when talking and exhaling. "It was cold, man," Liane Curtis vividly remembers. "And at night I was in that little spring dress, but I at least had the boots I was wearing. But even with those conditions, and how hard it was, I think everybody really loved the script. Mick loved the script. You know, we were having fun. Even the not fun things were kind of fun, like those cold nights." In fact, the brutal weather prompted an unusual (but practical) cast and crew gift: *Critters 2* embroidered woolen socks.

Another complexity involved the amount of daylight shoots involving the Krites, a feature that was nonexistent during *Critters*, which mostly took place at night. "It's very hard to do in the daylight," assesses Rupert Harvey. "I mean, I wasn't, as you know, involved at all on the set of *Critters 2*, that was Barry's baby, but it was a big challenge, I thought, to take it on and to take it into a daylight environment like that. That's tough."

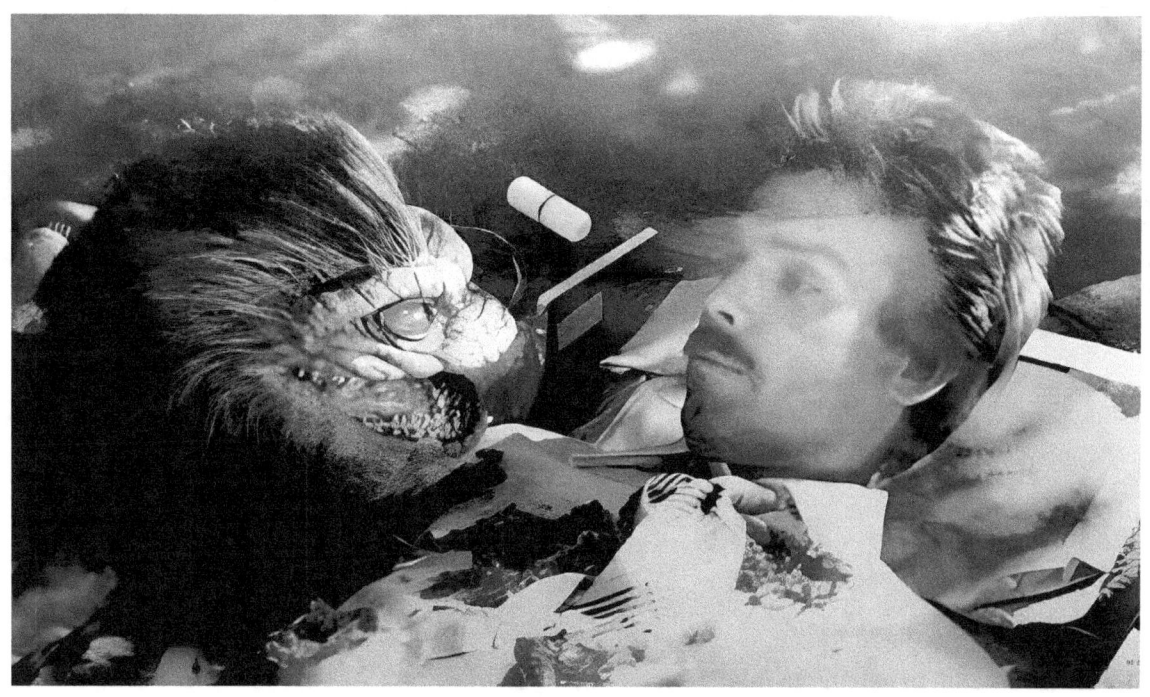

Fabricator and mechanical genius Dwight Roberts and his teammates bore the chaotic weather to make sure the Krites came to life on the set of *Critters 2*. (Source: Dwight Roberts)

The miniatures team worked from a variety of sketches to recreate a scale version of Grover's Bend and the Krites, which included this sketch.
(Source: James Belohovek)

FROM CRYSTAL LAKE TO GROVER'S BEND
An Interview with Charles Bornstein
(Editor, *Critters 2*)

How did you end up getting involved with *Critters 2*?

I was working on some things just prior, for instance, right before they were previewing it, I took over editing *Friday the 13th Part VI: Jason Lives*. And, because the editor of that, who I knew, got a chance to get out of horror movies and he got a chance to work on a legitimate film. And so this was right before they were going to preview. I took over the picture and did some more director's changes and the big thing there was I had to track music in for the preview. You know, that we, to this day, we're called picture editors, but we do everything. And one of the big things we do, if we're lucky enough to have enough assistants, we can get the assistant to work on the sound, the basic sound effects while we kind of figure out what music we're going to put in there. Usually when we went, not just me, but when you start a picture you kind of get a feel of what kind of music is going to go in there and you sort of rip off either classical music or scores of pictures that were kind of like what you were working on. Luckily, I had access to anything they had in the Paramount Music Library, which was really cool. Because it was about the scores that were not available on CD or LP at the time. I don't even know if CDs existed then. And so I got a bunch of stuff. And I always loved Jerry Goldsmith. So one of the scores that I really kind of borrowed a lot from was *The Swarm*, which is a great score for a really bad film.

But the score is unbelievable. It's a great score. Jerry Goldsmith basically would score these shitty films with this amazing music and he elevated all this stuff many levels up. So anyway, I worked with Tom McLoughlin. I tracked, it's called tracking when you put the music in, we tracked the whole thing and we had a big, big preview at the theater at Paramount. And they invited, look, it was the weirdest crap, first of all, the movie, the theater was packed, it looked like Hell's Angels and all kinds of odd people. And it really was, it was scary. The people that showed up for this *Friday the 13th Part VI* preview, and I even remember my assistant had these great stereo headphones that could record, it's like 3-D headphones that you could record with. And so, and I had mixed this, because we do a little temp mix. I had mixed this pretty hot, but man, oh man, I had control over the volume in the theater, and the audience just sucked up all of that sound. I couldn't crank this stuff up enough, and they went fucking apeshit over this stuff. They went apeshit from this preview and wanted more kills. Somebody had to basically be killed every four and a half minutes or else, like, the audience would not stand for somebody not being killed every four and a half minutes. So they shot all kinds of new stuff and I edited all that in and we mixed it and it was a really great relationship with Tom. Tom is a great friend of mine. At that time I had just met him, and so, Tom recommended me to Mick.

So I had a good interview [with Mick] and then I got hired. And on *Critters 2,* it was the same thing with the music and the previewing and all that. On this one, when I was at Paramount, one of the scores that you could never get at the time was John Williams's score on *Black Sunday,* and the stuff with the big critter ball going through the town, and Scott Grimes with the car, and trying to bounce it and all that, that was all music from *Black Sunday,* and it worked really well. Our composer, Nicholas Pike, he basically very successfully took the tempo and very, very creatively borrowed from that music here. That's usually what happens with good composers; if the score from the temp score works, they're crazy and everybody's in love with it, the really good composers can successfully reinterpret it in a way that nobody's going to get sued. So anyway, that's how I got to work on it. I never met Mick before that and Mick is a delightful guy and I'd say that part of what I think that you as an eight-year-old kid was responding to, and all the other people who watched *Critters 2* at the time, that Mick just has a very wonderful sense of humor. He's really quite funny and I always kidded him about that. I think that, I said, '*Mick, I'd love to see you make a really scary, dark film because your sense of humor is just always coming out and it's just fun and delightful, but I'm not sure that it's ever really scary.*' And so I would always tease him about that. I think that Mick made the second picture more delightful for you eight-year-olds than even the first one.

I think that and the second one had more of that than the first one did. And Steve Herek, who did the first one, had a very good career. He did big Disney movies and stuff like that. He used to be an assistant editor. He went from being an assistant editor to basically becoming a director. You know, Welles did that with the Coen brothers.

Yeah, it really did have such a totally different tone to it. I have an early draft of *Critters 2* after he had taken over the writing or rewriting of it and you can just see how much lighter that he was able to make it and given the fact that he was a first-time director for that picture.

Well, he actually directed one thing before that. There was a Disney movie called *Fuzzbucket*. It was a Disney straight-to-video or it was a TV movie. And it was light as well, and then he had written a couple of things that became big movies before, before all that. He did that thing about a 40s jazz, like a swing music thing, and you'd have to look it up. But he wrote that. James Horner did the score for it. But he had directed before.

From all intents and purposes, the second *Critters* was really scaled up. Everything was scaled up from the first one. Everything was kind of bigger in terms of the critters and the kills and the cast even…

I'm sure the first one they spent zero dollars on and it still was a low-budget thing, but we could actually afford a composer that had live instruments and we went to a scoring session in the middle of nowhere in Gardena or something. I mean it was, I'm sure that Nick Pike, that was his name. I'm sure that Nick Pike made zero dollars on that. He probably put all the money that he got paid, which wasn't much, into that scoring session. But it's a nice score.

Do you recall any, you know, in terms of editing *Critters 2*, was it a pretty straightforward process for you or did it stand out being unique or particularly challenging or anything?

It was a big scene in the church, it was like a high noon kind of scene. There's a lot of coverage there, but I mean it wasn't that big of a deal. The critter ball and all the stuff with the critters because you know they were just little puppets and stuff. There were little challenges here and there. The one thing I remember was that when we mixed, you know, did the sound mixing, that Mick did it right on the mixing stage, he did all those voices and things like that. There was a thing with Scott Grimes, and I think it had to be picked up by the foley [artist] because there was a sound that was needed like a chirp for his sneakers. And Mick did the sneaker chirp. I think he just maybe even did it with his mouth. He had a great time. He had a lot of fun. And the producer, Barry Opper, was a great guy. And Don Opper was his brother. And I think that Barry's assistant, Cara Tapper, went on to get a very good career working on big pictures. So it launched a bunch of careers. This was when New Line Pictures was just kind of in its infancy, and it got, with the Freddy Krueger films and all that, they made a lot of money and then Warner Bros. kind of bought them out. New Line got more ambitious and more ambitious and more ambitious. But when they made that first *Critters* film, they were just a little art house thing. They probably said, '*Hey, we better start making harder films. Because there's sort of instant money to be made there.*'

In your experience, going back to that era of the mid-80s up until the early 90s, what do you think the difference is between horror pictures from that era and what the market is now? Is it still similar in that case where it's a good launch pad for cast, crew, and production houses?

There's so many of them. Basically, yes, but I'd say that the big change between pictures of the 80s and now are that what were the B-movies in terms of mostly the budget. When we were doing these pictures, first of all, most of them, if the studio was making them, they spent as little money as humanly possible. Those *Friday the 13th* films were made for very, very little money. They were really low-budget. And then there would be probably some bullshit negative pickup, which is all bullshit, because they really made it. I mean, those things were produced by Frank Yablans's son. Frank Yablans at the time was the head of Paramount. I mean, it was all bullshit. But the smaller pictures, all these, even *Halloween*, all these things were all itty-bitty little companies. The difference is now these pictures are made by big companies, either spending very little money, or they go full on prestige and spend millions and millions and millions and millions of dollars. That's the big difference. And also, I think it's a difference of the audience, because when I was a kid, the general movie audience was much more literate. I mean, people read books and bestsellers and all kinds of stuff. And usually, movies were, with the properties that became movies, were usually books or plays or something literary, you know, the written word. Now it's all comic books.

Well, the one thing that at least gives me a little bit of faith, you know, is like we had mentioned with the fan base and kind of the new generation of viewers that can still appreciate it. This was still a period where films were shot on film stock. And that 35mm, or in certain cases, 16mm, but that aesthetic is very, very hard to replicate. And there we have it in its prime, in its pure form. In terms of editing film stock, were you cutting on things like Moviolas and flatbeds?

But editing is editing, really. The one thing that working on Avids and those kinds of machines, it really freed you up to try doing it eight million ways if you had to. And you didn't have to undo it to recut something. You didn't have to rip open a splice. And what used to happen, I was an assistant editor for an editor, Lynzee Klingman, who had just finished working alongside Dede Allen, a very famous editor. So the way Dede Allen did it was she had a million assistant editors and Lynzee did too. This is before there was computer editing. So if she wanted to try something different and she had already edited something, before she would start ripping open the splices, you know, to now do something different, she would make what we always would make for going to sound effects, a black and white copy of the picture. So there was a reference. So, if she had to go back to a cut scene and say, 'Well, that was nice,' when you'd completely broken open all of those splices and tried it this way, 'But I liked it better the way you had it before.' Then it's like, 'Oh geez.'

Well, she had a record of it, because there was a black and white copy. It had all the edge numbers and everything on it. Then she would also take the soundtrack, and she would make a copy of the soundtrack and the assistance. Because I had to do this when I worked for Lynzee on *True Confessions*. I had to put it in a synchronizer with the actual edited track, and I would have to write every code number so that, God forbid, we had to go back to the way it was, there was a record of it. Very labor-intensive. Now with Avids and all that you don't have to do that bullshit. So really, editing is editing. It really is. It doesn't matter. What you have to really kind of take your hats off to salute are the guys in the previous generation when there wasn't even what we call the splicing tape; they used what they call hot splicing. In other words, this is how they still cut negative, if they cut negative anymore, that you put it in a machine and you whack off the preceding frame. Or you actually cut into, in order to make the splice, you have to cut a half of a frame before the actual splice on either side. You put it in the hot splicer, you put glue, you scrape the emulsion off, and then you put glue on, and then the machine goes '*Ka-chunk*,' and you just now basically lost two frames. You lost a frame from the outgoing piece of film, and you lost a frame from the incoming piece of film. So, every splice that you made was a commitment. And if you had to go back and now add anything to that, either the head of it or the tail of it, you had to slug a piece of black leader, because the frame doesn't exist anymore. Now you're the editor and you're running a thing and you're seeing all these black spots and all that and you go, '*Well, this guy can't be very good. Look how many times he had to figure out how to do that.*' So those guys really had a plan, they looked at the dailies and they kind of figured out '*How am I going to put this together?*' and they did it and oh, you know nine times out of ten those cuts stayed.

On *Critters 2*, was it still Moviola or something a little bit more advanced than that, that you guys used to cut?

I probably used both. In a lot of pictures, I used both. I would look at the incoming cut. Everything would get broken down like a Moviola show, where every take is a little spool of film. As opposed to on chem roll, they're all just, they're all together on a roll. And then I would, I think I probably built it onto the incoming, so that once it was all together, if I wanted to make a change, now I'm on the flatbed, and now I open up the thing and I'd say to the assistant, '*I need the tail to EE 4732*' or whatever and then the assistant would go get the box and find it and hand me the piece of film. With digital editing, that doesn't exist anymore. Everything's there.

I know you worked on a ton of projects, but do you recall if you have any particularly favorite sequence from *Critters 2* from an editorial perspective?

Just some random thoughts. I might not be answering the question. Mick's wife, Cynthia, was the big alien. She's early in the picture, she's like the head of an alien [Warden Zanti]. And she got claustrophobic in that thing. She was freaking out. And Mick had to calm her down. She's in the head of an alien, and I can imagine, it was very claustrophobic. She did not enjoy that. I think I liked working with the puppets, all the Chiodo brothers stuff, the critter ball and the shooting of the cannons and the Hungry Heifer. That was a lot of fun. It's not like it was a difficult film to put together. I've had much more difficult things. I've had pictures that had even worse schedules than that.

One of the last pictures that I edited on film was for Tom McLoughlin. It was a TV movie. Hearst was the production company. It was based on a book, a true crime book called *Murder of Innocence*. And it was a true crime. It was a hideous situation where a mentally disturbed young woman, you know, in her twenties or early thirties, who failed at marriage, hated her in-laws, and they had kids, she didn't have kids. She was really messed up. She collected stuff. She collected an arsenal. She went into the school that her ex-sister-in-law's kids were in, oh my God, and she shot up a classroom and then there was a huge manhunt for her. So Tom made this picture and Tom was a real family man. How am I going to, you know, I will never ever show any kid actually getting shot. So if you ever get to see *Murder of Innocence* with Valerie Bertinelli, he did it in a very brilliant way because he sets it up when she was a kid and the kids would make fun of her because there was something odd about her and she would squeeze her hands. She would squeeze her hands when she got really upset. And then when she actually commits her crime, so we have this shot of the kids from the park in a flashback with the kids running and all that, faking being killed, and then in the actual murder, Tom did things in silhouette. You see the school kids freaking out, running in silhouette, and then you see that little girl who was young, squeezing her hands and then you see the kids dying. So you never ever really saw the actual crime. Until it was all over and then you see the school teacher with a dead kid in her arms and crying and all of that. So anyway, that was done in very little time. It was all shot on film. He shot a lot of film, a million setups. She had these episodes of doing crazy things, and I had to edit them in a particularly jagged way. I mean, I won an editing award for that film. I also worked on *Howling II: … Your Sister is a Werewolf*, which, you know, has a following, and that clearly is the worst movie that was ever made.

I was curious, with all the awesome things you had worked on over the years, where would you kind of rack and stack *Critters 2* in your repertoire?

Oh, I had fun. I don't denigrate that picture at all. It was kind of an early thing, and it was fun. I mean, I got to do a lot of things with Mick and more stuff with Tom, so that was great. Fond memories all around.

UNLESS THIS ONE IS A TOTAL DISASTER . . .

During production, director Mick Garris jokingly told *Fangoria* when discussing the prospect of a third *Critters* installment, "Unless this one is a total disaster, in which case, there will probably be no *Part 3* in the career of Mick Garris." The preview screening for *Critters 2*, held at the former Burbank AMC 10, was a jam-packed affair, with a sold out crowd who laughed, screamed, and enthusiastically enjoyed the film. The surprise came when *Critters 2* opened nationwide on 29 April, 1988, nearly three weeks after Easter, which was observed on 3 April that year. "If the preview screening was a bang, then opening weekend was more of a whimper," Mick Garris recalled in his official biography after seeing the film opening night at the Universal Studios movie theater complex, which only had three people in the audience.

Despite enjoying *Critters*, film critics Siskel and Ebert lampooned *Critters 2*, with Ebert later trashing the film in a one-star review for its lack of style and sense of fun found in the original. The particularly mean spirited review also took aim at the film's larger cast, unlikely dialogue, and believe it or not, the creature effects. The film also faced commercial struggles, grossing $3,813,293 but failing to recoup its production budget of approximately $4.3 million.

"When it came out – you can't say '*disaster*,' because it only cost four million dollars, but it did not do well," Garris explains in his biography. "And it was so crushing to have gone through however long of making a movie, maybe it was six months, to put your heart and soul into it, everybody working their asses off, the hours are atrocious. Then you have this magnificent screening in Burbank, and you think the world is your oyster; well, mine had no pearl. Once it got out to theaters, it wasn't detested – it was ignored. It's painful. It's your baby. And New Line did what they could to make it happen."

DID YOU KNOW?

Despite featuring a topless Roxanne Kernohan, *Critters 2* only received a PG-13 rating. The Motion Picture Association of America (MPAA) assessed that her exposed breasts were revealed in a "non-sexual nature" and thus did not warrant a more restrictive rating. Sadly, the Canadian-born actress, who also appeared in *Fatal Pulse* and the 1988 remake of *Not of This Earth*, died in a car accident in 1993, only 5 years after her role in *Critters 2*.

Perhaps most devastating for both *Critters 2* and Mick Garris was the resoundingly negative impact it had on New Line Cinema. CEO of New Line Cinema Bob Shaye revealed for the first time during a 2017 episode of Mick Garris's *Post Mortem* podcast that he had been meeting with potential investors representing an investment fund from Connecticut at the time *Critters 2* had been released. Shaye, who was close to inking an investment deal with the firm worth several million dollars, met with the investor in L.A., eating at a restaurant on Sunset Blvd. and then invited him to watch *Critters 2* at the Hollywood Cinema. Shaye explained that New Line's latest film was a sequel to a very successful first movie and he couldn't wait for the investor to see it. After dinner, they arrived at the near empty theater, only 14 people had bought tickets for the screening, which was being shown in a 600-seat theater. The lackluster opener tanked the multi-million dollar investment opportunity for New Line Cinema.

Critters 2 marked the final *Critters* film to be released theatrically and the film was quickly introduced to the home-video market the same year it premiered. New Line Home Video first produced a VHS and laserdisc version of *Critters 2* in 1988 and New Line Home Entertainment later released the film on DVD in 2003, while Warner Bros. released a DVD box-set containing all four *Critters* films in 2010. The four-set of films were later treated to a Blu-ray release in 2018 courtesy of the Scream Factory label under Shout! Factory.

Although *Critters 2* floundered at the box office, it continued to play well on the home-video market and ultimately did not outright kill the potential for additional installments in the franchise. The film also did not cripple the career of Mick Garris, who would go on to write and direct over two dozen feature films and mini-series episodes, including *Stephen King's Sleepwalkers* and *The Stand* mini-series. Surprisingly, time has been kind to *Critters 2*, and since its 30th anniversary in 2018, *Critters 2* is widely shown at festivals and horror conventions, often accompanied by Mick Garris and various cast and crew members.

IN MEMORIAM: ROXANNE KERNOHAN

One of the most memorable aspects of *Critters 2* (besides the iconic giant critter ball) is the portrayal of bounty hunter Lee as a blonde bombshell *Playboy* centerfold played by the stunningly beautiful and talented Roxanne Kernohan. Born Roxanne Bridget Furman on 20 March 1960 in Canada, she first modeled in Europe in her early 20s, appearing in various commercials, music videos, and printed ads. Always intrigued by the arts – whether singing/song writing, modeling, or acting – Roxanne began her film acting career in 1988 with appearances in the slasher movie *Fatal Pulse*, the post-apocalyptic sci-fi film *Phoenix the Warrior*, Roger Corman's *Not of This Earth* remake, and of course her breakout role in *Critters 2*. Roxanne also had parts in the documentary *The Decline of Western Civilization Part II: The Metal Years*, the buddy cop action-comedy movie *Tango & Cash*, participated in the pilot for the TV series *Baywatch*, and revived her *Playboy* affiliation with an appearance in *Playboy: Sexy Lingerie*. She had a role in *Angel III: The Final Chapter* and made her final screen appearance as herself in the direct-to-video movie *Scream Queen Hot Tub Party*.

Roxanne, wife to Kevin Kernohan and the mother of a then-two-year-old, tragically died on 5 February 1993 after suffering traumatic injuries in a car accident eight days earlier in Santa Clarita, California, not far from the location of *Critters 2*. She was 32 years old.

Roxanne signed her acting contract for *Critters 2* on 13 November 1987 and reported for 6 days of principal photography starting on 14 December the same year, with an additional 3 extra days earmarked for photo shoots and body casting. Fellow cast and crew mates fondly recalled working alongside Roxanne, remarking how she took her role seriously and remained humble, focused, and dedicated to honing her craft while on set. Roxanne's introductory scene in *Critters 2* was shot in frigid 24 degree temperatures – the coldest winter in California for 100 years – but director Garris and special makeup effects artist Chris Biggs affirmed how committed and professional Roxanne remained despite the suboptimal conditions. For generations of fans, Roxanne's gender construct-breaking portrayal of Lee in *Critters 2* will forever be a cherished aspect of their childhood or adolescent cinematic experience and her performance undoubtedly assisted in making *Critters 2* a bonafide cult classic.

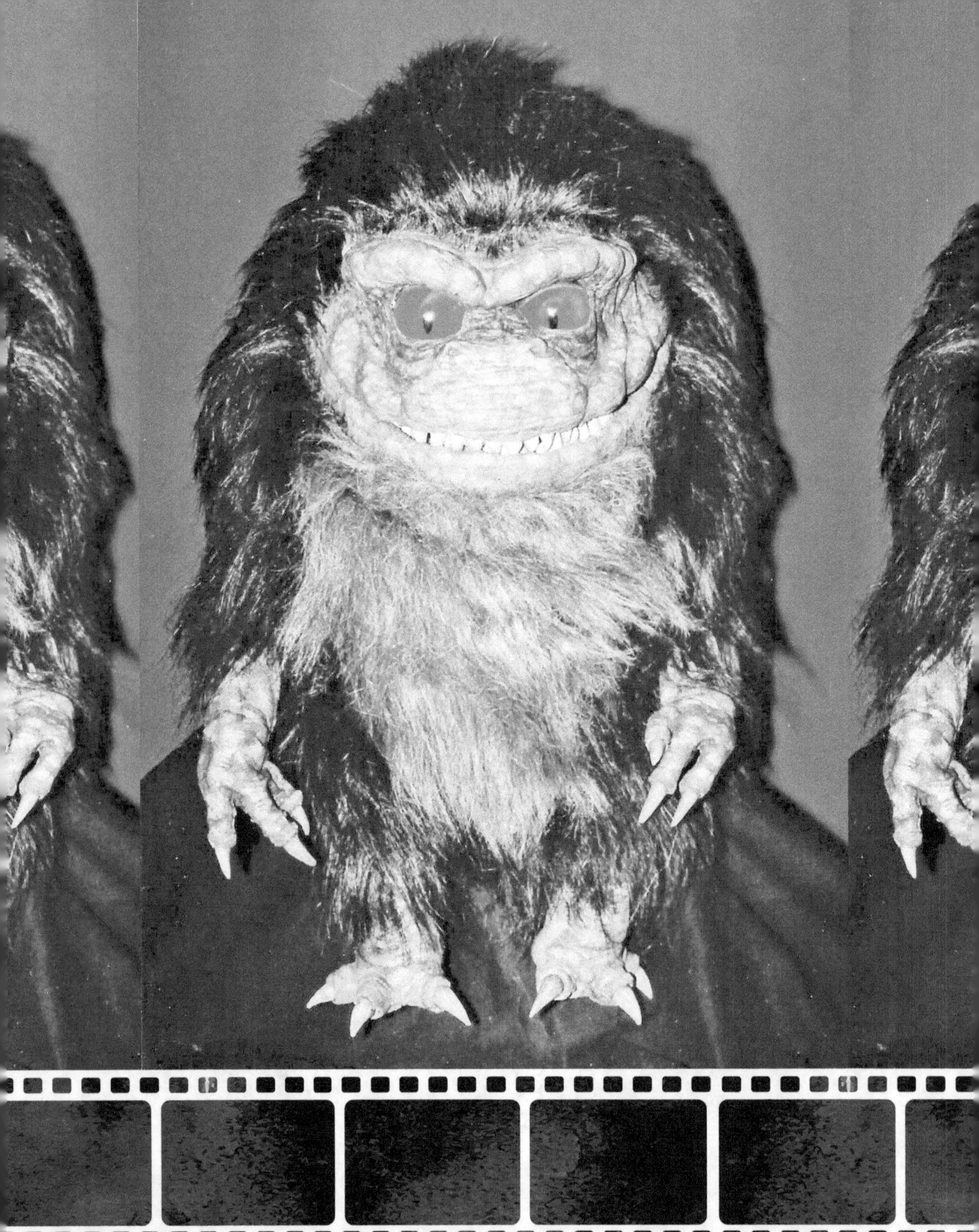

CHAPTER THREE
CRITTERS 3

LEONARDO DiCAPRIO KILLS KRITES

Producers Barry Opper and Rupert Harvey convinced New Line to finance the final two *Critters* installments by pitching a 'hinged' script that would link the two films together and shooting the productions back-to-back. Once greenlit, budding director Kristine Peterson was tapped to direct the third installment based on a script by David J. Schow. This time, the Krites wreak havoc against residents of a rundown tenement in the inner-city. *Critters 3* also marks Leonardo DiCaprio's first feature film, who stars as the titular adolescent hero, Josh.

PRE-PRODUCTION

"Now here we were in the early 1990s, just a few years after *Critters 2*," says Barry Opper. "Rupert and I said, '*It would be fun to do another Critters movies, but why don't we devise something that could be done very inexpensively, two movies that could be shot back-to-back, so we could do* Critters 3 *and* 4 *very inexpensively*,' and we brought that to New Line. We actually took it to their treasurer, a guy named Steve Abramson. And I think he told Bob [Shaye] that he thought it was a good idea. Anyway, they decided to go ahead and make *Critters 3* and *4*. Their executive, New Line's executive, for *Critters 3* and *4*, who worked very closely with us on doing the movies, was a guy named Mark Ordesky. Now Mark went on to do the *Lord of the Rings* movies with Peter Jackson and New Line. The two movies were made with the same formula that we shot *Critters 3* and *4*. In other words, what I'm suggesting is Mark learned from us how to do two movies back-to-

Opposite: The redesigned puppets used in *Critters 3* and *4* were the largest
of the standard puppets made for the franchise. (Source: Paul Salamoff)

187

back and essentially almost did two movies for the price of one, except we're talking about the difference between a few million dollars and multi, multi-million dollars with *Lord of the Rings*."

This time around, Barry and Rupert provided New Line with a treatment for the scripts that the pair had co-written together. Initially, the scripts were intended to be less comedic and much grittier and edgier. "I mean, the *Critters 3* I originally envisioned was much darker than, in fact, it was. I had something much more George Romero in mind," recalls Rupert Harvey. "I just saw this very claustrophobic rooming house or apartment house that Romero did in *Dawn of the Dead*, but I wanted it in a very confined, city environment. We'd done the bucolic art in the country, middle America stuff. I wanted to go back into an urban environment. I think if, in retrospect, if I had the chance to do it over again, I wouldn't cast it for two kids so young, and blue-eyed, blonde kids. Even though one of them was Leo. I don't think that served it very well. But I think it probably did as well, if not better, than *Critters 4*."

"The stories for both *Critters 3* and *4* were written by Rupert and myself together," says Barry Opper. "And then we hired writers to actually write the scripts to our story. We knew exactly the movies we wanted to make so we did outlines of the two movies and then we hired writers to write to those outlines. Kristine [Peterson] added a goofy element to *Critters 3* that was not in Rupert's and my initial story, similar in a way to what Mick did with *Critters 2*. We had about a 175-page script that was the two movies, you know a total of 175 pages. So *Critters 3* was one half; *Critters 4* was the other half. We shot *Critters 3*, took a short break in between to move over to the space set, and then we shot *Critters 4*."

Critters 3 takes place after the events of *Critters 2* and follows a family of three: father Clifford (John Calvin), daughter Annie (Aimee Brooks), and her younger brother Johnny (Christian and Joseph Cousins), who are returning to an unidentified "big city," presumably Kansas City or Topeka, following a road trip to Arizona. While pulling over at a rest stop to change a blown tire, Annie and Johnny meet Josh (Leonardo DiCaprio), who turns out to be the stepson of the slumlord who owns the tenement where Clifford and his family live. While waiting for the tire to be fixed, the kids lose their frisbee and encounter Charlie, who has returned to Earth in search of the remaining Krites. Incredulous about Charlie's explanation of the danger posed by the ferocious alien lifeforms he's tracking, the kids reluctantly take Charlie's early warning transponder crystal, which he explains will turn green when the kids are in harm's way. A Krite sneaks under Clifford's truck and stashes several eggs but soon Clifford and his family hit the road and unknowingly take the eggs with

Producers Barry Opper (left) and Rupert Harvey (right) were instrumental in garnering interest in additional
Critters installments including the idea to shoot the sequels back-to-back. (Source: Paul Salamoff)

them. After reaching the tenement, the eggs hatch after Clifford's truck sustains a minor fender
bender and eight critters (same as the first film) begin wreaking havoc on the building's remaining
occupants and caretakers, including sleazeball maintenance man Frank (Geoffrey Blake) and
Marcia (Katherine Cortez), the building's courageous telephone repair woman.

DID YOU KNOW?

In the script, Charlie's crystal transponder was originally described as a "disc the size
of a silver dollar, totally smooth, shiny, and featureless." Charlie informs Josh that once
it starts to glow green, he should "look out for himself," implying it would indicate the
presence of Krites. The decision to use a glowing crystal was almost certainly a practical
choice, since it would've been easier to rig a crystal to glow green rather than a flat disc.

After the Krites feed on Frank, attack another resident, and cut power to the building, Annie and her family band together with Josh and Marcia and flee to safety by reaching the building's rooftop. Charlie arrives in time to save the remaining survivors and obliterates the Krites but is stopped before eliminating the last two Krite eggs. Ug (Terrence Mann) appears in a holographic form to inform Charlie of the consequences of destroying the remaining eggs and dispatches a space pod to collect the specimens and ends on a "to be continued" cliffhanger, hence teeing up the sequel (*Critters 4*).

"David J. Schow, who is a dear, dear friend of mine and a great writer, I called him up and I said, '*Listen, we're gonna do two movies,* Critters 3, Critters 4, *they have to be done lower budget, they have to be done quickly*'," says producer Mark Ordesky. "We basically need the scripts in a matter of weeks, both scripts. And they need to be containable. So he said, '*All right, I'll call you back*' and then he called me back and said '*I've got it: critters go to outer space; critters go to the big city.*' I'm like '*No, no, no, contained.*' And he said, '*No it will be contained. Critters go to outer space on a spaceship and critters in the big city are gonna be critters inside an apartment building inside a big city.*' So at that point in David's life, he lived a vampiric existence. He basically lived by night. So he started writing and what would happen is, he and I would meet for what was breakfast to him and what was sort of like late night snacks for me. We would meet, we would talk, he would put pages on his doormat, essentially, of his home, and I would drive by in the morning, like, not every day, but whenever there were pages to get, and that's how it went. And ultimately, the conceit to do them simultaneously or back-to-back, I think that was very much Barry and Rupert's way, like, '*Okay, well, if we need to do them quickly, and they're both largely interior movies, we should just get a warehouse and do them that way with the same crew, different directors, obviously different casts, and do it that way.*' So that whole conceit, it was like necessity was the mother of invention. That's how it started."

The ambitious and rapid pace for a two-film production resulted in a crash course of script revisions and tweaks to ensure the production could be executed on a meager budget and on time. "Joseph Lyle is someone that did a rewrite after David, and that's a pseudonym, by the way, hence the extra writing credit," says Barry Opper.

"I know there were tons of revisions because the cover page of the script had this critter sketch on it, and in those days we would still issue hard copy pages to people," production manager David Witz explains. "And every time we'd have to have different colors for all the different

screenplay by
DAVID J. SCHOW

from a story by
RUPERT HARVEY & BARRY OPPER

REVISED DRAFT
11 JANUARY 1991

The *Critters 3* script cover page featured this sketch of a hungry Krite. (Source: author's collection)

versions. So I used to keep the cover page and I would pin them up in the office so we knew what color we were at. And it was a script page and it had on the cover half like the outline of a critter. It had all these different colors going around the top of the office. I can still remember that – that was a fun thing."

DID YOU KNOW?

The idea of setting *Critters 3* in an urban environment, though novel, followed in the footsteps of *Friday the 13th Part VIII: Jason Takes Manhattan*, *Gremlins 2: The New Batch*, and *Predator 2*, all of which plucked their respective mayhem-causing and murderous villains from rural or remote environs to the big city. Three years later, *Leprechaun 2* would shift its main locale to Las Vegas, proving the trend had not yet run its course.

CASTING

Though the story takes place in the big city, the location is primarily restricted to a single tenement building but the cast members (25) are fairly numerous (though the body count is minuscule). William Dennis Hunt (*Flesh Gordon* franchise) plays Briggs and twin child actors Christian and Joseph Cousins (*Kindergarten Cop*) were used to play Johnny. Character actor Geoffrey Blake, who appeared in over 155 productions including *The Last Starfighter*, *Forrest Gump*, and *Cast Away*, hams it up as Frank, a New Jersey-accented sleazeball of a maintenance man. The lovely Katherine Cortez plays a hard-charging telephone repair woman, Marcia, and Nina Axelrod (*Motel Hell*), an actress and the film's casting director, plays a bit part as Betty Briggs. Frances Bay, best known for her role as Grandma in Adam Sandler's *Happy Gilmore*, rounds out the cast of secondary characters. The film's lead, of course, Leonardo DiCaprio, needs no further introduction, though *Critters 3* marks his first screen credit and Aimee Brooks plays his budding romantic interest, Annie.

"Now a lot of the actors were also once again, besides my brother Don, from my background in theater," explains Barry Opper. "For instance, José Luis Valansuela, the Latino renter in the apartment in the beginning, he was out of my theater world. In fact, he still has a huge theater in the downtown Los Angeles area."

"I recall auditioning for the part," says Katherine Cortez. "I remember I went out somewhere off Olympic in a kind of a warehousey kind of building. It had offices in it in an area that was probably not as populated as it is now. It was kind of sketchy, it wasn't where you would normally go for auditions. It wasn't Fox, it wasn't any of those places; it wasn't on anybody's lot. It was a little off the beaten path in terms of the business as usual, and I just remember Kristine [Peterson] and doing my reading, and I remember how warm she was and that she really seemed to like it. And you know, as actors, you're always so in-fucking-secure. And you often think that just because that happened doesn't mean they're going to want you, right? So you learn to be there and yet save some part of your soul so that it's not killing every single time you don't get the part, right? Which happens much more frequently than when you do. So you really have to develop some skill around that. I remember Kristine [Peterson] and I remember being in the room with her and I don't remember what I read or anything, but I remember liking her and I remember we had a really good rapport. I felt very relaxed with her. Whatever she did and whatever she said to me, I remember she really relaxed me. The rapport was really good in the room and I think because she did that, my reading was undoubtedly better. You know, because she took the time to do that. Not every director does that."

ON LEONARDO DiCAPRIO

Perhaps the most memorable aspect of *Critters 3* is the casting of Leonardo DiCaprio as the unlikely hero Josh, a role similar (but not as likable) to Scott Grimes's Bradley Brown in *Critters* and *Critters 2*. Notably, the young soon-to-be megastar's presence on set, although he was variously described as being a bit shy at the time, became immediately obvious to those around him.

"When you're looking at auditions, it's funny how when you see something really singular, that sort of moment, like, '*Oh, that's it,*'" says executive producer Mark Ordesky referring to DiCaprio's audition for *Critters 3*. "'*That's the one.*' It's exciting when it happens. That was exciting for sure, getting Leo for that role."

"I remember coming home from the first day of shooting and I said how there's this kid and he's really got something, I think this kid's going places. Well, *that* was Leo," recalls Katherine Cortez. "You know, he was just a kid. He was in high school. He went to the school that my kids ended up eventually going to, the Los Angeles Center for Enriched Studies (LACES). I remember liking him so much. He was so open and he didn't have any *anything* yet. You know what I mean?

He was just a kid who was open with a lot of good in him. He had a good nature. And he was very friendly and wanted to learn everything and had this wonderful presence. He was so real, even at that young age."

"*Critters 3* was interesting because it was Leonardo DiCaprio's first feature film," says David Witz. "He was just a kid and an interesting side fact is my mom, she wanted to get into the business, so I explained to her at that time, '*If you want to make a little more money, if you get your EMT card, you can be the craft service* and *medic.*' So she had gotten her EMT and she was the craft service medic on the show. And she became like everybody's mother, taking care of everything. But she remembers taking care of Leonardo on the set because he was still a teenager. She would always make sure she was keeping track of him."

"Well, nobody knew who he was yet because he wasn't famous yet," chuckles cinematographer Thomas Callaway. "He was kind of real quiet and didn't seem like he wanted to be there, which was a bit strange. The young girl [Aimee Brooks] who played opposite of him, there was this sort of teenage love interest thing going on. I think she really liked him but his body language was such – that when standing together, he was leaning so far the other way. I told him, '*Leo, you gotta stand up straight or you're not going to be in the shot.*' He was really cooperative though, he was just quiet and shy. I didn't get the sense he was happy to be there. I later saw or read somewhere that he has pretty much disowned this movie (laughs).

"Leo would hang out with us," fondly recalls special effects fabricator and puppeteer Paul Salamoff. "He was really into the effects stuff. I think that the Chiodos had worked with him on something else. I remember he got the job on *Growing Pains* when we were working on *Critters 3*. He was a good guy, really nice, and cool to work with. I mean, who knew? Who knew he'd go on to do such great things?"

TOURING THE TENEMENT
An Interview with Geoffrey Blake
("Frank," *Critters 3*)

How did you end up getting on board for *Critters 3*?

Kristine Peterson, the director, was very nice. I'm not sure if I auditioned or if it was offered. All I remember is I played a building maintenance guy. There were two jobs where I did it as tongue-in-cheek. I basically, one of my dear friends, and still to this day is one of my dear friends, is a wonderful character actor who also was my neighbor in Venice Beach at the time. And he actually won an Emmy for *The Sopranos*. His name is Joey Pantoliano. He's "Guido the Killer Pimp" in *Risky Business.* He's the bail bondsman in *Midnight Run* with De Niro and Charles Grodin. You know who he is. Joey Pantoliano is his name. Joey Pants is what he's known to all of us character actors.

So Joey Pants, he has a very distinct voice. *'It's very much like 'dis. He talks like 'dis.'* He's from Hoboken, New Jersey, and that's exactly how he talks. And he won the Emmy for playing Ralphie on *The Sopranos*. But he has a very distinct voice. And I used to mimic him all the time as friends. So two projects around that same era, I jokingly in the audition, just mimicked Joey Pants. So for my character, Frank in *Critters 3*, I did the voice. I went in and I basically did Joey Pants. So when you watch the movie, I've never seen the movie, but when you watch the movie, you'll hear this voice. And so that's actually a tribute to Joey.

What stands out to you from your experience on *Critters 3*?

I remember an incident that's kind of right up there with legendary lore of how on the fly, you know, whatever you need to do to make the movie, just make the shit up as you go along. Adapt.

Anything that comes up, you know, they had no budget, so whatever came up, you just kind of, you flew by the seat of your pants to do whatever you needed to do on the day to get the day done. I do remember that. And the two incidents I remember the most is, the critters were kind of a mechanical puppet, but that was supposed to operate, you know, there was supposed to be a person who operated it with a kind of a remote control or something, and it was supposed to control it. Now, I remember the day that I had my death scene, where the critter attacked me and killed, that the critter that was supposed to do that actually broke down. So it wasn't operating. So, basically, I had to put my hand up its wazoo and I basically had to pretend like I was dying and screaming and writhing in pain and doing all that while I was using my own hand to chomp at my neck. I was operating the critter as a puppeteer. Using my own hand manually while simulating that it was killing me. And that was fun. So when you see it, that's what's happening there.

I do remember particularly liking Kristine [Peterson]. I don't know what she ever went on to do, but I did like her. I do remember her shocking blonde hair, and she was very tall. And it was still the first time I met Leo, Leonardo DiCaprio. And then the next time I ran into him, I ran into him and he was doing *Growing Pains*, I think, on the Warner Bros. lot. And he was at the Taco Bell that's no longer a Taco Bell. I ran into him and his crew of teenage misfits. And he had just gotten the De Niro film, *This Boy's Life*. And that was going to launch his career. He was telling me about all that. And then, the next time I saw Leo was at a screening on the Paramount lot, and we both had the same acting coach, a guy named Larry Moss. And he's still Leo's on-set acting coach. He's my mentor as well. He's kind of the most famous acting teacher on the planet.

I then remember running into Leo at the Paramount screening on the lot at the Paramount Studios screen. *Forrest Gump* had just come out. So there I am, standing in the back of this theater next to Leo. And the credits came up and I turned to Leo and I said, '*Listen man, buckle your seatbelt, buddy.*' And he goes, '*Why?*' And I say, '*You are about to become a major movie star.*' I mean *The Boy's Life* movie had already come out, and he goes, '*No, I'm not. This is Johnny Depp's movie.*' And the movie we were screening was *What's Eating Gilbert Grape*. And he got an Academy Award nomination for it. And he was amazing in it. And from that point on, that's when Leonardo DiCaprio really became Leonardo DiCaprio. And so look at him now.

You have such an impressive array of credits to your name, and *Critters 3* is just a drop in the bucket. What are your reflections on having had a role in this American cult franchise?

Critters 3 to this day does have quite a cult following. I do get invited to these conventions... I haven't done a lot of horror movies. I've come to think of it as really the only horror movie I ever did. I was offered a lot of them, but I never did them. I don't particularly like horror movies. I don't watch them. I didn't see it. It does get me invited. That movie, because of Leo... I get invited to these conventions all the time. These horror conventions. I don't go to them very often because they're kind of bizarre. But, the last one I did was the L.A. Horror Convention. And, I sat there and you print up pictures of the movies you were in and you sign and sell them to people. We weren't getting much business. Eric Roberts was there for something. But I do remember sitting there and the main attraction that was lined around the building was whoever the woman is who was the star of Chucky. I couldn't tell her name, but she had the actual Chucky doll in her booth. And people were lining up to take pictures with Chucky. And I was thinking, you know, I should have thought ahead. I should have, you know, should have found a critter. Had an actual critter been there with me, I probably would have done a lot more business. Maybe the one I put my hand in. So that's *Critters 3*. That's the gift that keeps on giving. And I still haven't seen it (laughs). Maybe I'll get my 14-year-old to watch it here soon.

LOCATIONS

The budget-conscious production kept to a strictly limited array of locations mostly in downtown Los Angeles and Santa Monica. The exterior shots of the tenement building were filmed on location in downtown Los Angeles at 1220 S. Olive Street. A picnic spot and parking lot in the Santa Monica Mountains National Recreation Area represents the rural Kansas rest stop seen in the film's introduction sequence when Clifford changes a blown tire and the kids encounter Charlie in a wooded ravine. The entirety of the interiors were shot inside a rented out former Smart & Final warehouse located at 2233 W. Pico Boulevard in Santa Monica. (The warehouse location has long since been demolished and repurposed as a green space today.) New Line Cinema had rented the former warehouse months prior, established a small suite of offices and even shot the Martin Lawrence comedy *Talkin' Dirty After Dark* on the premises.

"What was really interesting about that warehouse location was it kind of had these offices where New Line Cinema was set up in," says David Witz. "But they had another show in there just before *Critters 3* and *4*. So we swooped in after this other show that was called *Talkin' Dirty After Dark,* and it's funny. I remember this news article in the local paper that was speculating about the set. People thought that porno films were being shot there (laughs). But what was crazy was, we had this office, and I can still picture it in my mind, it was this long corridor and we had offices going down a line and in the middle at the very end was a restroom. Many times the toilets would overflow and drain down the middle of the hallway and it was just the most absurd, disgusting office setups I've ever been in (laughs)."

To create the interior of the Iris Arms Apartment complex, production designer Philip Dean Foreman constructed hallways, faux staircases, a crawlspace, a basement laundry room, Frank's office, an elevator and lobby, and multiple apartment rooms inside the Smart & Final warehouse. However, the warehouse did not have a particularly high ceiling, which posed additional challenges and created a cramped environment. The sets were also built approximately four feet off the floor to accommodate the team of puppeteers needed to operate the variety of critter puppets. "Philip [Foreman] was really great to work with," attests cinematographer Thomas Callaway. "He was the first production designer that really had drawings and paintings of the sets before they even started building them. He would show Rupert and I these designs and I was just always impressed with his work. Really well done."

"The ceiling probably wasn't even 12 feet, it wasn't really high," Edward Chiodo explains. "Philip did an incredible job. Tom Callaway did an amazing job. They all did an amazing job lighting it all. I remember a funny story. We had one day on set when a light blew up and caught fire and the sprinklers went off. The sprinklers went on for quite a while because nobody knew how to turn them off (laughs). Electricians were running to kill all the power, the camera crew throwing tarps over the cameras and all the equipment, and everything was soaked, totally soaked."

"I was just driving by it recently," says Paul Salamoff. "Off of Cloverfield Drive, off the Tech Freeway as you're going to Santa Monica. There was this shopping mall, it was a defunct shopping mall that they turned into studios. But we shot there, which was really interesting. It was basically gutted and they built all of their sets in there. It was so great, it was really cool because *Critters 3* and *4* had these very immersive sets, especially *Critters 4*, because you felt like you were in a spaceship. Everything was closed off and that was kind of fun. For me, being a huge movie geek and being a big sci-fi fan, to actually feel like you were in the bowels of a spaceship with nothing to ruin that illusion was amazing."

REVAMPING THE CRITTERS

The Chiodos's crew on *Critters 3* and *4* were originally tasked with building mostly fully grown Krites with an expectation that the baby Krites would be restricted to a cameo appearance, not a main feature in either film. The production's minuscule operating budget also prompted the Chiodos to hire a much smaller, less experienced crew of puppeteers and fewer fabricators, a decision that caused tension between the Chiodo brothers and the producers. In terms of design, the Krites in both *Critters 3* and *4* were even larger than those in *Critters 2*, mostly to accommodate an even more intricate array of servos and cables.

"Some of the demands they made on us for *Critters 3* and *4*, impacted the ability to make performable puppets," Edward Chiodo explains. "They were coming down really hard on us for our failure to execute, but at the time, they didn't seem to take any responsibility that the asks they had were too big, and their expectations were beyond. And then like any creative person, it would grow. They'd want more and more and more, and they'd forgotten what the plan was. Again, we were going to build a certain amount of critters that were going to be used in both movies and babies were going to make a cameo appearance. The thing is, in *Critters 3* and *4*, one of the things they wanted to do was upscale the puppets. They were saying, '*Animatronics have*

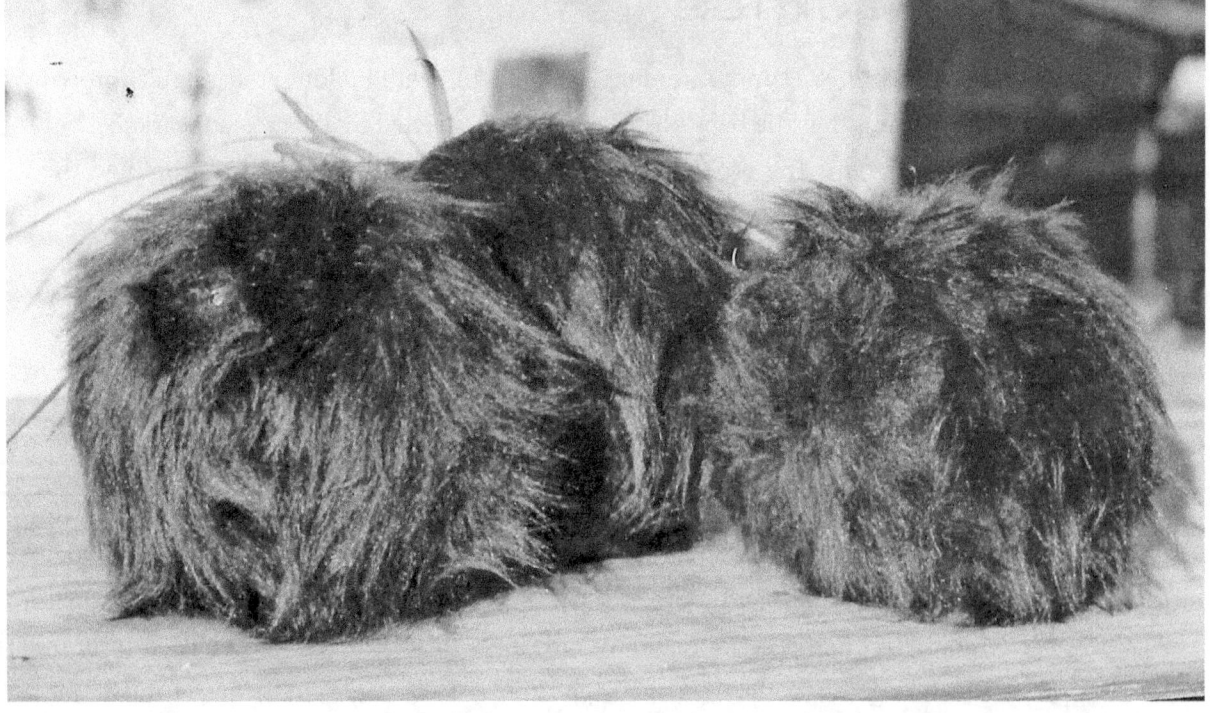

A limited variety of critters were designed and built to be used in both *Critters 3* and *Critters 4* (top), including conventional "rolling critters" (bottom). (Source: Paul Salamoff)

gotten really sophisticated and we want to up the sophistication of the critters – we want them to do more with their hands and their fingers and things.' Well, we reminded them that they were kind of useless appendages. They were just kind of there. They didn't do a lot with them. It was not about the hands and they said, '*No, we want to up that aspect.'* So we brought in Tim Ralston, an amazing designer and engineering mechanic. He designed these really sophisticated critter arms that had full movement. We had cable control arms and elbows and then circle controlled wrists and fingers. So, they were able to, with these telemetry gloves and the telemetry cable control, really create sophisticated movements. But to do that, we had to make the puppets bigger. The puppets in *Critters 2* were the perfect size. Those in *Critters 3* and *4* were too big. And then to put all the servo motors, then we had like five or six servos now in the body of the puppet. Plus all these additional cables coming out of them. They weighed a fucking ton. It was like holding a *fucking* bowling ball up (laughs)."

"I did some of the critters for *Critters 3* and *Critters 4,* and the critter eggs. Yeah, I was a critter egg guy," laughs Paul Salamoff, who was just 19 years old when working on *Critters 3* and *4*. "Critter balls, baby critters. I did the growing baby critter. I did the blown up critter head from *Critters 3*, the flattened bleach critter from *Critters 3*, the frozen laser critter from *Critters 4,* and a space creature specimen from *Critters 4*. And I designed three of them. I designed the blow up critter head, the flattened bleach critter, and the space creature specimen. One of my jobs I had was making a lot of the critter eggs and painting them. And that kind of painting I could handle. It's not so much detail painting as it was making things look real and so forth. So we had a lot of different eggs we had to make because some of them had to be really sturdy and strong and stuff like that, and some of them had to break, because there were scenes [where they] would break and there would be goo inside.

DID YOU KNOW?

The Krites possess the ability to launch quills at their prey. The quills, which are strong and sharp, contain a sedative-like venom that can quickly incapacitate an adult human. But what to do if spiked by such a prickly alien quill? Per an early draft of *Critters 3*, a mixture of burnt toast ("for the carbon") and milk reverses the most severe effects from the quill's venom, though the victim would still suffer from mild nausea.

"So, you know, one of the things that I really became was a proficient mold maker, and actually, I still have the picture of the glitter mold because that's one of my molds that I have. Yeah, and that was a matrix, silicone matrix mold, because the stearic acid, you know, you had to brush it in, in layers. And it couldn't be too strong, because then it wouldn't break. But it also couldn't be too light, because then it would be too fragile. So I was trying to figure out that happy medium. But the thing is, not busting it when you're trying to take it out of the mold. So I made a mold that, you know, the silicone could come off of the matrix part, the jacket of the mold, easier so you could pull it out separately and then pull the egg out without damaging it. And then just having to clean up the edge, which was fine, making a hole at the bottom and injecting the goop that we had to put in there and then sealing them up again and then painting them.

"That's one of the things that I was sort of involved with figuring out and I was sort of in charge of that problem set. When we had to do the critter that gets frozen, that was one of my gags because I got so good at working with stearic acid. So that critter literally had guts in it. I made it with internal organs that were made out of stearic acid. Different colors and different things. So when it shattered, it wasn't just a hollow thing. It actually had an internal structure in it that shattered as well. It was hard just keeping this thing from getting destroyed because it was so fragile. It was a one-take wonder kind of thing. I always consider myself more of a technician, an effects technician than an artist, even though what I was doing was very artistic, but it was more of the behind-the-scenes aspect of these creations. But I still like the fact that the Chiodo brothers trusted me enough to work on some of the more cosmetic kind of details to it."

DID YOU KNOW?

In March 2024, a screen-used Krite egg prop from *Critters 3* hit the auction block. It eventually sold for $1,150, which is considerably cheaper than what a full-sized Krite prop tends to go for. (Source: VIP Fan Auctions)

Fabricator Paul Salamoff created various Krite eggs
used in *Critters 3* and *Critters 4*.
(Source: Paul Salamoff)

THROUGH THE LENS
An Interview with Tom Callaway
(Director of Photography, *Critters 3* and *4*)

How did you get involved with making *Critters 3* and *4*?

Well, I had a camera assistant named Giles Dunning who is actually a DP now. Giles is British and I believe he lived with Rupert and his wife for a little while; I think they might have been family friends or something. Giles didn't want to be a camera assistant anymore and he was moving on to other things at this time and he told me about Rupert and Barry's films and encouraged me to interview for their upcoming projects. I set up an interview and scheduled an appointment to meet them. What's interesting is, Rupert is a car guy. He had this old Austin-Healey Sprite 'bugeye' that he had suped up; it had a V8 engine in it. At the time I had a De Tomaso Pantera, which is kind of a rare car, and I had parked in the parking lot and Rupert was late for the meeting. So, Rupert comes in and asks, *'Hey, who owns that car out there?'* I said, *'I do,'* and he kind of acknowledges and walks off down the hallway. I didn't know that it was Rupert at the time. So, when they call me back for the interview a few minutes later, we recognize each other from the lobby and we start talking and then we start talking about cars, and just really hit it off (laughs). Rupert ended up hiring me and then later on I interviewed with the director of *Critters 3*, Kristine Peterson, and she wanted to use me as well. It all ended up working out well. Rupert was a lot of fun to work with. I think *Critters 4* was the first movie he directed, but he was very prepared. We watched a few movies as part of our preparation. Because it was set in space, we really wanted it to look like *Alien*. That's what we were pushing for, that kind of feeling.

That's the striking thing about *Critters 4*, the aesthetic is just so different from the third one. Was this because of Rupert's role as director?

Yeah, I think so. Kristine was a more traditional director with an eye for coverage and the types of shots needed to complete the film. I had gotten to know Rupert a bit more while shooting *Critters 3* because he was on set every day and he would stop by to ask questions, show me things, and I would suggest things. He liked the idea of shooting at low angles with wider angle lenses and having big things in the foreground and that sort of stuff. He got really into that sort of thing and that is what I was really into as well. Sort of a film noir feeling to it. It ended up being sort of a film noir-space movie (laughs). The whole time I was shooting *Critters 3* I couldn't wait to shoot *Critters 4*.

It was *Critters 3* that you came up with that really awesome in-camera trick for the hologram...

That was an interesting day. They didn't have enough money to do the optical effects that were needed, but I had a friend who worked with laser technology at a company called Laser Media at the time... I talked to him about what I needed and he said '*You just need to pay for the laser rental and I'll come out and do it.*' I convinced Rupert to go with the in-camera effect and I'm surprised he ended up going for it. Then I thought, '*God, I hope I can pull this off,*' (laughs). So, we have this beam splitter set up in front of the camera and the laser is off to one side and Don Opper on set, and we did all of these cool shots with it. We also used an additional fiber optic light for the stone that lights up green when the kid holds it – we had a fiber optic cable that ran up his sleeve to light up the crystal. These days it would be much easier to do of course, but it was pretty cool at the time. So, after we finished shooting these two sequences, New Line just loved them, but asked '*Why are you spending money on optical effects before the movie's been cut?*' They didn't realize they were in-camera effects! That was pretty cool. I still use a few clips from these films on my reel because I think they still hold up, still look good.

Did you shoot the infamous critters going wild in the kitchen scene, with the beans and flour?

I shot parts of that scene, but we left a few shots for the second unit. We didn't do a whole bunch of second unit work on these films, there just wasn't the budget or crew for it, but we did use a second unit for this sequence because it was messy. I think I shot the master portion of that sequence and left some of the close-ups for the second unit. We shot both *Critters 3* and *Critters 4* with the latest high-speed stock that was available at the time, I think it was 5294. It was *very* light sensitive. We ended up shooting in very low-light level environments for these films.

How was it working with the Chiodo brothers and their crew on *Critters 3*?

The Chiodos were on set a lot. They did some of the puppeteering but not all of it; they had a crew. They were probably less hands-on for *3* and *4* but they were totally there building and designing the critters and had a lot of input on the gags and setups. Both directors listened to the Chiodos because they had the most knowledge and experience in how to pull these kinds of effects off. I absolutely loved working with the Chiodos and I would work with those guys any day. We did some fun stuff with the critters. They had this critter ball that rolls and I got this device from an engineer at Panavision – he actually built it for something else – and it was this scooter-type device with one wheel and a handle sticking out the back. We mounted the camera on the front on a platform and then we mounted the critter ball in front of the camera. The critter ball was mounted on an axle thing. It allowed me to drive the camera down the hallway with the critter ball moving. It was pretty cool. We also used it a lot in *Critters 4*.

The idea was to shoot the films back-to-back and then release them over time?

Yes, that was the plan. We would shoot them back-to-back and then they would be released over time. Because the end of *Critters 3* and beginning of *Critters 4* overlap, we shot those segments together before we left the set to go shoot on location (rooftop sequence) when the set was demolished and rebuilt for *Critters 4* in the same space. The first part of the day was directed by Kristine and then the second part of the day was directed by Rupert.

Kristine Peterson was from the Roger Corman school of filmmakers like Barry Opper and Rupert Harvey that was focused on getting the shot, cutting costs, and moving on rapidly. How rapid of a pace was *Critters 3*?

Not that we had a big budget, but it was more than the Corman movies. I felt that she settled too easily as opposed to having a little more time or a little more money. I think she did a good job though. She got along well with the actors and seemed to know what she wanted. I kind of had that feeling she didn't like me that much because I kept talking to Rupert all the time (laughs). I hope that's not the case. She pretty much let me do what I needed to do. There were a few things she absolutely wanted. There was this one shot she wanted, in which one of the critters opens its mouth and she wanted to push the camera inside its mouth and see that little dangling thing in the back of its throat. It was kind of a weird thing, because the Chiodos had to build an oversize critter in order for the camera and lens to fit inside there. We eventually did it. That was one of the few things she was really pushing for and she really got into it. I'm not sure how well we were able to pull it off.

The third one ended up being more comedic than anything, even hammy. Was that something teased out more in editing or was it premeditated?

I think it was something that evolved while we were shooting. And then the editor felt like the comedic aspects were working better and decided to play it up. Like the woman who lived in the building and wore the big floppy rabbit slippers. She ended up becoming more of a character in the way she was cut in post-production rather than the way we shot that character. I think they thought she was funny and likable and just played her up a lot more. I think this tone really came from the way it was edited along with some of the music.

Were there any gags you were particularly proud of?

In *Critters 3*, we did this cool shot that had a critter come lunging up this laundry chute. We built a chute and laid it on its side and rigged the camera to it and the woman who closed the chute was laying on her side. Just when the critter gets to the top she slams the door on it. That was pretty cool. We dropped the camera down the chute to make it look like a POV and it comes out the other end. We didn't have much of a budget so we were constantly coming up with these goofy ideas to keep it looking interesting.

Did you use a special lighting rig to get the eyes of the critters to glow?

The way that is done is, we made a special matte box that had a beam splitter in it and then we mounted a light on the side of the camera that shot right down the path of the lens and back at the subject. The Chiodos cut out little pieces of Scotchlite, a reflective tape-like material, and glued them onto the eyes of the critters. Then when the light hits the Scotchlite, it reflects right back at the lens and it gives off a glow effect. If it falls off angle, it doesn't really glow. It was kind of a pain to get it right. They had a much larger budget and more time when shooting *Critters* and *Critters 2* than we had. The Scotchlite effect using the beam splitter was so tedious and time consuming that I ended up buying a new light rig at the time called a data light and I was able to take off the matte box and put this light right next to the lens and it ended up working just as well as the beam splitter. We used this same technique in *Critters 4* as well. These days you could get the eyes to glow much easier or just use digital effects for the glow.

When you wrapped shooting *Critters 3* and took that 2 week break, that was just enough time to get the sets ready for the next shoot right?

Yeah, they scheduled it that way so they would have a few weeks to get the sets ready for *Critters 4*, the spaceship interiors. They were just barely able to get it done on time and I believe they were still painting some of the sets while we were shooting on others.

Were there any big mishaps or catastrophes on set that you can recall?

Well this is kind of strange, but this was the beginning of digital editing. Avid had just come out and there were two other systems. One of these used this stack of VHS decks. We ended up using a similar system but instead of tape, it was on Laserdiscs. So during editing, our footage was transferred to Laserdiscs. I remember this system and process being crazy. There were tons of these Laserdiscs to sort through and it was also expensive at the time. That system pretty much died out after *Critters 3* and *4*. They were competing with Avid, and lost.

Was there a big difference between working with Kristine on *Critters 3* and then with Rupert on *Critters 4*?

It was. Rupert and I had very similar tastes in movies and not so much with Kristine. Kristine and I got along minus that last week. I'm proud of the work I did on both films. It was tough on *Critters 3* because you're stuck in these small apartment room sets and an attic space. But shooting on location on the rooftop was a lot of fun. The building was downtown L.A. somewhere and after 9 p.m. we were unable to enter the building. The only way to get to the roof was using a scissor lift that took you up about five stories, and it just barely made it. It was a bit of a time consuming issue and a safety issue. We were shooting with the underage actors and the young boy had a twin that allowed us to maximize the time we could have them on location. It was a challenging 3 days worth of shoots. And they were all night shoots too. Super low-light conditions as well. Philip [Dean Foreman] had built this faux skyline that we brought up there and because the building was supposed to be on fire we had rigged some flickering lights and some tube lights to make that burning effect. The roof itself was kind of flat and blank, so antennas and other objects were brought in to dress it up a bit. On one side of the roof there was a building that was pretty close but they didn't want us shining lights on it and disturbing the occupants and the other side was kind of wide open with very few lights; it was just a dark space. It was a challenge to frame it in a way that you felt like you were in a city.

Do you remember seeing either *Critters 3* or *4* for the first time? What was the reaction?

Well, during the color timing process I saw them both a bunch of times. But it was cool because we watched them on a big screen at FotoKem so we were seeing 35mm prints. There was a screening and I'm pretty sure we screened them both on one night in Westwood. We had a cast and crew screening I believe. In terms of reactions, I think everyone had high hopes for *Critters 4* because it was so different. *Critters 3* was kind of run-of-the-mill, just another low-budget creature movie. I always wondered that if somehow *Critters 4* had come out first that they might have given it a little bit bigger of a release. The cast was great and the production value just seemed so much bigger. I don't know how *Critters 3* ultimately made out. I know fans of *Critters* don't seem to care too much for the sequels, from what I've read.

PRODUCTION

The 25-day shoot began on Wednesday, 27 March 1991 with the first day of shooting tackling the scenes in Frank's office. While most of the principal photography would be shot first (and out of sequence), the second unit and hero puppet work was saved for last and shot at the end of the schedule during what the crew dubbed "Critter Week." But, with almost no budget and little room for error, the production grinded on with few compromises and much frustration.

"Well, I think that getting the critters action, that was always tricky," production manager David Witz explains. "I don't remember anything that stands out other than the typical issues with night shoots and working with child actors and being confined to the interior sets. They thought that there were some efficiencies doing a back-to-back shoot, but it also caused some problems too because we didn't have as much downtime as we probably should have in between finishing *Critters 3* and starting *Critters 4*. It would have been better if they both would have been in space or they both would have been in an apartment, but they were both completely different."

The first day of principal photography on *Critters 3* started out rough. Script supervisor Julia Kohlas stuck her fingers in the animal handler's rat cage and was bitten, requiring a tetanus shot and bandages. Within the first hour of shooting, the crew's generator malfunctioned and needed to be replaced. While the crew waited, attempts were made to shoot close-ups of the critter's eyes reflecting through the grate in Frank's office, but technical difficulties prevailed and the shot was pushed back to Critter Week. A new generator arrived after the lunch break, but an animatronic hero puppet then broke down. Despite the rocky start, the mishaps did not cause any serious schedule setbacks for the production.

"The production designer was this guy, Philip Foreman, who's a very eccentric, interesting guy. And he was up for the challenge," notes David Witz. "I remember that some of the things he used to build the sets at the space station were like dish drying racks that, you know, they bought hundreds of them and put them in the ceiling to get this look. It was interesting. But yeah, it was a challenge. For instance, we were shooting on the roof of this building in downtown L.A. that was next to one of the busiest fire stations in all of downtown L.A.. Constantly having sirens go off. And so it was a bit of a nightmare, but luckily I had one of the, at the time I didn't know, but as it turns out, he's one of the best sound mixers out there, this guy named José García. And I think I had worked with him on something else before and it was one of my best arranged marriages where I hooked him up with, because I had worked with him before and he had a really bad boom operator and I had worked with this other sound team who had a really good boom operator and so I introduced them and I think to this day they still are a team. José García and Jonathan Fuh. So I hooked them up. It's one of my most rewarding crew achievements. But José, he's from Mexico and he has a great attitude. He's one of my favorite sound mixers. If I'm ever working anywhere where I can hire, I always call him first because he's the best at dealing with stuff and going with the flow and everybody always gets along with him. So I've worked with him several times. I remember he was challenged with all the sirens all the time there."

DID YOU KNOW?

Dan Bradley, the second unit director and stunt coordinator on *Critters 3*, was originally cast to play Jason Voorhees in *Friday the 13th Part VI: Jason Lives*, but was replaced by C.J. Graham shortly after filming started. A top talent in his field, Bradley later worked on films such as *Independence Day*, *Spider-Man 2* and *3*, *The Bourne Supremacy*, and *Indiana Jones and the Kingdom of the Crystal Skull*, among others.

"Kristine Peterson was eager to learn how the critters worked. She had come from an AD background," Edward Chiodo recalls. "So again, more about the organization, but she was really eager to learn how the critters worked. She wanted to work with the critters, but then again, even then, we ended up doing a lot of second unit type stuff. Kristine didn't always get to shoot the critters, but she was fine. I mean, she had stepped into a machine. People that had already kind of been there, done that. I found her generally pleasant to work with. I don't think I had any real issues with her. We learned from *Critters 2* that there were a bunch of specialty gags that we were going to be building, and the closeup of the critter mouth happened to be one of them. And in another one of the gags, a flare gets shoved down the throat of a critter, and then it illuminates the inside of it."

Shooting special effects sequences and working with puppets is often unpredictable. The fragility of the working motors and power sources of the puppets and the intricacy of the designs leaves wide open the likelihood of encountering technical issues, usually at the most inopportune times. However, bad decision making, minuscule operating budgets, and accelerated schedules can also lead to catastrophes concerning those same special effects sequences.

A rare photo of Charlie Chiodo (left), Edward Chiodo (middle), and Stephen Chiodo (right) on set during the production of *Critters 3* and *Critters 4*. (Source: Paul Salamoff) (Publisher's Note: Apologies for the image quality here!)

"The first night of shooting for us on *Critters 3* was a disaster," says Edward Chiodo. "Stephen was there with Jarn Heil who was our lead on set. They're shooting this sequence with the food fight, and they have the flour all in the air and they have candles going and then Jarn turns to Stephen and says, '*This is how silo explosions happen.*' And then a split second later – *woosh* – it blows up in a flash of flames. The puppets got singed and they had flour and all this stuff caked inside of them. *Critters 3* and *4* was a rough show all around. Everybody bit off way more than we could chew on that budget. I mean, the concept of doing two movies back-to-back with essentially the same budget we had for *Critters*. It was tough. And that was like the first argument I had with Rupert and Barry that night. I remember when the puppets got back to the shop that night, I called them and I got into a rip-roaring argument with them saying, '*Have we learned nothing?*' This is our third and fourth movie and I told them, I said, '*We're going to be here all night fixing these.*' You know, we had like an eight o'clock call. I said, '*I can't guarantee the puppets are going to be there at eight. They're going to be there when they get there.'* Because now the people that were working all day now have to work all night to fix them so they can be ready for shooting. And that just started off a real rocky relationship in those movies. And it all came out, we've reconciled, we're all friends and stuff, but the circumstances at the time made it really tough."

In a pre-shooting script version of *Critters 3*, the Krites throw cherry tarts at each other while a *Muppets* segment featuring the Swedish Chef baking pies plays on the television. After a few splats to the face, the Krites take off to hunt down Josh and the remaining survivors as they make their way to the building's crawlspace. This scene of course was later rewritten as the now infamous pork n' beans food fight among the Krites, which caused significant damage to the hero puppets much to the chagrin of the Chiodo brothers and their team who spent 24 hours working to clean up the puppets before the next scenes were to be shot.

"I do remember that because yeah, it was crazy, but when flour gets into the air it can be combustible," says special effects fabricator Paul Salamoff. "I remember it being a big concern. But I also remember the fucking baked bean fight - the baked bean fight which fucking ruined our puppets (laughs). Which was so hard. I mean, it was one of the last things I remember doing, but that was a fucking nightmare getting that stuff out of the puppets." Fabricator Deborah Galvez concurs, noting: "They wanted to use a hero puppet on the scene where they were dunking it in a pot of pork and beans. I told them, *'Don't use the hero puppet because it's animatronic – use the stunt puppet instead.'* But they wanted to see full articulation. And I said, *'Don't use it because you're going to ruin the mechanics of the RC servos in there.'* But they wanted to use it and they ruined the puppet. And I remember I had to spend an all-nighter repairing that. And I was really upset. They should have used the stunt puppet."

Besides causing serious damage to some of the various hero and stunt puppets, the Chiodos's critter crew also faced close calls concerning their health and well-being following some gags gone awry. "Funny, the flare gag, when we shot that, it was almost a catastrophe" recalls Edward Chiodo. "In the movie, the lights go out in the apartment house, and they're going through and the female electrician or lineman [Katherine Cortez], she's walking with a flare. A critter comes out of the laundry shoot and she takes the flare and puts it in its mouth. And we rehearsed it. I was puppeteering that. And we rehearsed it several times. And she was always supposed to stop short of putting the flare in. But when cameras were rolling, in the heat of the moment, she stuck the live flare down the throat of the critter's mouth. And so it was only, you know, just rubber between my hand and a lit flare. So I saw it coming at me on the monitor. And I freaked, you know, I came out, I was just yelling. I said, '*What are we doing here?*' Because there were little safety things like throughout, we were like, '*No, what are we doing here?*' I could have gotten seriously injured."

Although Katherine Cortez did not entirely recall melting the stunt puppet with a live flare, she did recall shooting the darkened scene with Leo. "I don't quite remember all of it, but I do remember it was tricky," Cortez says. "I remember that it was dark and those flares were live."

The infamous flare gag and flour dust incidents were not the only mishaps involving fire safety. "So, on *Critters 3*, the sequence involving the ladder going up to the attic, it was a squib setup involving a critter," explains Paul Salamoff. "When the squib exploded – the puppeteer, not realizing the squib actually caught on fire – it caught the stand on fire, and I was puppeteering it, and the critter was on fire. It wasn't like, you know, we're not talking like anything crazy, but, my hand is in the fucking puppet. That was a little terrifying. I get PTSD every time I see that scene. But, you know, that was fun regardless. We weren't really feeling a lot of fatigue. I mean, there were long hours, of course, but I didn't feel abused by that show. It was hard, but I felt like we were treated well. I just really enjoyed that show because we were given, Mark [Villalobos] and I, were given so much responsibility, you know, and we really embraced it. And the heroes really trusted us and we really earned that trust, you know, and it was a real, how do I put this, confidence builder, I guess, in regards to being professional. I really felt like I was being trusted and I was earning that trust."

Opposite: A smiling Deborah Galvez poses with a Krite hat and critter puppet during the lead up to "Critter Week." (Source: Paul Salamoff)

REMEMBERING *CRITTERS 3*
An Interview with **Kristine Peterson**
(Director, *Critters 3*)

During the late 1980s, you had come off this really, really intense schedule of filmmaking. Do you recall how you got attached to the *Critters 3* project?

Well, one never knows really why you're hired because I was a hired director. I was a hired hand. But I had been interviewing and talking to Barry Opper for probably a year or two about various projects – things I brought him, and was he interested, and who was he, and who was I? I think we really liked each other. I liked him a lot, and I think he liked me. He liked the films that I had made. Because by that time, I had, well, I don't know which sequence that was, but was it my third one? Anyway, I had done *Deadly Dreams*. I had done *Body Chemistry*, which had done very, very well. So he was interested and he called me up and just said '*Will you come and interview?*' That's how it happened. I went and talked to New Line. I actually did a phone interview and I don't even know that it went that well. I was up in Seattle and my father had just died and I think the producer said, '*Barry, you know, she seems a little flat.*' And he said, '*Well, her father just died. So when she's coming back to L.A. next week, will you give her an interview then?*' I think I lost the job and then got the job. So then I went in person and I was in a little bit better frame of mind and I was very excited about it. A bad interview and then a decent interview. But Barry was my champion. I mean he championed me here. Barry was really wonderful to work with, great producer, wonderful to work with. And anything he could do to help.

So he was kind of hands-on, like on the set?

Yeah, he was there all the time. He worked a little bit with the second unit and did some work with them. And he'd say, '*Oh, we got you some extra shots. You wanted this and this, but we got this and this too. We added some shots.*' It was nice. He was very good.

Did you get a chance to work with Barry after *Critters 3* or was that it?

No, uh-uh. Well, you know, it's very hard sometimes to find projects that come together. But I'm sure he would have and I would have because it was a very good experience.

Do you recall the particular shoot that involved the critters with the beans and the flour? So there was a story going around that the flour dust and with the lights hooked up, that it almost caused an explosion or there was a flash fire or something.

Oh, that's fantastic. I actually did not know that (laughs). That's funny. That's very funny. Well, those are actually two things I didn't know about, so that's interesting to hear.

I can appreciate how difficult the shoot must have been for you all on *Critters 3* with the night schedules, the children, underage actors, and the amount of visual effects and puppets, it was like the trifecta of challenges, and I'm sure the tight schedule and a very limited budget didn't help either. But the fact that you were able to pull it all off and make it work, I just knew that there would be some fascinating stories, how you tackled all those challenges.

I don't know how fascinating that is (laughs). Night schedules, I'll just say, I don't really have anything new to contribute. They're always a little bit difficult, but you just kind of turn off the rest of your life while you're doing it, and that's what you do. So it's not so horrible unless you're shooting outdoors and the sun is coming up and then panic sets in. But otherwise, nights are just, you know, they are what they are. They're difficult, but you just kind of adjust to it. And you know, the kids, we use the twins, which a lot of people do.

So Christian and Joseph [Cousins] were very sweet kids, and they just alternated and they were both very good and tuned in. I mean the parents were on top of things, they did their schooling. I don't really have any super difficulties to talk about them except which can happen to anyone who's directing scenes with children – and I don't have a specific incident – but it's very hard if you want to change a line or change the way they're delivering a lot because they kind of become, they're taught by usually a parent or a tutor and then if you want to change that it's really hard for them sometimes to kind of do that. Not always, but sometimes, because they're kind of prepped for it. So I would say that's the only major difficulty I would find with it. Which I just want to say didn't happen very often.

How was it balancing the amount of creature effects and the actors? Was that second unit or did you kind of do both?

We did both because a lot of those creature things happened with the main actors. There was almost always an interaction. So definitely hands-on with the Chiodo brothers. Total hands-on.

And at that point, I think with the creature designs, they had kind of, in a way, perfected some aspects of them?

They had. They were very, very good with them. I will say, I contributed two things to the movements or the attributes of the critters. And one was, I said, '*Well, can't you get these to move differently?*' because they would just roll the balls through the scenes, right? And I said, '*Well, three things.*' One was, in order to get their takeoff, when they're kind of spinning in place before the takeoff, we put a bit in them and attached it to a power drill. So just behind the critter, there was someone with a power drill who would power the bit and make them spin before letting them go. It was really fun, innovative and a lot of fun. And then I said, '*Can't you make these critters go around corners?*' And they just looked at me like I was crazy (laughs). And I said, '*Well, it would be really nice if they could chase someone kind of around the corner.*'

The Chiodo brothers were very inventive. So they came back the next day and said, '*We figured it out. What we're doing is we're going to weight one side of the globe. And when we roll it, it will head towards that heavy side and it actually goes around corners.*' You can see it in the basement in a laundromat where it goes around the corner and chases Diana Bellamy. It was fun. And then the other one was just kind of a weird little touch that I had a bug about, which is I wanted them to scream, you know, break a glass. What I had them do was, I said '*Can you build a close-up of a uvula and then you can put your finger in it and wiggle it?*' And that's what they did, they made this special throat of a critter and when it screeched, you could see the uvula wiggling (laughs). I really enjoyed those moments where you had to get inventive to make them come alive.

The Chiodo brothers did a great job. They were very inventive. They created the whole thing. It was fun to be able to add something.

I'm not sure at what stage you might have shot in this part, but when Charlie talks to the other bounty hunter Ug, Tom Callaway mentioned bringing in a team that had a laser and did the entire effect in-camera, which is awesome. Do you recall that particular setup?

Oh right, right. I mean, I was there. We shot it. I did not invent the process, so if Tom is saying he kind of invented that, I would have to say yeah, he probably did. It was probably great. I was very upset during that shoot because we didn't have time to have any practice and I couldn't figure out the positioning; I didn't know where the eye line was supposed to be. When you watch the film, you can see the eye line is off. It's not right. He's [Don Opper] not looking in the right place. So, I was very distressed by that. I didn't know that it was going to be off, but I didn't know where it was supposed to be. So, I was saying, '*Tom, where's the eye line? Where does he look?*' And no one knew, you know? So we just made a choice and I just wish that we could have done better with it.

But, you know, listen, there are flaws. There are flaws. We know there are flaws. But that's hard. I mean, that kind of thing where you're doing things in pieces is very difficult to do without money to be able to prep it and redo it and do some changes and experiment. My one regret is not having enough money to do it right.

I could imagine that the continuity aspect will be really difficult. Trying to not only shoot but edit the various scenes, especially the attack scenes, if the critters aren't rolling right or flying through the air right…

Our problems were actually bigger than that (laughs). They were bigger than that. Not having enough time is very difficult. Very difficult. Because you lose things that need to be in the film to make it stronger and better and more powerful. And sometimes you have to drop things and it makes it a little bit weaker. So that's the difficulty of it.

Do you recall viewing the final product for the first time?

Well, when you're in the editing room, you're seeing the different products every step of the way. We definitely had some surprises because we were going from film to video, and there was a shot in the sky that I think was one of the critters that went up and exploded. And we edited on video and then when we cut the film, the negative, and put it together, you could see all the wires and lines. So we had to back off. That was a period of time where video editing was just coming in, rather than cutting on either a flatbed or a Moviola. And the experience of the story and of the cuts is very different on video than on film. Okay, well let me just, I don't mean to be didactic, but I'll tell you the huge difference that I learned between cutting film and editing on video. In video, at least back then, not as much information is on each frame, right? Each frame has less information than film. Film has a lot of information.

And I mean by that, the pixels and everything, what your eye takes in. So in video, what you see, you take in very quickly and your eye kind of gets tired of it. So you tend to cut faster, meaning you end the shot sooner, right? Whereas in film, your eye lingers because there's so much depth to it and detail to it compared to video. And that sort of feeds into the explanation of why MTE and the fast cutting works so well, right? It doesn't work so well with film because you're still trying to take in the image when if you cut away, right, you cut away too soon. So what happens is if you cut in video, and I mean video, I don't mean like high-def or anything, but if you cut in video and then go to film, you have a sense of everything happening too quickly. It's just out of your grasp. You're like, '*What, what, what?*' So you have to consciously know that and then back off and let things linger a bit longer.

So it's huge, it's very, very different to do something in video and then take it to film. If you keep it in video, it's okay because your eye gets tired at the time when you're cutting. But if you go to film, your eye is still hungry. And so you are playing catch up. It's like, '*Wait, wait, wait.*' Anyway, it's just a funny thing that I learned on that film is that you have to be very careful if you're going from one to the other. It doesn't apply anymore, but it applies to the older films. It's a little bit like, you know in the 30s and 40s when they made films, everybody talked too fast, right?

Okay, well it's the same thing. It's because when you speak it in film, it comes off faster than in real life. So, film actors actually speak more slowly than they do normally. There is a style. They often think, '*Oh, there's a style for stage and a style for film, but there IS actually a style for film.*' Because it's less, but it's also slower. Even though most directors say do the same thing again, but faster. They mean something different. They mean action. It's speaking, it's not saying it faster.

Ultimately, Rupert Harvey goes on to direct the fourth one. Was there any talk in the beginning to have you do both *3* and *4*?

No, never. It was always going to be two different directors. It wouldn't have been a bad idea to have one person do them both, but that wasn't what we were doing. And also Rupert was one of the producers, so I think he wanted to do one. I don't think it was a decision, '*Kristine can only do one, I think Rupert wants to do one so who will do the other?*'

What was your take on Leonardo DiCaprio being part of the cast at that time? A couple folks had mentioned that you could just tell that this kid had this raw, unbridled talent. Did you kind of feel the same way, that there was something special about him, even at that stage?

Well, it was not unbridled (laughs). He knew exactly what he was doing. He was terrific. And I said to him, I mean, as soon as he walked in and started reading, we went, '*Oh, this guy is a star. He's fantastic.*' I mean, you knew it instantly. I said to him once, I think early on, I said, '*You know, you're a good actor.*' And he said, '*Well, at least all those lessons weren't for nothing.*' So he worked at it. He worked at it very hard. And I think he was a great actor. You could tell instantly. And that was the same way for Rupert when Angela Bassett walked in. I don't know how she came off in the movie, but in the room she was spectacularly good and could do anything. Same with Leo. Leo could do anything. He was great.

So it's kind of safe to say that it was, you know, from a director-to-actor perspective, that there was definitely a comfort level that you had with him and his role and his abilities.

Oh yeah, absolutely. The older woman who played the grandmother [Frances Bay], she brought a lot of her grandkids, who were around Leo's age, and when he came on the screen, everybody else started screaming in the screening room. I was like, '*What is going on?*' I didn't know he was such a heartthrob. I hadn't watched his TV show, so I didn't really know him from that. I only knew him from the auditions. It was hilarious. I thought, '*Oh my God, he already has a following.*'

So, absolutely no surprises on your end that he had gone on to do exactly what a lot of people thought he was going to do and just ride that trajectory forward through his career?

Yes, I think that's true. I think you could say that.

Director Kristine Peterson in action on the set
of her hit thriller, *Body Chemistry* in 1990. (Source: Kristine Peterson)

So many people dismiss *Critters* 3 and 4, you just slide it to the side. But there are so many aspects to both of them that are extremely interesting for the period in which they were made and some of the talent that was involved with both productions. It's just such a great story.

Yeah, I think there's a reason that it's swept under the rug a bit. It really did not have... I hate to go back to the budget. It's the one thing I regret. It did not have the budget that it needed. That would have made it sharper and would have made the critters stronger, more dangerous, more forceful. I think as it plays now, it plays more like a kid's movie rather than an adult movie. And I don't know that it originally was supposed to be that.

So, that's a great point. Script-wise, did you get the sense that it was perhaps a little bit darker, maybe not darker is the right word or not, but a little more intense than the final product?

I don't know if I'd call it darker, but I would say it held together better, it was more action-oriented, and I think it moved along better. Let's just say the script was really good, and I wish that we had had more money to really fulfill all of its potential.

I can imagine too, having it set inside an apartment building is, to me, it just sounds so difficult with the tightness of the spaces. Did you find that particular set design particularly difficult to work with?

Oh yeah. We were supposed to be in an apartment building that had floors. So every time they were doing something in a stairwell, I had problems. I had to figure out how to shoot it because there were no stairwells. We could go up only half a floor. So we had to fake all of the stairwells and floors. It was terrible. I didn't like that. That is tough.

I had a feeling that it was going to be really, really tough. Once I had heard that it was inside a facility like that, I was like, '*Ah, I can't imagine that.*' Well, it worked better for Rupert because he didn't have to deal with verticality. His was all horizontal. Mine was vertical. That made it really difficult. You always figure out something. And that made it really difficult. You always figure out something. But that's another thing where you go, '*We could have made it a little better if we'd actually had some verticality.*' So things like that. That has to do with time and money. I hate to say it. Because the intention is there. The intention is to do that. And there was the rooftop scene at the end. I had a problem with the props because we were supposed to be throwing things out at the beginning and I couldn't. And we didn't have the right props. We were throwing things that were fluttering away in the wind. That was a little bit difficult.

The scene I do like is where Marcia [Katherine Cortez] is hanging upside down on a rope. And I actually often think about that, where she goes... She's hanging there, and she sees a phone, but she goes, '*One step at a time, Marcia, one step at a time.*' And whenever I'm in hot water in my life. I think, '*One step at a time.*' I thought she was a really wonderful actress. In fact, I used her in *The Hard Truth* where she plays a police detective.

CRITTERS 3
SHOOTING SCHEDULE

Schedule-wise, *Critters 3* unfolded mostly according to plan. Limiting the number of locations, splitting duties between units, and shooting most of the puppet sequences over a dedicated week helped to increase efficiency. Below are some highlights of the original schedule based on call sheets and production notes.

Day 1: (6:30 AM Call)
Int. Frank's Office - Frank fixes a broken window, gets gooed, and talks to Briggs on the telephone.
Int. Elevator - Frank counts tenants.
Int. Lobby - Rosalie thanks Frank, helps Mario.

Day 2: (7 AM Call)
Int. Basement Laundry Room
Int. Second Floor Hallway

Day 3:
Int. Basement Stairs / Laundry Room

Day 4: (7 AM Call)
Int. Basement Stairs, Lobby - Annie finds Rosalie, fights critter; dislodges critter from Rosalie's leg, and calls Dad. Rosalie drops laundry down chute.

Day 5:
Int. 2nd Floor Hallway

Day 6:
Int. Clifford's Hallway/Apartment Dining Room
Int. Crawlspace

Day 9: 2nd Unit Stunt Day (6 PM Call)
Ext. Iris Apartment's Exterior - Marcia climbs onto cables and falls down to the phone booth.

Day 10: (7 AM Call)
Int. Third Floor - Marcia with flares; critters block landing; Dark critter almost gets Marcia.

Day 11: (7 AM Call)
Int. Clifford's Apartment Dining Room

Day 12:
Int. Clifford's Hallway (dark)
Int. Clifford's Apartment Dining Room (dark)
Int. Crawlspace (dark)

Day 13: (7 AM Call)
Int. Third Floor/Crawlspace - Josh pokes his head up into the crawlspace; the gang struggles to pull up Rosalie; Annie and Josh crawl to the elevator; Josh and Annie climb a ladder.

Days 14 and 15:
Int. Crawlspace
Int. Elevator

Day 16: (7 AM Call)
Int. Crawlspace, Elevator - Josh kills critters; Mr. Menges's jacket mysteriously moves; Annie sees a rat and falls to the elevator roof; Josh and Annie think they killed Marcia.

Days 17 and 18:
Ext. Rest Area

Day 22: (9 AM Call)
Ext. Iris Arms Apartment Building - Marcia pulls up; Rent-a-truck arrives; movers move a mattress; Clifford crashes into Rent-a-truck; everyone runs to the front of cars after the crash; Josh and Briggs enter the building; critter POV shot.

Day 25: (5:30 PM Call)
Ext. Roof - Aimee and Josh look for a way out; Charlie arrives
Ext. Street in Front of Iris Arms Apartment

DIRECTOR: KRISTINE PETERSON
PRODUCERS: B. OPPER/ R. HARVEY
UPM: DAVID WITZ
1ST A.D.: JOHN VOHLERS
2ND A.D.: LAURA GROPPE
213-315-4900 OFFICE
213-828-3341 FAX

"CRITTERS 3"
CALL SHEET
CALL TIME: 630A

SHOOT DAY 1 OF 25
DAY/DATE: TUE. 27 1991
SUNRISE: 5⁴⁷ AM
SUNSET: 6¹⁰ PM

SCENE	PGS	D/N	SET/ DESCRIPTION	CAST	LOCATION
31	1/8	D	INT. FRANK'S OFFICE: FRANK LOOKS OUT BROKEN WINDOW	7	2233 PICO SANTA MIRWICH, CA
33	1/8	D	INT. FRANK'S OFFICE: FRANK GETS GREEN GOOED.	7	
B33PT.1	2/8	D	INT. FRANK'S OFFICE: FRANK CACKLES TO HIMSELF.	7, D-2	
3A	2⁵/8	D	INT. FRANK'S OFFICE: FRANK TALKS TO BRIGGS ON PHONE	7, (RATS)	
21	4/8	D	INT. ELEVATOR: FRANK COUNTS TENANTS.	7	
22	7/8	D	INT. PARADISE LOBBY: ROSALIE THANKS FRANK & HELPS MARIO.	7, 8, 10	
	TOTAL = 4⁴/8				

CAST	CHARACTER	PU	MU / REH	ON SET	REMARKS
A. JEFFREY BLAKE	FRANK (SW)		6:30A	7:15A	R.P.T. TO STAGE
D. MARIE BELLAMY	ROSALIE (SW)		10:30A	11:45A	J

STANDINS / ATMOSPHERE X S.I.'S	CALL	ON SET	IMPORTANT NOTES
TINA ARVANITES	6³⁰A	6³⁰A	
ROBIN BOYD	6³⁰A	6³⁰A	**NO SMOKING ON STAGE**
			PLEASE DRESS WARMLY - STAGE IS CHILLY

DEPARTMENT	MISCELLANEOUS & SPECIAL INSTRUCTIONS
PROPS	MATTRESS; FISHBOWL; GOLDFISH; SCREWDRIVER; COFFEE MAKER; DESK JUNK; OLD BOXES; CRITTER EGGS; EVICTION NOTICES; GREEN GOO; RAG; CAGE W/ TARP; TELEPHONE; COFFEE MUG; BROKEN EGGSHELLS; CARDBOARD BOXES
ART/SETS	PRACTICAL ELEVATOR DOOR; BROKEN WINDOW; GRATE
MAKE-UP/HAIR	
WARDROBE	DBLE. CLIFFORD PANTS & SHOES SC. B33
GRIP/ELECTRIC	
SPFX/ANIMALS	SPARKS; ELEVATOR JOLTS; (6) RATS W/ WRANGLER.
CRITTERS	ONE PAIR GLOWING EYES

QUOTE OF THE DAY: We have no children-only adults...

UPM: DAVID WITZ   1ST A.D.: JOHN VOHLERS   2ND A.D.: LAURA GROPPE
213-957-9170

CRITTERS 3

CRITTER WEEK

Day **SATURDAY MAY 25 1991**
FIRST _____ Day out of **8**
Crew Call **7A** _____
Shooting Call _____
Location **Critter Studios**
 2233 W. Pico Blvd. Santa Monica

Day 1: (7 AM Call)
Int. Crawlspace - Charlie's POV bubbles come up from crack between elevator wall; Charlie's POV N.D. critter near Annie wriggles up from elevator housing; closer of above threatening, "Ah, smorgasbord;" N.D. critter leaping and leaving frame near Annie; Bleach critter threatens Mr. Menges; critter unfurls toward Mr. Menges; Mrs. Menges's POV bubbles critter watching, it balls up.
Int. On Ladder - N.D. critter lands on ladders, stands and turns; push in on critter's eyes, teeth; critter rears back, goes for Charlie (to proceed shot from gun); Ladder critter gets his; close-up of explosive into critter's chest.
Int. Table Top - Bleach critter in a blanket being beaten - insert needs to go as if he died; Bleach critter stirs, emerges from blanket (dead Bubbles critter in the background); Bubbles critter stands up in frame; Bubbles critter being cut in half, aftermath with bubbles coming out.

Day 2: (7 AM Call)
Int. Top of Elevator - Annie falls toward camera.
Int. Elevator Shaft - Critters group up at the bottom, looking up.
Int. Crawlspace - Annie pulls a bullet from pocket.
Int. Frank's Office - Critters's red eyes thru grate.
Int. Frank's Office - Critter knocks off the phone and gives it a raspberry.
Int. Basement Stairs - Rosalie POV critter goes for leg; critter grabs bunny slipper.
Int. Basement Laundry Room - Eruption of teeth and eyes as critter goes for the camera.

Day 3: (7 AM Call)
Int. Basement Laundry Room - Critters bows to launch quill; reshoot quill going into bunny slipper; critter fights mop head; critter pops up in dryer, sees bunny slipper and freaks out.

Day 4: (7 AM Call)

Ext. Rest Area - Truck tire rolling toward critter.
Int. Menges's Kitchen - Five critters bust through hissing and chattering; critter hits floor; critter attacks foot, bites ladder rung; lunges into camera.
Int. Menges's Kitchen Critters Jamboree - Critters turn the kitchen upside down; food fight; critter comes thru hatch and Marcia hits it back down.

Day 5: (7 AM Call)

Int. Menges's Kitchen Critters Jamboree - Critters turn kitchen upside down; food fight; aftermath, the kitchen is a disaster area.
Int. Second Floor Lobby - Bleach critter in foreground and two critters in background stand up in frame; Bleach critter eyes Cliff then Rosalie; Bleach critter bows, shoots quill into Cliff's hand; N.D. critter bows and shoots quill toward Rosalie; Bleach critter bows and shoots quill toward Rosalie; close-up of N.D. critter shooting more than one quill at a time; extreme close-up of quilling; critters grouping in bowling pin formation, get knocked over by ashtray can; critters regroup.

Day 6: (7 AM Call) 1st and 2nd Unit Day

1st Unit, Int. Second Floor Lobby - Continue shooting sequence of critters getting bowled over, scattering, flying into the air, and regrouping.
2nd Unit, Int. First Floor Foyer - Close-up and extreme close-up of uvula (screaming) critter; as Annie leaves stairs, Bleach critter and Kitchen critter roll into lobby; critter bows and quills.
2nd Unit, Ext. Iris Apartment Roof - Close-up of roof hatch, won't give.
2nd Unit, Int. Laundry Room/Laundry Chute - Critters spin out or leap out toward the camera.

Day 7: (9 AM Call) 1st and 2nd Unit Day

1st Unit, Int. First Floor Foyer - Critter roles out from the corner, screams, and bows; four critters react to the explosion; Charlie's POV: critters look up at Charlie after explosion; three critters respond "LOOK OUT" as Charlie tries to fire his weapon; Bleach critter and others stand ready to attack; one critter turns with Charlie as he turns toward elevator; critters react to Pillar critter explosion.
1st Unit, Int. Elevator Crawlspace - Explosion!
1st Unit, Ext. Iris Arms Apartment - Critter pieces landing, critter goo, green slime, green flames.
2nd Unit, Ext. Iris Arms Apartment - 25 shots (Flagpole) - Close in on bolt, giving, giving gone; Charlie POV wire; Johnny's POV on the roof looking at the ground.

Day 8: (9 AM Call) 1st and 2nd Unit Day

1st Unit, Int. Third Floor Hallway - Laundry Chute - Marcia's flare lights up a critter's insides.
1st Unit, Int. 3rd Floor Hall - Menges's Door - Critters attack door, Bleach critter spits splinter.
1st Unit, Int. Menges's Kitchen Critters Jamboree - Reshoot; critters continue to destroy the kitchen.
1st Unit, Int. Crawlspace Near Elevator - Charlie says "Everyone be quiet!"
1st Unit, Ext. Iris Arms Apartment St. (Night) - Charlie reactors to critter crushed by truck; Marcia notices antenna; inserts of truck exploding when Charlie lands, windows - tires.
2nd Unit, Reshoot anything not done on Day 7.

POST-PRODUCTION

Principal photography for *Critters 3* ended on 24 April, 1991, culminating with a week dubbed "Critter Week" for the series of visual effects sequences shot by the crew. Though the "week" was spread out, it consisted of several shooting days beginning on 25 May and ending on 15 June, which overlapped schedule-wise with *Critters 4*. (The "Critter Week" for *Critters 4* began the week after on 17 June) The cast and crew wrap party for both *Critters 3* and *4* was held on 24 June (a Monday, oddly) at the DC3 Restaurant, a restaurant and jazz bar formerly located at the Santa Monica Airport (even more oddly).

"I remember going to the wrap party," says Edward Chiodo. "And again, we worked really hard on those movies. And I had a lot of friends on it. And it's funny, when I walked into the venue where the party was being held, it's kind of like people, I sort of noticed people turning toward me and whispering, '*I can't believe he showed up*,' that kind of mentality. And it really, really hurt. I mean, I remember Barry [Opper] came up to me and gave me a big hug. Kristine [Peterson] came over to me, gave me a hug. But other than that, it felt like, '*Oh, I'm not wanted here.*'"

"Yeah, I think he might have been the brunt of a lot of the troubles that were on the film," explains Stephen Chiodo. "And I guess, you know, maybe it was the budget, it was the pressure… There were a lot of things going on. But still, we were there, we provided the puppets, we did what we were asked to do. But it was a tough, tough shoot."

ADVANCED SHOOTING SCHEDULE					
DATE:					
SCENE #	PGS	D/N	SET/ DESCRIPTION	LOCATION	
			THE PRODUCTION STAFF WOULD LIKE TO THANK EVERYONE FOR ALL OF THEIR HARD WORK — AND REMEMBER CRITTERS IV STARTS SHOOTING MONDAY MAY 6 —		

EDITING WITH E-PIX

An Interview with Terry Stokes

(Editor, *Critters 3* and *4*)

How did you end up as the editor on *Critters 3* and *4*?

I was connected with New Line Cinema. I did a feature for them, *A Nightmare on Elm Street 3*, I think it was. So, I had a little history there. Barry produced several films for New Line. He solicited me to do the trailer for the first *Critters*. And then I was working on another film for New Line called *Suburban Commando* and I was doing it the old-fashioned way with a splicer and scotch tape and so forth on a 35mm work print. And Barry Opper called me and he said, '*Terry, I want to get you on this project I'm doing.*' I said, '*What is it?*' He said, '*I'm doing* Critters 3 *and 4 and I'm shooting it all at one time and I want you to edit both films.*' I said, '*Well, that would be great.*' He said, '*Yeah but Terry, you're going to have to go learn a whole new way of editing. We're going non-linear digital on these shows.*' I said, '*What's that?*' He starting telling me about this new system out that's called E-Pix, digital format stuff, and he said '*You have to get into this, you have to learn this system in this digital world or else you're going to be left behind. You're going to be an old guy and you're going to be out of business in no time at all.*'

So I asked him how it all worked. He said, '*What we're going to do is going to be cutting dailies on Critters 3 and then when we wrap that we're going to roll right over and start filming Critters 4 and you'll be in director's cut on Critters 3 and cutting dailies on 4. After half a day on.*' And I said, '*How am I going to do that physically? I don't think that's possible.*' He said, '*Here's how it's possible. You're going to learn this digital system. You're going to have to do some training.*' So I got to it and he got the name of this gal who was a rep for E-Pix out of Toronto. And the system was, if you know digital discs, these were like 78 RPM discs, so bigger.

And you got three discs per length of time. I think it was like 20 or 30 minutes of material you could get on that. And all three discs had the same material on it. So that if you needed a quick cut of something, you could do it by sourcing another disc. You know, that's the way it was. All the digital dailies were digitized into a set of three discs, probably 30 minutes of dailies or whatever. And so I went and I took the training, and I didn't think I was going to be able to do it. I taught old dogs new tricks, but I couldn't even remember how old I was. But I did learn it. So I went to the first day of work, the dailies were in, and I got all kinds of people around from the E-Pix company representatives, the representatives through the, I can't remember what the company was, but they were with us too. And the thing plugs in and I plugged it in and I hit this button that I knew how to hit and nothing happened. The system wouldn't work. So finally after a few hours with people from local technical sources who were there trying to figure it out. They said, '*Well, why don't you go home and we'll have it fixed by the time you come back in the morning*.' So I went back the next morning. Now, of course, I have 2 days to deal with it and I plug it in. I hit the play button and it still wouldn't work. And now they're sweating. I can see the perspiration of the crowd scratching their heads. And next thing I know, there's a guy coming from Toronto who invented the system, flying down non-stop from Toronto, and he's going to be there in the evening and he'll have it fixed the next day.

So, I show up on the third day (laughs), ready to catch up on, you know, two days of dailies plus the third day of dailies, and I sit down at the console and I hit the start button and the picture comes up, and it was there for about five seconds and all of a sudden everything went dark – all the monitors, all the machines, everything – and I realized the lights are out in the room as well. It happened coincidentally when I pressed the button to start it. I get up and I say, '*That's fucking it. I'm out of here. I'm not doing this*' (laughs). I called Barry, I said, '*Barry, I'm going to film. I can't do this stuff because the machines don't work. This is a lousy system*.' And I'm out in the parking lot stomping around, mad as hell, threatening Barry on the phone. '*Get me film. I want film in here. I'm going to get a Moviola and a KEM* [editing machine] *and I'm going to do this stuff like the way I know how to do it*.'

And all of a sudden, they all come out running to me and in the parking lot and they say '*Terry, Terry, it's okay, it's not your fault and it's not the E-Pix's fault. Some guy on a cherry picker down on the corner of Sepulveda and Pico Boulevard hit the transformer on a television pole. The whole west side of L.A. is down without power*.' About an hour later it was all restored and I got back on it and everything started working fine and I got caught up real quickly and the rest is history. I was in director's cut with Kristine and then I was in dailies with Rupert on *Critters 4*, and finished both films. And unfortunately they went to video. They didn't ever release it in a theater. They never made it to the screen. I don't know why, whether a New Line decided they didn't think it was going to be worth trying to distribute it or whatever. That's the *Critters* horror story (laughs), from an editor's standpoint. And I still have to chuckle about it. I remember stomping around in that parking lot, just fumes coming out of my ears. And they came out and said, '*Terry, Terry, it's okay, it's okay. It wasn't your fault. Oh my goodness. The whole area is blacked out.*' I said, '*You mean when I hit that start button I blacked out everything?*' '*No, no, it wasn't your fault. It was the cherry picker, the transformer.*' Simultaneously, I mean, it just couldn't have been any more timed any better.

Was that one of the first features cut on E-Pix?

I think so. I think it was. And, yeah, I'm in some kind of book, I remember reading a book, and this was the first, I'm one of the first editors to do a feature film, or two in this particular case, but the first one was *Critters 3* on this type of non-linear digital system. At the same time, Avid was there. And Avid took over the industry, so E-Pix didn't stick around too long.

What was your experience like working with Kristine Peterson?

She was a delight. She was easy to work with and we got along great as far as I know. I don't know if she remembers me, but we did have a good experience in the cutting room. She was delightful to work with, very creative. And also, in that film, one of the stars of the film was Leonardo DiCaprio. He doesn't like to talk about it (laughs). When reporters or whoever is trying to interview him, they say, '*Do you remember your first screen role?*' And he'd say '*Yes*'. And then he'll mention, you know, the film he did after *Critters 3* (laughs). But Barry and Rupert saw what he was and what potential he had. And also, *Critters 4* had Angela Bassett,

How difficult was it to be cutting *Critters 3* while also working the dailies from *Critters 4*?

Well, it was a challenge only in as much as really learning how to really quickly use the system in an efficient way. The thing is that you'd be working on one section of the film and then the dailies wouldn't fit on the first three discs or whatever the three disc level, so you had to do some disc changing. And we got pretty proficient at doing that. My assistant Marnie, whose last name is, it was then I think Marnie Pope but her last name now is Bellingham, and she got very good at that. So, I could shut the system down, we could eject the disc, she had the other three discs right there and we loaded, and we could do that within about 10 minutes, which seems like an awful lot of time, but if you consider that in film, in the old days of film, you know, you'd need a trim of some kind to extend a scene, or somebody would say '*I'd like to see the tail of that scene or that piece of film you cut there, physically cut,*' and you'd have to say to your assistant, '*Go find me the trim on blah, blah, blah,*' you know, using edge markers, actual film to find it. So I'd say I need a tail trim on 1495 and she runs out into the room and all the trims are hanging on like paper clip kind of things. And they would be hanging there and they would be categorized as to what reel and number that they were on that pin. But that would take easily 10 minutes and sometimes they couldn't find it and they had to do a thing called "dumping the bin." And they'd clip, they'd use rubber bands to secure all the clips to those pins and then actually physically pick up the bin and dump it upside down. And inevitably, three or four little pieces of film would fall out that had come falling off the pins down into the bottom of the bin of film. So sometimes you'd be waiting for a trim for a half an hour and if you couldn't find it or so, sometimes you had to order a reprint of it.

Even E-Pix is sort of clumsy now in retrospect to what Avid was all about. It was still faster and it still afforded a lot more creative options than how you went about cutting a scene. A director could say, you know, '*How about we use da-da-da take and move that here and so forth?*' You could do it just bam-bam-bam, you know, a couple of punches of a button and it was there and you could look at it and see what it was like. '*Oh, I like the original better. Oh, no, I think that's better. I think this is better.*' But that could be done in just a matter of minutes, less than a minute you could do it. So, you know, it was a great advance, but it didn't last long once Avid hit the road and everybody was into that because you didn't have to do all this disc changing. It was all in a digital format on a giant, you know, database that you could access.

How did the sound get synced up with the E-Pix?

With E-Pix, it was simultaneous. The format, the film and the sound were transferred onto the same disc, well, it looked like an old, large LP. If you turn the disc upside down, you can see the tracks. And sometimes that was problematic if somebody put a finger on it, and that fingerprint, you had to take the soft cloth and rub it off and so forth. But you know, the sound was transferred simultaneously with the picture. It was already in sync. And that by itself saves even more time.

That is a really remarkable time period in that transition…

Yeah, it was. After that, it became Avid and Avid was even like the supernova train. It was a high speed rail after that. What's interesting is that in terms of filmmaking time, it still took the same amount of time to do it as it would have been film. One of the reasons was it gave you all this flexibility to be able to try, '*Oh, let's try this as an ending*,' or '*Let's try this ending to that scene*,' or '*Let's reverse that.*' The director, knowing he had all this time, speed, could try all kinds of different creative options that he or she wanted to try and so in essence just giving a director at that amount of time he took it.

How was it working with Rupert Harvey on *Critters 4*?

That one was pretty good, too. I mean, Rupert was, he had been sold on the system at the same time Barry was. He had the demonstration that's done to do it digitally. And that's how they sold the projects to New Line, is that they could do it and deliver it and so forth and do it back-to-back. That way they're not tearing down and trying to hire a new crew. They're not having to change locations for set pieces, they're not having to do, you know, if they have any locations. So for most of *Critters 4* was rather done on set pieces, you know, because it was all inside spaceships and I can't even remember, but it was mostly all able to be handled at the same soundstage. Rupert was very impressed with the system. He was not a jovial, bubbly kind of guy to work with. Like, Kristine and I had a lot of laughs. Rupert's not a laugher (laughs). Very intense and serious, but that's okay. It was working and we flowed along and got it done. Didn't have any technical breakdowns of any kind so that's the way that was. Not as much fun as working with Kristine though.

It was another interesting thing, I'll just flash back on this. Anytime we had a little problem, like one day it wasn't working and functioning right, and I'd call up the technical advisor who was attached to the company that had signed the contract with Barry and Rupert for the machines. And I'd call him, his name was Dave, and I'd say, '*Dave, things aren't working here, da da da.*' The first thing he would say to me is, '*Terry, is it plugged in?*' (laughs) '*David, I wouldn't be calling you if I hadn't plugged it in, if the machine wasn't powered up. Come on.*' And he asked that question every time we ever had to call him. He'd say, '*Is it plugged in?*' It's a joke in the cutting room. '*Did you remember to plug in the machine?*' '*Yes, it's all plugged in, Marnie.*' I'd say, '*Marnie, did you plug in the machine today?*' '*Yes, Terry, it's all plugged in.*' And then we'd giggle about it (laughs).

RELEASE AND RECEPTION

New Line Cinema premiered *Critters 3* during a cast and crew screening on 16 September at the now closed United Artists triplex on Westwood Blvd. in Los Angeles, California. New Line Home Entertainment released the PG-13 rated *Critters 3* direct-to-video on 11 December 1991 and included the tagline "You Are What They Eat." Following DiCaprio's breakout role in *Titanic* in 1997, newer VHS releases of *Critters 3* prominently feature DiCaprio on the cover art with a black banner with his name in large font followed by "Starring In His Film Debut." DiCaprio and his staff were reportedly infuriated by the inclusion, as DiCaprio has famously shunned *Critters 3* from his repertoire over the years and lampooned it as "possibly one of the worst films of all time." Despite DiCaprio's hyperbole about the film, *Critters 3* marks another goofy, family oriented and tonally lighter entry for the franchise, though it falls short of having acquired a rabid fanbase.

"I think *Critters 3* did as well, if not better, than *Critters 4*," posits Rupert Harvey. "I don't think that's entirely because of Leo. I think it's just whatever. It was more palatable to a wider audience, even, dare I say it, a segment of a family audience."

The film later enjoyed a DVD release by New Line Home Entertainment on 5 August 2003 and was re-released on 7 September 2010 as part of a multi-disc DVD set by Warner Bros. that included all four of the original *Critters* films. The four films finally received a proper Blu-ray release on 27 November 2018 courtesy of Shout! Factory.

---

1. Will Leo DiCaprio replace co-star Kirk Cameron
on Teen Beat's October cover?
2. Did half the crew really tour with Elvis this summer?
3. Do Barry & Rupert sleep in the nude?

You and a guest are invited to
hear all the answers at a special screening of

CRITTERS 3

Monday, September 16th - 7:30 P.M.

UA Coronet - Westwood
10889 Wellworth off of Westwood Blvd.

Please RSVP with Jeff or Julie: (213) 315-5378

CRITTERS 3 DELIVERS THE KIND OF RENTAL FIGURES YOU CAN REALLY SINK YOUR TEETH INTO!

They're orphaned, they're hungry, they're multiplying and they're CRITTERS – back for another helping of humankind in this swift and scary sequel. This time Critters are moving up in the world: straight up the elevator shaft of an urban tenement, in search of the snack they like best – *us*.

SELLING POINTS

- They're back...the latest course in the CRITTERS franchising feast!
- Produced by thrillmasters RUPERT HARVEY (A NIGHTMARE ON ELM STREET 5, THE BLOB, CRITTERS 1) and BARRY OPPER (CRITTERS 1 & 2).
- Special effects by Critter creators: The Chiodo Brothers (other credits include ROBOCOP, DARKMAN, GREMLINS).
- Directed by Kristine Peterson (BODY CHEMISTRY, DEADLY DREAMS).
- Written by David J. Schow (LEATHERFACE: TEXAS CHAINSAW MASSACRE III).
- Theatrical-sized color poster.
- Broad cross-genre appeal: thriller, adventure, humor and suspense.

CAST: DON OPPER *(CRITTERS 1&2, SLAMDANCE, ANDROID.)* CHRISTIAN & JOSEPH COUSINS *(KINDERGARTEN COP)* FRANCIS BAY *(NOMADS)*

COL 75273
Sugg. Rtl. $89.95 **$65.30** Dealer

Available on VHS
COLOR/APPROX. 86 MIN./
ISBN# 0-8001-0977-5
PRINTED IN U.S.A.
CC Closed Captioned for the hearing impaired by Captions, Inc. Los Angeles

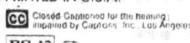

PG-13

NEW LINE HOME VIDEO

rca Columbia Pictures HOME VIDEO

Sold exclusively by
RCA Columbia Pictures Home Video.

BE KIND PLEASE REWIND

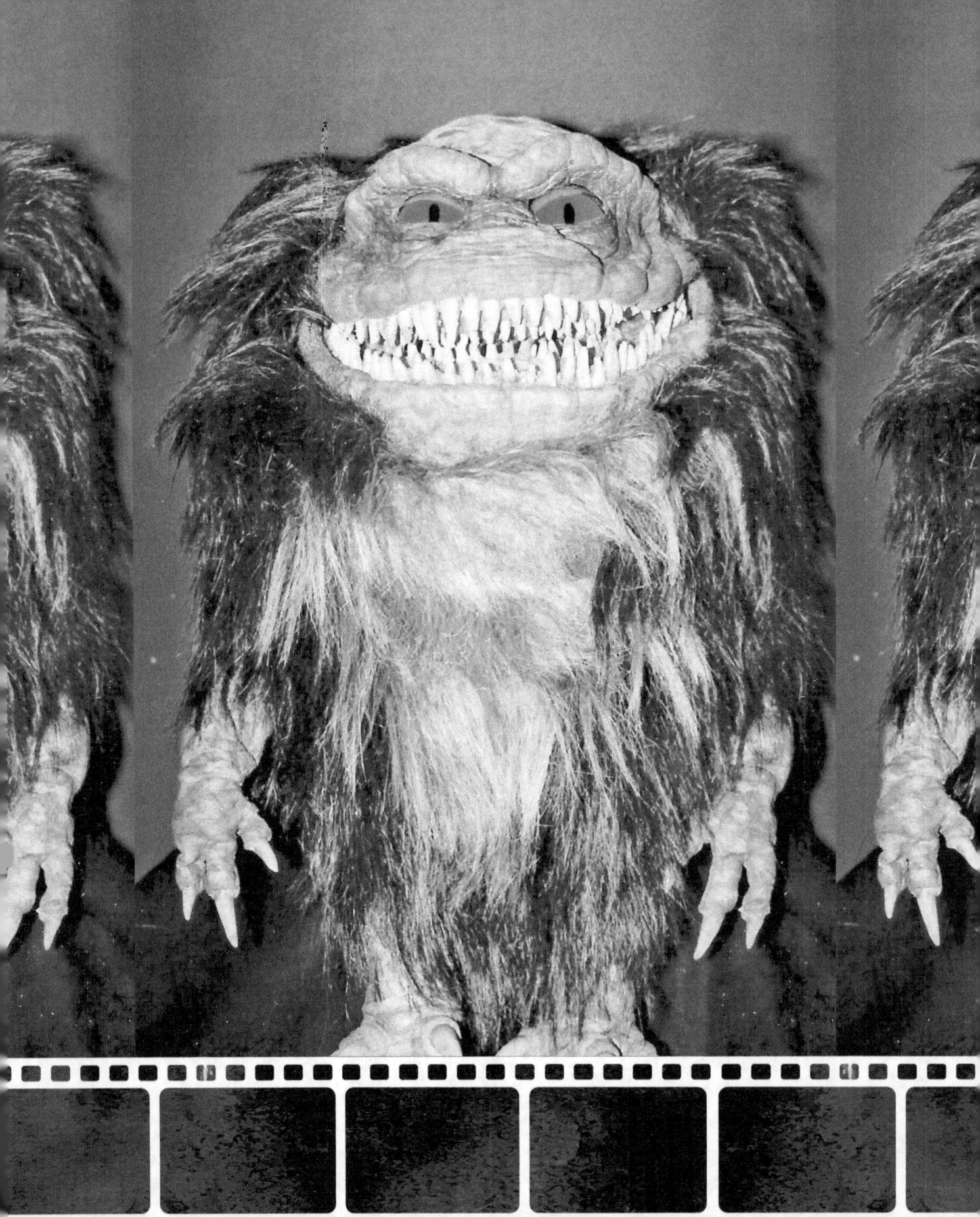

CHAPTER FOUR

CRITTERS 4

KRITES IN SPACE

Immediately following the production of *Critters 3*, many of the same crew members returned after a 2-week pause for *Critters 4;* a tonally darker film than its predecessor and this time directed by Rupert Harvey. Set in outer space and almost entirely onboard a salvage ship called the RSS *Tesla*, the story takes place in the year 2045 following the events at the end of *Critters 3*. Remarkably, cast members include Oscar nominee Brad Dourif, future two-time Golden Globe Award-winner Angela Bassett, Anders Hove (*Subspecies* series), along with recurring roles played by Don Opper and Terrence Mann.

"The crew was essentially the same for *Critters 3* and *4*," explains Barry Opper, "but the tone was totally different for *Critters 4*. The tone of *Critters 4* was definitely brought on by Rupert. Much edgier and like a neo-noir. I think that there is an edge that you found in some of the British quasi-horror movies that hadn't hit the U.S. yet. It's kind of like an intellectual edge."

The movie begins following the end of *Critters 3* with Charlie examining the destroyed basement of the Iris Arms tenement building where he discovers the last two remaining Krite eggs. Before he can destroy them, Charlie is contacted by Ug (in hologram form), now a member of the Intergalactic Council, who prevents Charlie from terminating the Krite eggs citing Zoological Mandate E-102, which prohibits bounty hunters from destroying any transgalactic life-form if it means total extinction of that species. A collection pod is dispatched to Earth and Charlie is obligated to load the remaining Krite eggs aboard, but Charlie becomes stuck in the pod as it locks and launches back into outer space.

Opposite: Another "Baldy" puppet was created for *Critters 4* and served as one of the film's only two hero puppets. (Source: Paul Salamoff)

The story jumps ahead to the year 2045 as the pod aimlessly drifts through the Saturn Quadrant near the flight path of a salvage ship, the RSS *Tesla*. The ship is led by Captain Rick Buttram (Anders Hove) and supported by navigator Fran (Angela Bassett), engineer Al "Albert" Bert (Brad Dourif), his apprentice Ethan (Paul Whitthorne), and cargo specialist Bernie (Eric Da Re). The crew interdict the pod and bring it aboard but are contacted almost immediately by Ug, now known as Councilor Tetra, the head of the intergalactic agency TerraCor who offers the crew a handsome cash reward in exchange for the pod. A deal is arranged for *Tesla* to deliver the pod to TerraCor Station 44, a 3-day voyage away. Once there, the crew is greeted by a malfunctioning voice-activated artificial intelligence computer system known as "Angela," but the station is otherwise devoid of life.

Greed and mistrust spread among the crew as Rick tears into the pod to steal whatever is inside for himself but is interrupted by Ethan. Rick manages to open the pod and is met by Charlie who emerges from a cryogenic slumber as do hatched baby Krites who quickly dispatch Rick in an orgy of violence. After meeting the rest of the crew, Charlie explains the danger posed by the Krites, which are now running rampant throughout the abandoned station. We learn that TerraCor had researched alien species for biological warfare purposes but determined a species with the ability to rapidly reproduce was needed, hence the intergalactic quest for the missing pod with the Krite eggs. As the station begins leaking radiation, which will result in its total destruction, the Krites continue picking off crew members and have laid a new batch of eggs as they prepare to flee the station for the closest planet (Earth). Charlie manages to shoot and kill some of the Krites but destroys the ship's flight control panel. As the crew faces a race against time to repair the damaged controls, Ethan discovers Krites in the bio lab are accelerating the growth rate of baby Krites using various equipment. As Ethan warns the others, Councilor Tetra and his stormtroopers board the station and demand the remaining Krite eggs. The face-off turns deadly, with Albert being shot and killed and Charlie's heartbroken over Ug's villainous manifestation into Councilor Tetra. Ethan lures the stormtroopers into a trap in the bio lab who are killed by the Krites and a showdown over the remaining eggs ensues, with Charlie killing his former friend and the surviving crew members fleeing the station for Earth shortly before the station explodes; the Krites now extinct.

"What inspired me then? I don't know because things change," ponders Rupert Harvey. "Things that inspire me now build on the basis of what inspired me then. I can't really tell you, except for in terms of drama, not in terms of production value or production design or lighting or anything like that. I mean, bear in mind, when we shot *Android*, I didn't think *Blade Runner* had been made. I think *Blade Runner* came out after *Android* did, which was where we all met up, Don Opper and myself and Aaron [Lipstadt] and everyone. But the world of English horror probably thematically and dramatically inspired me as much as the kind of clunky world of English sci-fi. For horror, things like Quasimodo and *The Pit and the Pendulum*, the original versions. Definitely, I remember them clearly. *Doctor Who*, now, that really wasn't the *Doctor Who* that we know today. It was just this really clunky TV show that had a really cool premise. And it really was the world of English movies that informed, and English comics that informed me."

PRE-PRODUCTION

"We had shot *Critters 3* and *4* back-to-back and it had always been my intention to do them both at the same time," notes Rupert Harvey. "When New Line first talked to us about doing another *Critters*, I said '*Yes*,' but only if we can do two and make them back-to-back. New Line went back to their primary customer for more *Critters* at the time, which was Japan, and asked '*Would you like two films for the price of one?*' (laughs) I don't recall what the price was, but two films for the same price they said, '*Yeah, sure, let's do it.*' So, knowing the project was for Japan, primarily, I immediately went ahead and hit them below the belt, as they were among the most racist of movie-going purchasers in the business, at least, that I'd ever come across, which gave me the perfect excuse to hire as the captain [navigator] of the spaceship on *Critters 4* as a.) a woman, and b.), a black woman. The Japanese investors were particularly notorious, but it was very general. I always had quite a bit to do with knowing and understanding the foreign sales market because that's how we could finance ourselves in those days."

screenplay by
DAVID J. SCHOW

from a story by
Barry Opper and Rupert Harvey

REVISED DRAFT
26 February 1991

"It was a very racist and sexist world," Harvey continues. "You couldn't sell, I mean, it's not hard to believe, but you couldn't sell a movie with a black guy as a lead. And you look at every other movie that's made these days, it's completely normal, it's completely straightforward that you want Will Smith or, well, you name it. You don't think twice, but back in the day you *did* think twice because the business, the business perhaps rather than the audience, was still sticking with this attitude that you couldn't sell a movie with a woman in the lead or a black person in the lead. And New Line didn't bat an eyelid. They raised, maybe raised a brow because they knew some of the difficulties but I guess they already had a contract signed for the big chunk of the funding that came from Japan. But it wasn't just Japan. I mean, the market for *Critters* was pretty broad internationally. It sold everywhere. They never had a problem selling it. So I'm not sure when this code of practice ended, but I remember running into it time and time again when I was setting up movies in the early days of my involvement in pictures and movies that you didn't even bother with. Don't go there if you're trying to cast a black person in the lead."

DID YOU KNOW?

Rupert Harvey forged a relationship with Rachel Talalay, the production accountant on *Android*, in 1982. Talalay had previously worked with director John Waters as a production assistant on *Polyester* and later as a producer on *Hairspray* and *Cry-Baby*. She also became a regular at New Line, working on the first *Nightmare on Elm Street* before directing the sixth. They married in 1990 with none other than Waters officiating the wedding. Talalay also had an uncredited role in *Critters 4* as an alien bodyguard of Terrence Mann's Councilor Tetra.

CASTING

Besides Terrence Mann and Don Opper returning in their respective roles as Ug/Councilor Tetra and Charlie, the much smaller cast as compared to *Critters 3* was composed of many new faces. New to America at the time, Danish-Greenlandic actor Anders Hove plays Captain Rick Buttram, Angela Bassett is Fran, the ship's navigator, while Brad Dourif serves as the eccentric engineer wizard Al 'Albert' Bert. The cast is rounded out with Paul Whitthorne as Ethan, an apprentice engineer, Eric Da Re as Bernie, a cargo specialist, and Anne Ramsay as Dr. McCormick.

"I remember Brad Dourif of course, he had been an Academy Award nominee and had won a Golden Globe for *One Flew Over the Cuckoo's Nest*, but he had disappeared off the face of the earth for years and years," recalls Barry Opper. "Angela [Bassett] was fresh out of Yale drama school. I remember the readings for those parts of course; there's a much more limited cast with it taking place on a spaceship. Anders Hove brought a similar kind of brooding quality that Klaus Kinski had on *Android*, which we really liked."

Perhaps not *everyone* remembered Brad Dourif. "I didn't recognize Brad Dourif at craft service, and I, in all seriousness, asked him if he was working with the lighting crew," recounts fabricator and puppeteer Jason Bakutis. "He gave me this utterly bemused look, like he was trying to gauge if I was fucking with him or not. I'm still embarrassed by it…"

For Anders Hove, the role as Captain Buttram was among his first cinematic appearances in America and just before he became a cult sensation following his role as the vampire Radu Vladislas in the Full Moon franchise *Subspecies*. "It was maybe '89, early 1990, when I had just come to town," Anders Hove says. "So it was all pretty new to me. It was a great pleasure for me to meet Brad Dourif. It was an honor to work with him. I mean, I was a big fan of him and I think he's a great actor. He's very different and has his own style, and he's quite a personality. And Angela Bassett, this was one of her first major speaking roles. It was just exciting for me to work on an American movie for the first time. I must have auditioned for it of course, but I don't really remember that. Almost 99 percent of the time you audition for something and never hear back. This was all new and very different. I mean, I had never been in a science fiction movie, anything close to it before. It was absolutely fascinating to me. Exciting."

When asked whether it was abundantly clear Angela Bassett was the perfect choice for the ship's navigator, producer-director Rupert Harvey remarked: "Yeah, because she had such – such presence. I don't know how much work she'd done before then. It probably wasn't the very first thing she'd done. But, you know, she hadn't done very much, she wasn't recognized. The fact that she came into *Critters 4* is indicative of that, but I know that when we met, that she just was kind of statuesque in her demeanor, not in her size or anything physically, but she just had a sort of authority to her, that said, '*Yeah, okay, this is right*.' I have to talk to Barry and I'm not sure if he would even remember when we came up with casting the captain [navigator] as a woman. I don't think we wrote the character as a woman originally. I think it was a guy. But wherever it came from, I'm very glad it did."

Paul Whitthorne plays Ethan, an unlikely hero similar to the roles previously played by
Scott Grimes and Leonardo DiCaprio (Source: Paul Salamoff)

DID YOU KNOW?

Don Keith Opper, who played Charlie McFadden in the first four *Critters* films, eventually left the industry to resume his work as a carpenter. Before his departure, Opper showcased his acting and writing talents, working with various studios. At one point, one of his scripts caught the eye of Clint Eastwood and entered development at Universal Studios. The studio's unending demands for tweaks and rewrites diminished Opper's patience and resolve, a pain associated with the industry that led him to exit altogether.

PRODUCTION

Production for *Critters 4* began on 8 May 1991, including the set construction inside the same warehouse on Pico Boulevard used for *Critters 3*. Principal shooting began on 27 May and ended on Saturday, 22 June, making it a 27-day shooting schedule. The crew finished a last day of pickup shots, consisting mostly of critter close-ups, on 23 August at a small studio located at 3521 Helms Ave., Culver City, California. Like on *Critters 3*, the Chiodos's critter crew met numerous challenges with last minute project changes and unrealistic expectations of the puppets and puppeteers.

"The concept of shooting back-to-back to amortize the costs of *Critters 3* and *4* was really great, if they stuck to the original concept of what we were going to make," notes Stephen Chiodo. "We made a certain amount of puppets, a certain amount of babies, whatever it was, but then in the fourth film, the concept changed to incorporate a bunch of characters that we had never planned to make within the budget. And that caused a lot of contention."

"Some of the points of contention on *Critters 4*, and really *Critters 3* as well, I remember clearly because again I was on the front line with Rupert. He wasn't happy with some of the puppeteering; some of the puppeteers we had gotten on *Critters 3* and *4* weren't professional puppeteers," explains Edward Chiodo. "Well, again you weren't paying professional puppeteers, it was not a SAG gig, it was people that worked on building the puppets. You know a lot of the people that had worked on the original *Critters*, they had gone on to other things. So again, it was a low-budget movie. So we kind of had a bunch of newer people that maybe weren't as experienced. So it was a function of their budget. I feel bad that some of the puppetry isn't better. But then, with some of the demands they made on us for *Critters 3* and *4*, impacted the ability to make performable puppets. Again, they were coming down really hard on us for our failure to execute, but at the time, they didn't seem to take any responsibility that the ask they had was too big, and their expectations were beyond. And then like any creative person, it would grow. They'd want more and more and more, and they'd forgotten what the plan was."

"I puppeteered on *Critters 3*, but then I wasn't available for *Critters 4*," says Stephen Chiodo. "And I think the puppeteering kind of went down a little bit with some of the people that we were working with. And I think they were upset about that. And I think rightfully so."

Nevertheless, the production grinded on and despite those existing tensions, the crew members exerted their best efforts and fondly recall working on set. "I remember trying to troubleshoot the critter balls," says Paul Salamoff. "There were many different types. We had soft ones for bouncing. We had ones that we put on a rubber ball. We had ones that were on bowling balls. And then we had ones that had weights in them so you could roll them around corners. And that was one of the things I became really good at. I was one of the good critter rollers, which was really fun. And then of course, the puppeteering. So Mark [Villalobos] and I were sort of like the main, you know, puppeteers. I had a good body for puppeteering, I guess. I think it helps that I had a performance background because that's the thing, you're not just a stick wiggler. There are people who just don't respect it. It's a little derogatory to call puppeteers a stick wiggler, but they just don't get it. It's not just like, '*Oh, I'm supposed to flap this wing or I'm supposed to move this tail.*' There should be agency. There should be a reason why movements are happening. It's a performance. It is a performance that you're doing. It's not being afraid to make noises, like making noises while you're talking to him because it translates to the puppet. It was Stephen [Chiodo] who really taught me that. That what you do, the performance that you give from your arm down, translates from your arm up. It translates into the puppet. And I did suit work as well. So, you know, like having to act through layers of foam and make sure the creature felt alive. You know, it's not just a little movement in the state, it's a living creature. And you need to always remember that and respect that."

"We had a pretty good time on *Critters 4*. It was really fun," remembers special effects coordinator Frank Ceglia. "For *Critters 3* and 4, I was both the 'one card' and the special effects coordinator. My wife did the makeup for *Critters 3* and 4. Rupert [Harvey] is an old friend of ours. His wife Rachel Talalay and us all worked for New Line Cinema back in that day, and my wife worked with Rachel on *A Nightmare on Elm Street 4* and 6. I came up with a gag on *Critters 4* where we launch a critter into the air and it explodes. I rigged it with some explosives with a long fuse and launched it out of an air cannon. As the puppet reached the apex of its trajectory, it blew up a little bottle of flash powder. We were experimenting with it a bit, but it turned out pretty good."

The most visually striking aspect of *Critters 4* is the intricate spaceship interior designs created by Philip Dean Foreman. Utilizing a wide range of carefully prepared plans to enhance the field of depth in the narrow hallways, Foreman relied on his experiences from the Roger Corman-era to achieve outsized results, and even reused some of the same artifacts from previous shoots, such as dozens of egg crates, as key design features.

"You know, we were all kind of playing on our home turf, because we'd all come out of the Roger Corman school of fine arts filmmaking," says Rupert Harvey. "And we'd made, I don't know how many movies I'd made with Roger by then that used those bloody egg crates for sets. I mean, all of us had been in that world and my friend, my old mate Philip Foreman who was the designer on both of the movies. I first brought him over from the UK to work on *Galaxy of Terror*. I brought Philip over to be a consultant on it, because it already had Jim Cameron doing sets for it. And I remember talking to Jim about it, and Jim was sort of resident art director for Corman at the same time that I was there and we were all there. And I remember talking to Jim about his philosophy of some of that set construction, in which you can see stuff on *The Terminator* and *Aliens* quite clearly. But Roger Corman's kludging school of set decoration stuck with us all. So we were, as I said, playing on our home turf when we started out doing a sci-fi picture for very little money, because every one of us, including those of us on *Android*, had been involved with Roger Corman's wilder productions. And *Android*, I think, we reused sets from a sci-fi film that he'd made just before that. But we basically, I think, literally physically reused the flats, painted them different colors and I did the same thing again on *Critters 4*."

Cinematographer Tom Callaway explains how Foreman's ingenuity also came into play when shooting several sequences involving POV shots: "We did some really long Steadicam shots in the spaceship set. The hallways were very narrow and Philip [Dean Foreman] had incorporated some humps in the flooring where the hallways intersected to give some spatial depth and texture but it was tough for the steadicam operator to maneuver walking backwards but the results turned out looking very good. We also did a few POV shots from the critters's perspective, which I liked. There's also a sequence in which the actors are stuck in a trash compactor and then they escape by crawling through some duct work and I thought that was pretty cool. They had baby ones and we did a flying critter gag that came right at the lens. All of these were of course pre-digital effects. And you look back at some of these effects, and they would be just so easy had we had access to modern digital effects. We did some in-camera, optical, and practical effects to pull all these gags off."

Principal photography ended on 9 June and the Critter Week for *Critters 3* began on 10 June. The Critter Week for *Critters 4* followed afterward on 17 June and ended on 22 June, registering only a 6-day shoot with an extra day for pickup shots, mostly close-up work, later on 23 August. The 9 to 11-person critter crew for *Critters 4* included Paul Salamoff, Mark Villalobos, Jason Bakutis, Barbara Meyers, Deborah Galvez, C. Mitchell Bryan, Jarn Heil, Dean Mercil, David Russ, and alternating appearances by Edward and Stephen Chiodo.

Philip Dean Foreman created striking visuals such as the space pod and the interiors
of the salvage ship and the docking station. (Source: Paul Salamoff)

Eric Da Re (Bernie) prepares to meet a grizzly fate on the set of *Critters 4*. (Source: Paul Salamoff)

Although the amount of potential safety issues were not nearly as omnipresent as those on *Critters 3*, the special effects crew on *Critters 4* did encounter a few close calls. "I played a dead body on *Critters 4*, and a baby critter puppet was on my back, and a small squib exploded and literally caught me on fire (laughs)," comically recalls fabricator Jason Bakutis. "I didn't even know until some production assistants started smothering me – and the flames – with blankets."

Paul Salamoff, who suffered his fair share of safety issues on *Critters 3*, escaped serious injuries on *Critters 4* during a sequence involving firearms firing blanks, though he admits bearing full responsibility for the mishap. "On *Critters 4*, we were in the control room of the spaceship, I think it was like the bridge of the spaceship. The critters are behind the computer, and Don Opper, he's the one who has the gun and he's shooting the critters behind this thing. So what I was supposed to do was, my critter is behind the thing and I'm making it do its thing, its movement and reaction. And then Don's going to shoot at the critter, basically shooting at me, with his weapon. So what I was supposed to do was go up for a second and then go back down. But I went down with a puppet and knocked my head really hard. The safety people on that show were great. This was not anybody's fault but mine, it was definitely operator error. I did have goggles on, which made it hard to see. But all of a sudden, as I'm still trying to bend down because we were timing it, I didn't go down all the way, and the next thing I know I just felt this blast. It wasn't too far away from him. And I was in shock. I was just completely frozen. Fortunately, I was okay and thank God I had the gauze on. Because I think that would have been a problem. I mean, who knows what would have happened. But yeah, I was stunned. And they took really good care of me, which was good, but boy, I'll never forget that. You know, that was completely my fault, because I was supposed to go all the way down with the critter and I didn't."

Although the Critter Week for *Critters 4* was shot immediately following the much more difficult Critter Week for *Critters 3*, the subsequent shoot was limited to 6 days with a final seventh day added for pickup shots later in August. With fewer gags and even fewer puppets, the 6-day shoot overall unfolded without too much fanfare or difficulties.

Special effects fabricator Paul Salamoff was instrumental on *Critters 3* and *Critters 4*; creating various Krite eggs and pitching in on puppeteering full-sized Krites. (Source: Paul Salamoff)

These two hero puppets were the only full-sized Krites used in *Critters 4.*
(Source: Paul Salamoff)

2233 W. Pico Blvd
Santa Monica, CA 90405
213/315-4900
213/828-3341 FAX

A

Producer B. Opper R. Harvey
Director Rupert Harvey
Title "CRITTERS 4"

Day __WEDNESDAY MAY 8TH 1991__
__FIRST__ Day out of __27__
Crew Call __7A__
Shooting Call __8A__
Location __Critter Studios__
2233 W. Pico Blvd. Santa Monica

SET # SET	SCENES	CAST	D/N	PAGES	LOCATION
INT BASEMENT LAUNDRY ROOM UG APPEARS · SAYS CHARLIE CAN'T KILL THE EGGS	2	1·6	DAWN	3 4/8	
INT BASEMENT LAUNDRY Room UG DISAPPEARS · CHARLIE DOESN'T KNOW WHAT TO DO	4	6	DAWN	2/8	
INT BASEMENT LAUNDRY Room H POD LANDS BEHIND CHARLIE	3	6	DAWN	1/8	
INT POD CHARLIE GETS LOCKED INSIDE THE POD	5 PT	6	DAWN	2/8	
		TOTAL PAGE COUNT		4 1/8	

CAST & DAY PLAYERS	PART OF	MAKE-UP CALL	SET CALL	REMARKS
1 TERRENCE MANN	UG	10³⁰A	W/N	
6 DON OPPER	CHARLIE	6³⁰A	7³⁰A	

STAND INS & ATMOSPHERE
Steve Boyd at 6³⁰A
uji Johnson at 6³⁰A

SPECIAL INSTRUCTIONS
PROPS · 2 BLACKENED COFFEE CANS · BOUNTY HUNTER RIG + BELT BUCKLE · CHARLIE'S GUN
CRITTER EGGS · GREEN GOO · SPACE POD
MECH EFX · CHARLIE'S GUN FIRES · DEBRIS · FULLERS EARTH · SMOKE · POD DROPS THRU
CEILING · GREEN MIST
LASER EFX · LASER FOR HOLOGRAM GAG SC #2
CAMERA · MULTIPLE CAMERA COVERAGE
SET DRESSING · LIGHTS TO BLINK INSIDE POD

ADVANCE SHOOTING NOTES

SET # SET	SCENES	CAST	D/N	PAGES	LOCATION
DAY 2 THURSDAY MAY 9 1991					
INT DOCKING BAY	115	1·4·6· ATMO	D	5/8	
INT DOCKING BAY	117	1·4·6· ATMO	D	1 1/8	
INT DOCKING BAY	118	1·2·4·6· ATMO	D	1/8	
INT DOCKING BAY	119	1·2·4·6· ATMO	D	1 3/8	
		TOTAL PAGE COUNT		3 1/8	
DAY 3 FRIDAY MAY 10 1991					
INT DOCKING BAY	127	4·6· ATMO	D	3/8	
INT CORRIDOR JUNCTION	135	1·2·4·6	D	1/8	
INT CORRIDOR OUTSIDE DOCKING BAY	A135	1·2·4·6	D	4/8	
INT DOCKING BAY	B135	2·4·6	D	1 6/8	
INT DOCKING BAY 42A	137·138·139	1	D	4/8	
		TOTAL PAGE COUNT		3 3/8	
DAY 4 SATURDAY MAY 11 1991					
INT DOCKING BAY	141	1·2·4·6	D	2/8	
INT DOCKING BAY	A141	1·2·4·6	D	1/8	
INT AIRLOCK IN 42B	143	2·4·6	D	4/8	
INT DOCKING BAY	145	2	D	3/8	
INT DOCKING BAY 42A	A145	1·2·4·6	D	1 6/8	

1st A.D. John Vohlers
2nd A.D. Stuart Hagen 213/874-8949
2nd 2nd A.D. Romney Pearl 213/463-1562

Production Mgr David Witz

STAFF AND CREW		STAFF AND CREW		EQUIPMENT	
Prod Mgr	D. Witz	Key Make-Up	S. Parker-Saunders	Prod Coord	E. Ervin
1st Asst Dir	J. Vohlers			Asst Coord	J. Berk
2nd Asst Dir	S. Hagen	Hairstylist	B. Buckner	Office P.A.'s	K. Yeage
2nd 2nd Asst Dir	R. Pearl				J. Schneewe
Key Set P.A.	K. Harpster	Costume Designer	J. Burrows	Prod Accountant	J. Guild
Set P.A.'s	T. Arvanites	Set Costumer	L. Kennedy	Asst Accountant	C. Susskind
	J. Stamback				
				Asst to Producers	J. Johnson
Script Super	D. Newman	Prod Designer	P. Foreman		
		Art Director	J. Wallace		
Cinematographer	T. Callaway	Set Decorator	L. Shorr		
Camera Operator		Set Dresser	C. Banker		
1st Cam Asst	G. O'Malley	Art Dept Coord	M. Alexander		
2nd Cam Asst	G. Kidd	Lead Person	S. Slusher		
Loader		Swing	R. Solo		
			B. Cole	Transpo Capt	G. Jacobs
Extra Camera					
				1 Fueler	
				1 Generator	
Gaffer	J. Spencer	Constr Coord	T. O'Brien	2 1Hole Trailers	
Best Boy Electric	D. Watson	Constr Foreman	J. Betts		
Lamp Operators	M. Gordy	Scenic Artist	S. Dietz	1 Wardrobe Trailer	
	K. Williams			1 Make-Up Trailer	
		Craft Service	B.J. Witz		
Key Grip	W. Allen	First Aid	B.J. Witz		
Best Boy Grip	D. Footman				
Grips	D. Arnello	Special EFX	F. Ceglia		
	J. Downing	Asst EFX	P. Haines		
		2nd Asst EFX	T. Ceglia		
		Critter EFX	Chiodo Bro's		
Sound Mixer	J. Garcia				
Boom Operator	J. Porrello				
Video Playback					
				MEALS SERVED -	
Laser EFX	S. Ritt/Mirage Prod			40 LUNCHES	
Computer EFX	B. Matzerath				

END OF FILMING

SPECIAL EQUIPMENT AND LIVESTOCK

COMMENTS — DELAYS (EXPLANATION) — CAST, STAFF, AND CREW ABSENCE

C. BERTAL ELECTRICIAN REPLACED M. GORDY
D. O'BRIAN GRIP REPLACED J. DOWNING

* AS PER SCRIPT SUPERVISOR D. NEWMAN: 1 PAGE WAS DELETED FROM SC# 69 DUE TO
CRITTER PAGES REWRITES (BLUE) 6/4 = EFFECTS TOTAL PAGE COUNT.
• SC #149 WAS ADDED BUT ONLY CHANGES TOTAL SCENE COUNT-NOT PAGE COUNT
BECAUSE IT WAS INCORPORATED FROM SC# B149
★. SC# A69 = 1/8 WAS DELETED = EFFECTS TOTAL SCENE AND PAGE COUNT
△ Per Director/Producers decision Scenes 124 + 136 are deemed complete.
⊙NOTE: REMAINING SCENE AND PAGE COUNT WILL BE COMPLETED DURING
CRITTER WEEK. Of the remaining counts, 13 scenes (2 pages) are OFFICIAL.

This day (DAY 25) is the official WRAP of LIVE ACTION).

CRITTERS 4

CRITTER WEEK

Day _MONDAY JUNE 17 1991_
FIRST   Day out of _6_
Crew   Call _8A_
Shooting Call _____
Location ____ Critter Studios ____
     2233 W. Pico Blvd. Santa Monica, CA

(Critter Week Begins June 17)

Day 1: (8 AM Call) 1st Unit Int. Spaceship
Int. TerraCor Ship's Bridge - Close-up of Charlie through the bridge's windows.
Int. Trash Tube - Charlie/Fran slide by vents in tube.
Int. TerraCor Cargo Bay - Rick in the pod (his POV of Charlie); close-up of Charlie as he reacts to Rick's death (two shots).
Int. Bio Lab - Close-up of Charlie as he pops out of duct at Ethan; Ethan climbing into trash tube, he looks back at the lab; close-up of Ethan as he says "No Way" and backs away from hatch; Ethan's POV scan of broken up bio lab, cracked Krite eggs; close-up of Ethan at the intercom; Ethan looks at Charlie; pan off of fully grown baby critter and over to laser critter.

Day 2: (7:30 AM Call) 1st Unit Bio Lab
Int. Bio Lab - Wide shot as mercs whirl around, close-up of merc #1 whirling around; closeup of merc firing his weapon at the door; door takes the first hit; merc lowers his gun and looks around; mercs back up, closer together; over-the-shoulder shot of critters popping up and mercs turn; slow pan becoming whip pan for POV of empty bio lab; whip pan to more critters popping up.
Int. Corridor - Reverse angle on mercs marching down the corridor (no Ethan).

Day 3: (7 AM Call) 1st Unit Bridge of the _Tesla_
Int. Bridge of the _Tesla_ - Angela's POV of wires sparking, critters in the hatch; a critter as it ducks from Charlie's shot; critters split and disappear around the bulkhead; critter casts a shadow behind Al Bert's console, Charlie's shot hits Al Bert's console; Charlie's second shot hitting _Tesla_ control panel; critter is electrocuted in a spray of sparks; Al Bert's POV of destroyed console.
Int. The Cockpit of the _Tesla_ - Critter slithers above the main console going left and right; the critter

drops onto a chair (Charlie in the background); the critter jumps onto the console, turns to face Charlie, and snarls.

Day 4: (7 AM Call) 1st Unit Pharmacy
Int. Corridor Near Pharmacy - Crittervision as they head toward the docking bay.
Int. Corridor Outside Pharmacy - two critters exit pharmacy and see heroes running toward them; Ethan and Charlie's POV of a critter blood trail.
Int. Pharmacy - Critter POV as it approaches the pharmacy door and on the door as it peers around; Bernie's POV as critter lunges at his face; tight shot on Bernie's back as critter lands on him; handheld tight shot on critter as it clings to Bernie's back and chews on him, repeat the shot with the critter on Bernie's front; critter active on Bernie's dead body.
Int. Main Control - Critters flip up buttons on the control panel; critters plot course to Earth.

Day 5: (7 AM Call) 1st Unit Docking Bay
Int. TerraCor Docking Bay - Handheld tight shots of Rick thrashing, crawling, and dying; baby critter on Rick's arm as he crawls and thrashes; critter shadow as it drops into duct access; over-the-shoulder shot of Ethan as he sees Laser critter; same shot as Laser critter lunges and impales on a hose; pickup shots of Ethan backing away from critter; Laser critter rolls and springs into frame; Ethan's POV of Laser critter uncurling at his feet; Laser critter bunching to lunge and lunging at the camera; close-up of Laser critter chewing into the nitro hose; Ethan's POV of Laser critter as he thrashes and freezes.

Day 6: (7 AM Call) 1st & 2nd Unit Pickup Shots
1st Unit, Int. Ethan's Cabin - (Reshoot) - Fran sits up when Rick calls.
1st Unit, Int. Docking Bay - Critter shadow as it drops into access docking bay; over-the-shoulder of Ethan as he sees the Laser critter; close-up of pre-kicked Frozen critter (two camera setup for wide/tight shots); Ethan: "Not bad for an apprentice."
1st Unit, Int. Trash Compactor - Ethan reacting.
2nd Unit, Int. Corridor Outside of Pharmacy - Ethan and Charlie's POV looking at critter blood trail; two critters exit the pharmacy to see heroes running toward them.
2nd Unit, Int. Trash Compactor - Close-up facehugger.

Pickup Day: (7 AM Call) Miscellaneous
Int. Docking Bay - Close-up of gun cocking, second closeup of finger on the trigger.
Int. Bio Lab - Close-up of syphloid growing; close-up of baby critter; closeup of preemie critter.
Int. Main Control - Close-up critter claw on keyboard.
Int. *Tesla* - Close-up of Bernie playback.
Int. Living Quarters - Close-up of graphics playback.
Int. Loading Dock - Close-up of pod door opening.

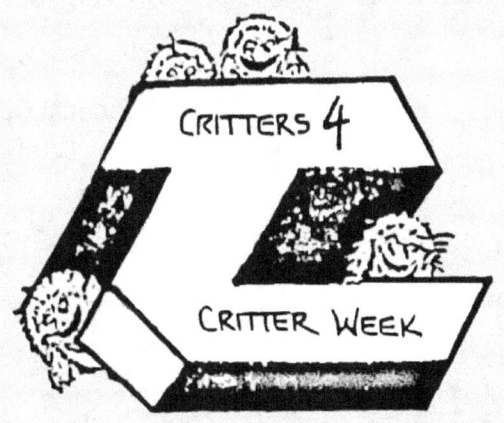

POST-PRODUCTION AND RELEASE

Only 2 days after wrapping the last day of "Critter Week," the cast and crew celebrated its wrap party at the DC3 Restaurant at the Santa Monica Airport. Although New Line Home Entertainment released *Critters 4* on VHS on 14 October, 1992, the cast and crew screening was held later on 4 December at the General Cinema Beverly Connection located at 100 N. La Cienega Boulevard, Los Angeles. (The theater eventually closed in 2004 and was demolished in 2006.) The film's tag lines included "In space, they love to hear you scream" and "They're invading your space." While tonally darker than *Critters 3* and beautifully shot, keenly highlighting the exquisite interior spaceship designs, *Critters 4*'s daring inclusion of Ug's character not only turning villainous, but being killed in the film's final act, has long left fans divided. Interestingly, the setting of *Critters 4* in outer space encouraged other horror franchises to experiment with similar ideas, such as *Leprechaun 4: In Space*, *Hellraiser: Bloodline*, and *Jason X*.

Like *Critters 3*, New Line distributed *Critters 4* direct-to-video and with a PG-13 rating. Warner Home Video later released *Critters 4* on DVD on 13 September 2005 and then re-released on 7 September 2010 as part of a multi-disc DVD set by Warner Bros. that also included the other three original *Critters* films. The four film-set received a Blu-ray release on 27 November 2018 courtesy of Shout! Factory.

Barry Opper & Rupert Harvey
invite you and a guest
to a special screening of

CRITTERS 4

Directed by Rupert Harvey

Wednesday, December 4th - 7:00 P.M.

General Cinema Beverly Connection
100 North La Cienega Blvd.
(Across from the Beverly Center)

Please RSVP with Jeff: (213) 665-9088

```
You and a guest are cordially invited
to the "CRITTERS 3 and 4" Wrap Party!

At:   DC3 Restaurant
      2800 Donald Douglas Loop North
      Santa Monica, California
      (213) 399-2323

      (at the end of 28th Street
       South of Ocean Park at the
       Santa Monica Airport)

When: Monday, June 24th, 1991
      8:30 P.M.

You MUST R.S.V.P. by Wed., June 19th
Contact Prod. Office: (213) 315-4900

IMPORTANT: You MUST present invitation
           at the door.
```

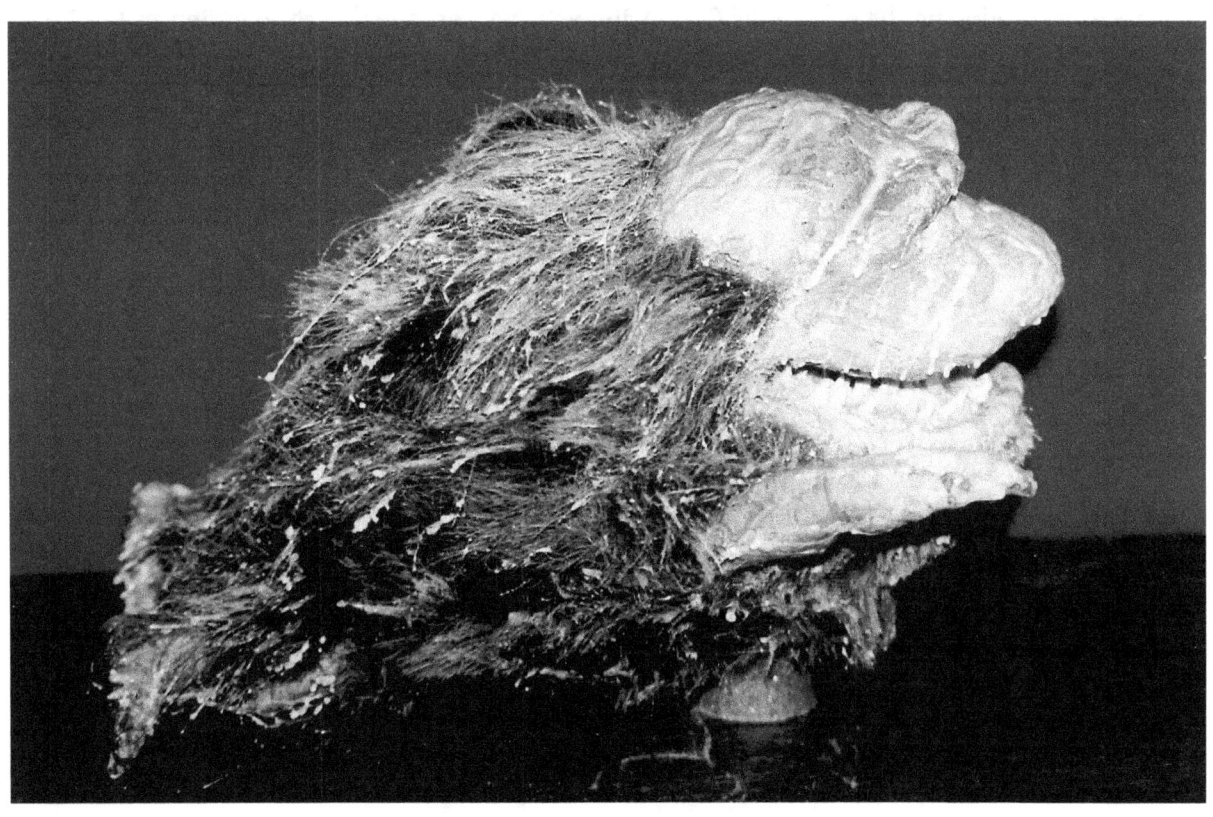

One of the specialty puppets used to depict "Baldy's" frozen death at the hands of Ethan in *Critters 4*.

(Source: Paul Salamoff)

FROM KRITES TO HOBBITS
An Interview with **Mark Ordesky**
(Associate Producer, *Critters 3* and *4*)

Critters 3 **and** *4* **were early parts of your incredible career trajectory, which has since included executive producing the** *Lord of the Rings* **trilogy. What were those early experiences like?**

I'm incredibly grateful, *Critters 3* and *4* were the first films that I got to work on. They were the first films that took me from behind a desk, so I'm unbelievably grateful. It was a wonderful experience, but beyond the fact it was a wonderful experience, I'm incredibly grateful because they were the first films where I was actually more integrated into the filmmaking process than I had ever been. I love that whole conceit of how things radiate outward, for sure.

I understand that there was this interesting aspect of a hinged script as well as the production being shot back-to-back, which I think is just phenomenal. And the set designs by Philip Dean Foreman were just incredible, especially how quickly that you guys were operating. How did this production strategy evolve?

The whole origin of why *Critters 3* and *4* sort of began to manifest from on the studio side is that there was a market, and particularly internationally, for these kinds of lower-budgeted genre movies. So New Line was looking to library titles that we might do like quality, lower-budgeted sequels, I guess, or for lack of a better word. And so Rolf Mittweg, who was running New Line International at the time, was a big proponent of doing this, so that was sort of the inciting incident from a business perspective of why do the films and why do them *then*. And at that point I was the low man on the team, I was the most junior executive on the development production team at New Line at that time. So that's how the projects came to me. And literally we were told, we had pre-sold certain international rights and there was already a delivery date. There was already a contractual date by which the movies had to be delivered. So, finished, completed and this goes to the point you're pursuing about why the films were done the way they were done. So, working backward on the calendar, we quickly realized these films would have to be done in close proximity to each other, and ultimately got to the point where they'd have to be done simultaneously.

How quickly do you think both scripts were able to be completed?

David [Schow] either wrote both of them in four weeks or he wrote each one in four weeks. I remember it was unbelievably fast. That was kind of the joys of the project because the financing of them had already been arranged, and they had effectively already been greenlit at a certain price and the studio New Line had approved the two concepts of the big city and outer space. We basically were a moving train pretty quickly, from the moment it started, we got everything moving very efficiently and very fast. They were almost like indie films happening inside the studio.

I think Rupert had noted too, his intention, I think for the third one was something a little bit darker than how it turned out. Maybe less on the comedic tone, but everyone kind of pointed to the notion that in post-production, *Critters 3* became a little bit sillier on the comedy end. But from your perspective, was that kind of the iteration for *Critters 3*, or was it always intended to be a little bit sillier than the other ones?

I always remember from the script that there was humor and also it was endemic to the franchise. There was always sort of this dark humor to it. So yeah, it didn't personally surprise me.

Given the tight scheduling and the budget constraints, was it a fairly efficient production?

Yes, that was my recollection of it, and that is a true testimonial to Barry and Rupert as producers and the fact that we really got the best of, because Barry and Rupert were so effective as independent producers, and then we had the best of the New Line studio apparatus in support of these movies. So it actually worked out incredibly well.

I was always really impressed not only by the design, but also by the speed in which the sets for *Critters 3* were deconstructed and the spaceship set for *Critters 4* was constructed. The production value for the fourth one, even today, really punches above its weight. I've heard nothing but great things about Philip Foreman. What was it like to kind of see that process?

Yeah, I have to say, my strongest *Critters 4* memory is the production design and the speed of it all coming together. It looked amazing. Phillip was using egg cartons for parts of the interior designs and I think some of the hallways. And it was just, it was so clever. Everything felt so innovative and clever, and basically, using limited resources in an incredibly smart way. When you see things like that, you know you're working with amazing people, because on camera, it just reads so beautifully.

Do you recall any specific challenges you faced on *Critters 3* and *4*?

I regret to say not specifically. I remember, I just remember more about the opportunities. I remember, on *Critters 4*, which features Angela Bassett in one of the roles, this is obviously very early days, but you know, just the fact that you could have actors of such talent in a fun genre movie, those kinds of things always made for excitement.

Does anything else stand out to you from *Critters 3*?

Yeah, I only remember my favorite because I was really new to film sets, period, like on these movies. But I remember when the sequence was being shot with the laundry chute, where the critters go up the chute, and I remember looking around the warehouse thinking how on earth is this going to happen? And then of course the kids patiently explained to me like '*No, no, no, the camera can't tell whether it's looking up and down or side to side, so we'll just do everything on the floor sideways for the camera's perspective to look like things are racing up and down but they're just going side to side.*' I had only been at New Line, I think, 2 or 3 years. And again, I had been mostly behind a desk doing development notes and various things like that. So to be on a set and see how things actually happened and to learn those kinds of things, it was invaluable.

I know that a lot of genre films present great opportunities for folks trying to look for work and build off of it. What would your advice be to actors or filmmakers when they see these

types of opportunities, even if it's a genre that they don't ultimately want to be working in? Is it still worth the risk to participate in such projects?

In these times, the advice I tend to give young people is make things and get noticed in an arena that means something to you. So if you like genre films, then that's an area you should be in. But really, that's the best way for everything. I learned that the film and television industry is one of those great things where you can learn an awful lot from study but it is also one of those things that if you don't have the opportunity to learn that way you can learn an awful lot just by doing it at any level.

Take Peter Jackson for instance. His first film was a 16 millimeter film that took him 4 years to make because he could only shoot it on the weekends because he had a day job, he had a 'job job,' and he made it with his friends. And whenever there was something he wanted to do, he had to innovate it. So when he wanted his character to hang off the edge of a cliff, but he still wanted that amazing shot, he had to build essentially his own little kind of, I wouldn't call it a crane, but it was essentially a camera rig that would go out, you know, like there was none to have. And that kind of innovation still happens today. So I always find that that's the most important thing because I remember the job I had before I went to New Line at a company called Republic Pictures. I saw Peter Jackson's first film, which was called *Bad Taste* in what would have been I think 1986 or 1987. And I was so gobsmacked by the innovation and the sort of kinetic energy of it and just how creative and brilliant it was. Like I took that videotape with me everywhere I went and I took it to New Line when I got to New Line. So my point is getting noticed and recruiting people who are fans and advocates for you. It's like that's the currency of the realm.

You're absolutely right, *Bad Taste* was something else. That was such a unique film. Some of the things he was able to generate in that were just remarkable, if not outright nauseating…

When you watch that film now, the energy, the way he shoots and the way he's, even, I can still remember, and he does this on everything, but on *Lord of the Rings*, he makes sure the camera always goes wherever it creates the most dramatic, dynamic storytelling opportunity. So if that means you've gotta build your own little crane, or that means you've gotta innovate in some way within your limitations, then you'll innovate.

CHAPTER FIVE
CRITTERS ATTACK!

REBOOTING A CLASSIC

In 2019, a *Critters* reboot written by Scott Lobdell was shot in the picturesque landscape of Cape Town, South Africa. Debuting direct to television via the Syfy channel, *Critters Attack!* was a surprisingly strong franchise installment featuring re-envisioned Krites made by the Canadian special effects team Amazing Ape. Unfortunately, *Critters Attack!* was released the same year as the micro-budgeted *Critters: A New Binge*, which debuted as a web-series for the horror streaming platform Shudder after languishing in development hell and later in distribution limbo. But how did we wind up with two unrelated *Critters* projects in the same year?

In October 2014, Warner Bros. launched its Blue Ribbon Content division, a short-form series production unit that aimed to develop and produce live-action series as well as animated series for burgeoning digital platforms. Sam Register, the then-President of Warner Bros. Animation and Warner Digital Series, headed this new division, while Andrew Mellett led Blue Ribbon Content's financial operations, business affairs, and distribution deals.

"Blue Ribbon was originally dreamed up as a way to develop original programming based on IP from the broader Warner Library for this sort of emerging digital short-form world," explains Ben Gigli, a producer at Blue Ribbon Content who later served as an executive producer on *Critters Attack!* "Platforms like YouTube Red and ABCd were tiptoeing into these 3 to 10-minute long episodic, digital first kinds of programming. So [Blue Ribbon] was the place to do those. For reasons I don't really know, because it happened before my time at Warner Bros., Blue Ribbon was set up with Peter [Girardi] and Sam running it, even though they were also doing live-action stuff. They were doing stuff for YouTube Red, ABCd, Go90, and some of these other big corporate studio initiatives to do short-form programming."

"When I got there, we were in this funny space where there were a lot of people at Warner Bros. trying to figure out which units had the rights to which programming. Within Warner, there was Warner Horizon, which primarily handled cable television programming. As platforms like Hulu and Netflix became bigger and more prestigious, the budgets also became bigger. Horizon was like, '*Well, I feel we should be the ones making hour-long series on these bigger properties.*' And Warner Bros. Television was also like, '*Well, we should probably be handling these.*' And Blue Ribbon was in this funny spot where we were getting to do things not claimed by any of the established television units inside the studio. And so one of the things that became our purview for a few years were short-form series that were appearing on Go90, which is where *Critters: A New Binge* lived, though it was not my project. I don't think it ended up there because, you know, Go90 got boxed up very abruptly, but it was made for Go90."

Blue Ribbon Content announced its intentions to reboot *Critters* with Go90 among its initial projects in October 2014, though it took several years to finally come to fruition. Ultimately, director Jordan Rubin, best known for the horror-comedy *Zombeavers*, was slated to helm the *New Binge* web-series, which was shot in Vancouver between late May and late June 2018.

"It was something we were expected to be involved with, and had we been involved, it would have been very different," laments Rupert Harvey. "Someone had someone's ear at Warner Bros. and they made it worse by having conversations with me and leading me to believe that this was going to be something that we were involved with and were regularly engaged in. But nothing was happening as far as I was aware. Nothing happened after a series of conversations I had with these particular people. Then all of a sudden, I hear that, in my own neighborhood in Vancouver, the show is in production and people start asking me when I was starting, when I was shooting, and all kinds of things. So it was very badly handled by the people involved. They had to sign checks and give us credits, but it wasn't quite done the way it should have been done. Let's just leave it at that. I think the product, the little I've seen of it, speaks for itself."

Rupert's production partner, Barry Opper, feels the same way. "The newer *Critters* installments, we had nothing to do with," he confirms. "Warner Bros. got the movies from New Line when New Line sold all of their movies. Warner Bros. did deals with other people to make reboots of the *Critters* movies and they were obligated by contract to deal with Rupert and myself, but they didn't do it. Someone in their legal department pointed it out to them at the eleventh hour and they tried to pacify us, having already started shooting the series. I actually saw an episode, Rupert didn't even look at it. I think he saw the first episode of the *New Binge* series, how they dishonored the critters in a way. He didn't look at any others, but I looked at them all. I guess maybe because I wanted to punish myself or something. They had no understanding of it. It was not a happy situation looking at any of those."

Back during the production of *Critters 2* in 1987, rumors began to circulate about a third installment. Of course, the underwhelming performance of *Critters 2* shelved that idea in the short term, but the Chiodo brothers felt a certain way about maintaining their role in future *Critters* productions. "Charlie designed the critter. It's our character," Stephen Chiodo explained to *Fangoria* in 1988. "The idea of somebody else doing it just doesn't seem right." However, given the passing of time and the third and fourth installments, the Chiodos have softened their stance.

"We had talked to them [Warner Bros.] for years, like 5, 6 years before *A New Binge* actually happened," recalls Edward Chiodo. "And yeah, it was interesting. They knew who we were, they knew what role we played. Initially, the call was, '*Hey, do you guys still have the critter puppets? And do you think we could reuse them for this direct-to-video version we're gonna do?*' And we said, '*No, we don't have them. And even if we did, they're so old, they couldn't be used.*' And then they kind of went away, but they did come back a couple of years later to revisit it. And then finally, it got into serious talks about wanting to do this. They had a new director, Jordan Rubin, attached and his writing partners, and they pitched this idea. And we thought it was kind of fun, you know, whatever. And we had really extended negotiations about doing *A New Binge* with them. But the money was extremely low and they were going to be doing it in Vancouver. As much as we love *Critters* and would have loved to continue it, it didn't make sense financially for us and them, really. And to siphon off money to do it here in L.A. when that money really needs to go on the screen, we felt it just wasn't right. We felt like we had had our time with *Critters* and it was time to pass on the torch."

"That's just it," agrees Stephen Chiodo. "You hire local talent to build it up there so you don't have to have it built down here [in L.A.], ship it, otherwise, all of that money would be wasted. And then who's going to operate it? You're going to have locals operate it. So right there, there's so many glitches for us being involved. It was better for the production to kind of just take it on with some Canadian production effects company."

"I pitched to them the idea of bringing us on as consultants," says Edward Chiodo. "Give us a fee, you know, we're negotiable, it's not going to break the bank, but we have so much knowledge. If they end up going to go to somebody else, they're going to want to do it their way. That's fine. But we can give them so many pointers on all the mistakes that *we* made and for them *not* to make. And yeah, they didn't bite."

With the Chiodos out of the picture, the *New Binge* series lumbered along in development hell for several years until Verizon's Go90 mobile-oriented "social entertainment platform" was disbanded in July 2018. Two months earlier, YouTube Red had been rebranded as YouTube Premium. And a year prior to that, the ABC network had significantly scaled back plans for its ABCd platform. Within just 4 years, the short-lived webisode fad had withered, leading to the dissolution of micro-content platforms and jeopardizing the future of *A New Binge*.

"We had this interesting window of a couple years where we were doing these types of short-form series," says Ben Gigli. "And we were also empowered to do movies with this interesting sort of approach. Warner Bros. used to do direct-to-video movies where they would bankroll a certain chunk of our budget. Then we would go out to our partners, be it the Syfy channel or Hulu or Netflix, and we would find the other half of our budget there. And as part of Blue Ribbon's DNA, we were encouraged to root through the vast Warner Bros. library of film and television and cartoons, which stretched all the way back to the 1930s, to find stuff that was like, '*Okay this is kind of cool and there's something here and nobody's remade it lately.*' It's not like we're asking, '*What about* Nightmare on Elm Street?' It's like, '*Yeah buddy, everybody at the studio wants to remake* Nightmare on Elm Street.' But you find something kind of cool and you're like, '*Well, this seems interesting.*' Or you discover a character that was maybe a little bit neglected, but like once upon a time had a big footprint. So oftentimes we'd be looking at the Hanna-Barbera library and we'd see something like Penelope Pitstop. People really liked her, but no one's really done anything with her in a long time. Maybe there's something interesting to do here. So we were empowered to do that through the broader Warner Bros. library, but that also necessitated a lot of making sure that nobody else in the broader Warner organization, which of course was very broad, wasn't also kind of thinking about it or working on it.

"Sometimes, we'd find something and get all excited about it, and then we find out that so-and-so big-name showrunner that we have an overall deal with really always loved the show, and they're already kind of calling dibs on it. We'd be like, '*Okay,*' and we'd have to walk away from it. Or we'd find something and we'd be like, '*Well, what about this?*' And they'd say, '*Well, that movie's really cool, but when the contract for the original movie was originally drawn up in 1984, we sort of promised Sylvester Stallone the perpetual first right to be an executive producer. And we have to pay him $200,000 an episode no matter what to make it, so it's probably not cost-effective. Also, good luck calling up Sylvester Stallone's people and trying to convince them to give you the time of day to talk about this small series that you need his permission to do.*' So it was this perpetual game of cat and mouse where we were asked, '*What about this?*' '*No.*' '*What about this?*' '*Nope.*' And we found a little bit of a groove with our partners over at Syfy channel, who have this long tradition of doing these fun, direct-to-cable horror movies. They have a model that works; they have a business that works, and they are looking to be more involved with known intellectual property. Warner Bros. has this big library, and we said, '*Let's start rooting through the horror library. Let's see what we can find.*' Fortunately, if I'm recalling this correctly, *Critters* is pretty much fully owned by Warner Bros., pretty much like 100 percent in-house. I'm pretty sure there were permissions that we did have to go and ask on from the former producers."

PRE-PRODUCTION

While Blue Ribbon continued to explore its options with the experimental *New Binge* series, producers simultaneously pursued a feature-length update to the *Critters* universe with *Critters Attack!* A chance encounter with filmmaker Bobby Miller, a Columbia University film studies graduate known for the horror-comedy short *Tub* and his debut feature *The Cleanse*.

"It all starts at Blue Ribbon," reminisces Bobby Miller. "I had been meeting there on general meetings for years, and in their bathroom was a tiny critter that they were using as like a toothbrush holder. I remember using their bathroom and seeing this critter in there and I was like, '*Do you guys own the rights to* Critters, *what's the deal with that?*' And they're like '*Yeah, we're trying to figure out what to do with it.*' At the time, they were going to do something like a web series [*A New Binge*] when I was first talking to them, and they even brought me in and showed me one of their original critter puppets. I was all geeking out. And then nothing happened and I didn't hear from them. Then I had heard rumblings about the *Critters* series that ended up on Shudder, called *A New Binge*. So I was like, '*I guess they chose someone else. Oh well, that ship has sailed.*' Then I was at Fantastic Fest, I think around September or October. I had a short that was playing there and I got a call from Blue Ribbon that they wanted to do *Critters* and I was like,

Blue Ribbon Content's choice to direct *Critters Attack!*: filmmaker Bobby Miller. (Source: Werner Pretorius)

'*Whoa, are you looking for pitches?*' You know, what's going on? And they're like, '*Well, we already have a script and we're looking to shoot in like two weeks in South Africa, of all places.*'"

"Another colleague of mine, Alex, she had gotten to know Bobby and gotten to know his work a little bit and was just really excited with him as the perfect choice for this approach, especially with the practical effects," says Gigli. "That was one thing that was really important to us going into *Attack!*, which we really wanted to do practical. In *New Binge*, the puppets themselves are much more stiff and not as articulated. I think they had a couple very articulated puppets, but they didn't have a ton. Most of it was augmented with CGI. And I think generally, based on the fan reaction and internal reaction, we all felt that going practical was really key. We wanted to bring back that kind of silliness that goes along with the puppet practicality, but also the fun visceral feeling of those 80s horror originals where you have these kind of grimy, grody, slimy puppets with their gross hair and shiny teeth and slimy faces and everything. And everyone was very keen on that. It was very much like, '*Hey, this is an important thing and we want to make sure that we stick to that in this one.*' And that was a feeling across the board, not only inside of Blue Ribbon, but also with the Syfy channel."

EARLY SCRIPT

To write the script, producers tapped Scott Lobdell, a well-known comic book writer and screenwriter respected for his award-winning work on several Marvel Comics series involving the X-Men in the 1990s and also for his work with DC Comics in the 2010s on series such as *Red Hood and the Outlaws*, *Superman*, and *Teen Titans*. Lobdell also wrote the script for the 2017 slasher-comedy *Happy Death Day*.

"We got Scott on board kind of early on," recalls Gigli. "We had been meeting with Scott, generally about work he'd been doing as *Happy Death Day* had just come out. Obviously that film [*Happy Death Day*] did extremely well and everyone was really pumped about that. And Scott was feeling great and wanting to stretch the comedy muscle a little more inside of the kind of horror framework of all that."

"I was approached only because of the strength of *Happy Death Day* at the box office," says screenwriter Scott Lobdell. "And the producer said, '*Listen*, Critters *has always been a franchise that's like 80 percent comedy and 20 percent horror. And we want it to feel like a genuine horror movie with some comedic elements,'* and I thought, *'Oh that's a really interesting concept.'* They said, *'We want to stay away from camp. No camp. Zero camp. Get rid of all campiness,'* and I'm like, *'Okay, you can still have humor without camp,'* and apparently that was obvious in their understanding too."

"It's funny because the difference between feature films and television films and television series is crazy in the sense that you can write a pilot in November and it's in front of the cameras in March. Whereas with a movie, we'll use *Happy Death Day* as an example. I wrote it in 4 weeks and then it took 10 years to get made. And that's not the most uncommon thing. And so when I was asked to write *Critters Attack!*, they already had their pre-production date established and they knew when they were going to be shooting. So I was writing on the back end of that, which made it very, very different from when you write a script and have 6 weeks to write it and then 3 weeks to do the rewrites and then 3 weeks to do the final polish. With this, it was so short that I was actually doing the rewrite and the final polish within my first 6 weeks of writing the script because they had a hard date. So in some ways, it was the most joyful experience ever. I had a meeting with them and they said, *'We just have a question about this and this'* and I answered the question and then they said, *'Okay, go ahead and write it.'* And then I just had like two very, very small notes. And so within that context, it was a really fun, joyful writing experience. So my orders were to treat it like a reimagining. And so that is, in part, how I came up with the idea that we've only ever met male critters, and suddenly we're going to meet this queen bee-type critter. But also one of the things was that there was a whole original subplot where they were learning how to communicate and learning English, so that was kind of fun. They eventually decided *'No, the critters can't talk because that makes them sound silly, so no talking.'* I'm like, *'Okay that's fine'* and again that was all towards this notion of trying to make them scarier, more primal, you know."

Lobdell approached the first draft with a grand vision of expanding the *Critters* universe, including a subplot involving the bounty hunters, while largely abandoning concerns for budgetary limits. Unfortunately, the extremely tight budget and pressing deadlines led to a rescoping of the draft and its subsequent revisions.

"Scott had this first draft. I don't even know what draft it was to be honest with you because when I was brought in I don't know how much was developed before or after. But Scott had a draft that was really big," remembers Bobby Miller. "I mean, it was not a shoot-a-Syfy-channel-movie-in-South-Africa budget. He had a big one and the bounty hunters were in there.

And I was super geeked about the bounty hunters being in there. Syfy, for whatever reason, didn't want the bounty hunters in the movie. So we were like, '*Okay, well, in a way that kind of works out for us because that story was just so much bigger than what we really had time or money to do.*' I said, '*Let's take this as a creative challenge.*' We have this big world and Scott introduced a lot of things that were new and maybe controversial in terms of how the critters were born and I was like, '*Well, let's try to just work on this stuff and make it as good as possible and just kind of bring the scope of the movie down.*'"

DID YOU KNOW?

While shooting *Critters Attack!* in South Africa, producer Ben Gigli wound up staying in Cape Town to work on another Warner Bros./Blue Ribbon project, *The Banana Splits Movie*, a horror-comedy movie directed by Danishka Esterhazy. Much like the creation of *Critters 3* and *4*, Gigli's productions were shot back-to-back with many of the same local crew members, albeit with different directors.

"Part of the challenge with making this movie in particular was that, because of the way the budget was constructed with part of it coming from Warner Home Entertainment and another part of it coming from Syfy, Warner Home Entertainment had very specific deadlines that it had to hit because of the way that its home movie system worked," explains Gigli. "So the way this was all set up to function was that Syfy would get a first window on cable, and then, after that window passed, Warner Home Entertainment could release it in like Redbox, and the DVD market is actually still, or was up to even size in other parts of the world where broadband internet doesn't quite have the same penetration that it does here. But because that Warner Home Entertainment really had to have the movie done by a certain date, they weren't going to provide the budget if we couldn't finish the movie by that certain date. So we had to get going with the script before we had a director in place to ensure that we could hit that deadline.

"There was some really big stuff in the earlier story build, and there was some stuff that I desperately wanted to keep in an earlier draft of the script that, unfortunately, once we got into actually scoping those things, we were just like, '*Oh man, we're not going to be able to do that.*' These were not in budget. And so there was some early story stuff that was very big. And a lot of that was very interesting and provided a lot of cool backstory to things. But it also was not totally core or necessary to telling a story that we were having occur at our primary location in the film. It was a lot of intricate, big universe stuff and just kind of beyond the scope of what we were going to be able to do in a 98-minute movie. And then there was other stuff that was really fun, like gory set pieces that would have been so cool to do if we had another three quarters of a million dollars to only spend on those three pages. For instance, there was this scene with a bus crash and all these critters begin working their way up the bus, eating people and everything. It was really, really fun. But when we got into scoping in with the production team, we're like, '*Guys, we need to flip a bus over and then light a bunch of fires.*' And this called for like dozens of puppeteers. There was just no way we were going to be able to afford doing this and also shoot the rest of the film."

In the version that was ultimately shot, *Critters Attack!* follows a struggling young woman named Drea (Tashiana Washington) who is still reeling from the recent tragic death of her mother. Barely making ends meet at a dead-end job delivering sushi, Drea will do anything to attend the same college her mother attended before giving up her higher education dreams after getting pregnant with Drea. After another failed application to the school, Drea accepts a job babysitting for a school administrator in a desperate attempt to influence her next application. Now saddled with watching Trissy (Ava Preston) and Jake (Jack Fulton), along with her younger brother Phillip (Jaeden Noel), the quartet take a hike in the woods where they encounter a bizarre skunk-furred animal they believe is injured or sick. The docile furry creature of course is a queen-bee alien of the Krite species whom the kids affectionately name Bianca. The kids are unaware that a spacecraft loaded with Krites has landed nearby and unleashed a hoard of insatiable hungry and aggressive critters that tear through the town, attacking and eating everything in their path. The kids and Bianca become acquainted with a mysterious bounty hunter, Aunt Dee (Dee Wallace), and face off against an army of Krites, including a giant critter ball, at Drea's dream college in a climactic battle for survival.

CASTING

"I was involved with all the casting," explains Bobby Miller. "It was all really quick. The kids were from Toronto and Tashi [Washington] had worked with one of my friends on an indie film and he recommended her. Again, you know, everything was so quick and I had reached out to some of my friends and asked who could play this role? There's so much to do when you're in prep and it's all so condensed that I just needed help from friends. And my one buddy recommended Tashi. Her audition was so great because she was just adding these bits to the role; she would improv stuff. And we were really jazzed on Tashi the entire shoot because I felt like she was just making everything better, able to ground the emotional material, but also really good at slapstick comedy. Like when she walks in and sees the critter, Bianca's killed that one critter. And then her sense of timing is really, really good. So I was really excited because I felt like if we could get someone good in that role and the critters looked good, we'd have a movie. And the kids were all aces too. I mean, kind of scary good. And again, challenging conditions. We're working a lot of nights towards the end of the movie. It really becomes a night movie. And where I think the critters look best, I think if we had more time on the script, I would have wanted to figure out a way to stage more scenes at night because they really look great at night. That first night sequence, which was the carnage scene in the parking lot of the sushi restaurant, I really loved how they looked in it and I love the scene overall."

"Dee Wallace was great. Who wasn't great? I mean, come on (laughs). Right before I left for South Africa, I met with her. And it was funny because, at the time, I don't think the script was finalized yet. It was getting rewritten or something, so we met just purely to meet. I thought, *'I'd really love to talk to her about the movie. That way she knows I'm not some goofball and it might prevent her from not wanting to do it.'* And we hit it off and she was really excited about the idea of being this bounty hunter character and completely flipping viewers's expectations. The cool thing about her on set was that, when she was there, everyone got serious, all the kids. We have a lot of young people in the cast. It was like, *'No, you can't slub around,'* because she would nail it. It would be like, *'One-take Dee.'* She was just great. And so it made everyone else have to be on their game. And also, she's like the perfect actor for a director on a budget because she has the quality of being fun to play around in the scene. And she has that spark of exploring different things. And at the same time, she doesn't F around. It's like, *'We gotta get this scene done.'* She understands that there's only so much time for an indie filmmaker to get this stuff in the can. She has this dual mode where she is able to play and give you great stuff while also being conscious of the time."

"They brought me the offer," says Dee Wallace, "and I thought it was an interesting reboot and it was shot in South Africa, one of my favorite places on Earth. I loved working with these people. I loved Bobby's directing style, but I wish Tashiana and I could have had more time to play and dine off-set."

ONE BADASS BABYSITTER
An Interview with Tashiana Washington
("Drea," *Critters Attack!*)

From what I understand, you guys had quite the adventure shooting in Cape Town given the speed with which the project took off…

Yeah, it was definitely a quick turnaround, but I had the time of my life filming. I had never been to South Africa before, and honestly, when I auditioned for the role, I wasn't expecting to shoot in South Africa. I thought it was going to be somewhere in America, so that was a pleasant experience. I absolutely had a blast shooting it. And even a few days prior, we had a little bit of time to talk and do some microphone rehearsals. But it was crazy because they should have probably had a few extra days to shoot, but certain people had trouble getting their visas in time, so that took like a week away from all of us being there at the same time. But we still got it done.

Bobby Miller explained that he was at a film festival in September or October when he got the call to make the project and, by Thanksgiving, he was already in South Africa?

Yeah, Bobby was there for a long time. If I didn't know any better I would say he just moved there. He was there from Thanksgiving all the way to around mid-February. He had a very nice time getting there and preparing and writing and editing scenes and things of that nature. I wish I'd been there since Thanksgiving. That would have been a great Thanksgiving and a Christmas present.

Do you recall how you were approached about this project?

It was honestly like any other audition. The audition came in, I had to do the self-tape. This was, you know, pre-COVID, so usually self-tapes were a little bit more rare. Usually, I would go into the casting office. But for this, I just had a self-tape. I worked on it with my acting coach. We sent it in. I actually had red hair at the time. And I mean, it's a small thing, but I've learned that sometimes different unique hairstyles that I have are attractive to casting directors, producers, and directors. So I had a specific hairstyle which I ended up having in the film. I dyed my hair black-brown but the two braids that I had, the fresh cornrows on the sides, I'm sure that no other girl that auditioned kind of had that hairstyle. So I think that, humbly speaking, aside from talent, that hairstyle made me stick out a bit. But I remember auditioning, I think they sent over some notes and then I sent another self-tape with the notes and I remember I was really sad because I wasn't doing any work. I was like, '*Where is my life going?*' I remember I was shopping in Victoria's Secret and my manager called me and said, '*You're going to South Africa!*' And I almost fainted at Victoria's Secret.

Were you familiar with the *Critters* franchise and the legacy of the original?

Absolutely, because my mom loved horror films. When she was pregnant, she was high-risk so her doctor told her no horror films or anything like that and once she had me it was like that's all that plays in the house. Because she was catching up on all the horror films she didn't see while she was pregnant. And it's like, you would think that she would show your kids Barney, but no, I'm watching Freddy Krueger, I'm watching *Critters*, I'm watching *Gremlins*, I'm watching and I'm just mortified, like, '*I can't look.*' She's like, '*Just look at it, this is amazing!*' So I was definitely familiar with the *Critters* films, not all of them, but definitely the original. I had seen it multiple times.

Do you recall the first time you had seen the script for *Critters Attack!* in its entirety?

I believe I saw the full script after I had booked the job. And I remember printing it out, just so that I could start memorizing lines while I was on the plane and stuff like that. But even still, it wasn't the quickest turnaround, only because I had the same issue trying to get a visa. I was supposed to get there maybe two days prior, but it was, you know, the visa issue. But at that time, I was just reading it over and over again, getting familiar. The scenes that I had rehearsed for the audition were very familiar to me. And I was even working still with an acting coach. I'm like, '*I feel comfortable doing these scenes.*' We already worked on them. But they were a little bit challenging. You know, there's a lot happening. '*How do I stay present and give my best performance for this?*'

So I was committed as soon as they told me I booked the job, I was just so committed to bringing Drea into life.

And you had not met the other actors prior to landing in South Africa, or was that the first time you had a chance to meet your fellow cast members?

That was the first time, yes. A lot of my cast members are Canadian. And you know, just being the age difference and stuff, we wouldn't go out for the same role, so it's not like I would see them on audition or anything like that. I did look up everybody's work and I got familiar in that way. My first time meeting them was on set. The first person I met was Jaeden Noel. We had a couple days shooting together. As the days progressed, I met everybody else. Jack, Ava, I met them later.

That's remarkable because together you all had such great on-screen chemistry that it seemed like you all had known each other from working together on other projects.

That's really just kudos to my co-stars, because even though they were young, they were so talented and so professional. They had worked on several projects before. It's not like this was their first time. They weren't green. They also weren't overly excited to be on set as if it was their first project. So, we had a lot of fun while shooting. It wasn't like it was just straight work for this. We had our moments of being silly on and off set and things of that nature, which I think helped build the chemistry. Because they would call 'Cut' and we're walking back to the trailers and we're still laughing and we're still discussing certain things. I think that would help it come across on screen that way.

You mentioned how strenuous the shooting pace was and the limitations with both time and budget. Were there any particular challenges that you faced and overcame on this project?

As far as challenges go, this is my first horror film. Because I had never played a role like this before; I wanted it to have a touch of humor. I wanted it to basically be convincing and believable. Because you are on set with puppets, which, believe it or not, are scary. When you look at them, even though they're not moving, they are scary in real life. When I was a kid, I was afraid of dolls because I was like, *'Mommy, I think the doll is alive.'* And I'm telling you, those creature puppets, don't sleep with one in your room because they will jump up and attack you. That's just how I feel. And Mom was like, *'Oh, I wonder if I could take one home.'* I would have to keep mine encased in storage or something because that is not sitting in my room looking at me. But I think the biggest challenge in general was the fast turnaround and just being able to give my best performance because we had limited takes.

And also the weather because it's very windy in Cape Town. If we were shooting the same scene broken up on different days, one day the weather would be so windy, like you'd hold onto a pole and you'd be in the air horizontally. But the next day, the wind would be kind of still. So the wind posed some continuity issues. But the biggest challenge for me, being in my head, was not overthinking it and just giving my best performance. I'm just so grateful that I had a director like Bobby Miller who gave me a safe space to feel comfortable and reassure me that I booked this job for a reason.

In prepping for the character, were there any particular inspirations that you drew from?

Oh, absolutely. I watched the original multiple times before I got to set. I also watched the third installment a few times. And, you know, it was... my mom was happy because a part of my prep, she was just like, '*You know what this means, scary movie time.*' And it was just a marathon of scary movies. And it's one thing to like kind of enjoy it as, you know, just like as the viewer. Like, '*Wow, this is a great film,*' but it's another thing for me to have to study. '*How are they reacting in the scene? Are they overly screamy? Are they kind of more so in shock and to themselves?*' You know, '*What's the best way to play it that's most realistic?*' Because another thing my mom likes to do is, she'll hide and jump out and scare the crap out of me. So I used my reaction from that in the film. And I thought about that. Because sometimes you'll see in films something jumps out and the person is like screaming for a really long time. Whereas, when my mom jumps out and scares me, it's kind of like a quick one. So I used that and the scene right before the first attack with Jack, it was a quick, '*Oh my god, you scared me.*' And then the bigger one came after. You know, his legs would get chewed out in the film. And so, on the plane, she would even suggest, '*Hey, I just saw this great horror film. You should check this out, you should watch this. You should watch that movie again.*'

Freddy Krueger in *A Nightmare on Elm Street* to this day, I cannot watch it. Even though I know he's going to pop out, I'm not going to sleep because when I go to sleep, he's going to get me. Freddy Krueger and the original *Candyman*, I refuse to watch them.

And of course, the moment Dee Wallace arrived must've been great. How was working with Dee?

Dee Wallace is very short, but when I tell you she is 7 feet tall with her energy and her presence, she is definitely a giant. Her energy, her spirit, her talent, and the way she carries herself. I was starstruck and I just took the opportunity to learn as much as I could from her in the short time that we filmed together. She is so professional, so witty. And I asked her, I was like, *'If you have any suggestions for me, please let me know.'* She came in and she forced all of us to step up. I came up with Jackie because she was so amazing. It's like, *'Oh, no, we have to be better.'* It was like a silent agreement that me and the kids had. We have to step it up to meet her where she is with it, with the scene. It definitely took the film to another level, just on set, the energy, the vibration was higher. She just brought such a light to the film on and off set, and I'm so grateful to have been afforded the opportunity to work with her.

And you had some pretty difficult shoots, like the soccer pitch show down and others with lots of effects. What was that like?

It was a lot of running, a lot of reset, do it again, reset, do it again. Me and the kids are running, so we're trying to keep our energy up. We shot and it ended up being late at night, but we would shoot into the morning. You can see in that last action scene with the (cannon) shooting — that was a great day to have the wind because it was kind of blowing in my hair. It was very movie star-licious and a lot of fun. The crew worked so hard to set up that shot in a quick and timely manner because we had so much to cover in such a short time. Sometimes, we would be sitting on set for an hour, just going over the lines. Bobby would be helping us figure out how we could make the scene better with some things that you add, what would make it as dynamic as possible. So even though that was challenging with all the running and the shooting, that was one of my favorite scenes to shoot. It was kick-ass critter time. So, yeah, that was a lot of fun.

When the critter ball is obliterated, the initial plan was to have buckets of critter blood and ooze spray you down but, for whatever reason, it was only little flings of goop coming at you…

When I tell you it was a disaster, it was one of those things where it's like one take and that's it. We had a great rapport with the crew. Everybody was friends. I literally knew everybody in the cast and crew. And the crew was so excited. We would joke about it, you know, with the week coming up too. *'Oh, we're gonna dress you guys in slime. We're so excited.'* Blah, blah, blah.

When I tell you Bobby called '*Action!*,' we shot the gun, and I just thought it was gonna be like Nickelodeon Slime Time. Then, one speck hit my cheek and like half a speck hit my shirt. And you know, it was hilarious, but we couldn't break character. So we're just there looking determined, like maybe there will be more slime because the critters are dead, and we're just standing here.

Then they were like, '*Cut!*' And we were like, '*Oh my God, what happened?*' And they were like, '*Just stay still! We'll have to kind of edit it.*' And they threw a little bit more slime on us. Then, you know, the way they did the editing, they cut back to us and we had even more on us. But, oh my god, I definitely thought I was going to be drenched from head to toe in slime. And I was not. And I was so disappointed. Because it was my childhood dream to be slimed at Nickelodeon. I was like, '*Yes, slime time, baby!*' But it ended up looking good on camera. They were able to fix it. And I think we had to get a little CGI slime. But yeah, that was a fail.

How come the guys with the buckets didn't slime you up, did they just miss?

I think maybe they just weren't close enough because it's only but so far they can get in front of us without their shadow showing on our face in front of the camera with the lighting. I just don't think that they were close enough or that they were positioned right to kind of slop it on us. So if someone is like 10 feet away from you and they kind of shoot it at you, maybe they didn't aim high enough. I don't know how. I don't remember how big the buckets were. It just didn't hit us the way it was supposed to. It kind of landed right in front of us and it was almost like, '*You're ruining the film! We don't have any more slime!*' So, Bobby literally took matters into his own hands and said '*Actors, stay put.*' So we're sitting there, super serious, and Bobby took slime in his hands and came in and rubbed it on our faces and said, '*Continue to look serious.*' That's how they cut and pasted it together. So the slime you saw on our face in the film that didn't even really touch us – that was later because Bobby was hands-on and was like, '*No I refuse to let this happen like this.*' Bobby's the one that saved the day with that one.

Were you a victim of stomach flu that ripped through the production?

I will say this. When we started filming, I was about 11 pounds heavier than I was by the time we finished filming. And when I tell you, even some of the South Africans got sick. Like our 2nd AD, his name was Lee. He was a native there. He got sick. Some of our makeup artists got sick. I don't know what it was, but it hit us like a domino effect. And... damn. I hate to be too graphic, but I

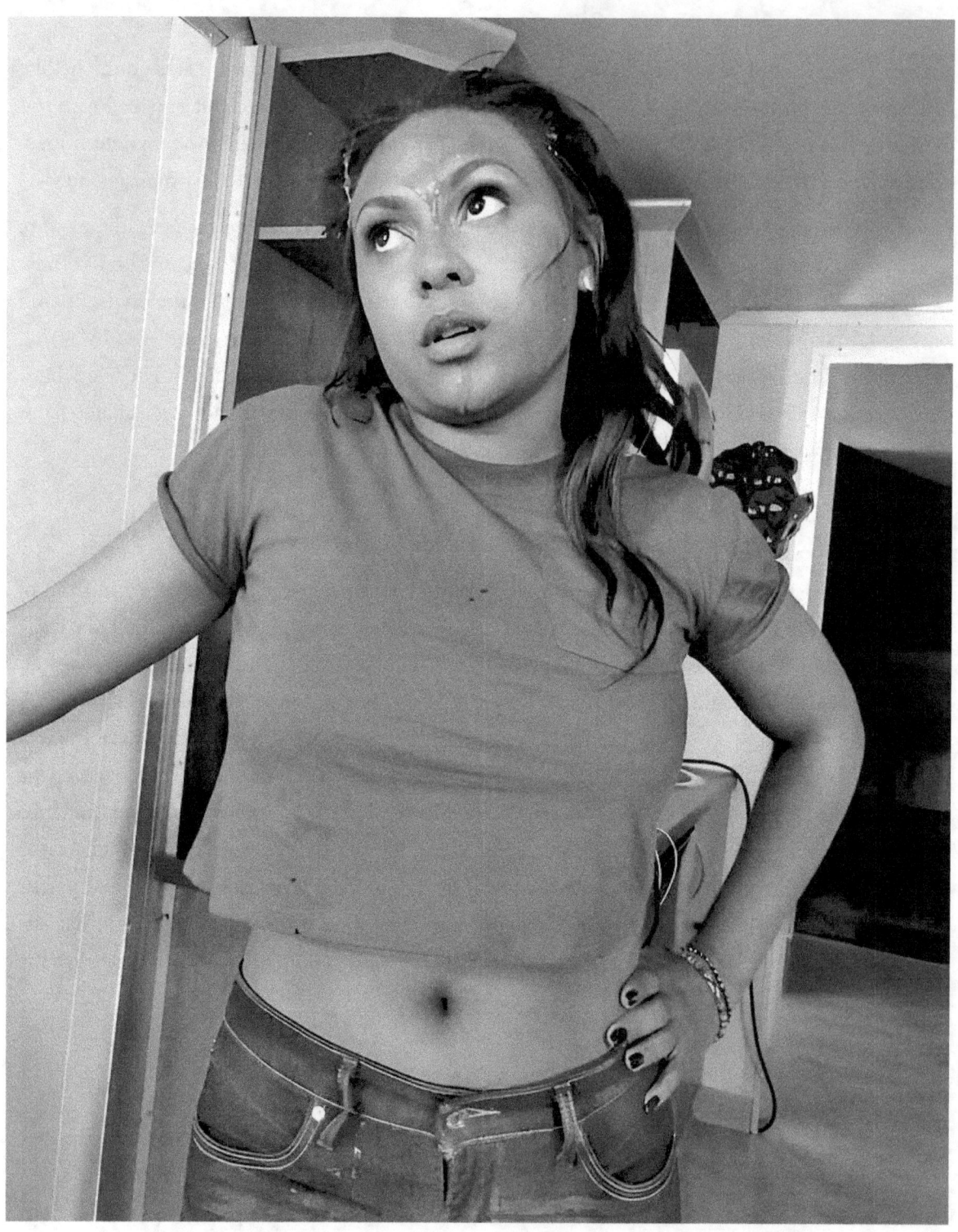

A svelte-looking Tashiana Washington lost a noticeable amount of weight after suffering from a serious stomach flu while on the set of Critters Attack! (Source: Tashiana Washington)

remember they were calling me on set, and I was in the trailer like, '*I'm coming!*' But in my head I was like, '*I'm not coming yet.*' I couldn't. And I was like, '*They're going to have to wait another 5 minutes because I have to take a shower because it's horrible.*'

And I remember them waiting outside the door like, '*Are you okay?*' And I was like, '*I'm fine.*' I was like, '*I hope they don't know.*' Then I was like, '*They know, they know, they know.*' But it literally tore us a new asshole, all of us. We all lost weight and came back to America slimmer and trimmer. But it was no joke. And then I remember when it first hit me, I was in the scene where I first come to the house and I'm being given the notes on like how to take care of the kids. I remember while I was filming with the mom I was looking at her I was like, '*No, no, no, what's happening? This can't be happening.*'

So I had to secretly go tell Bobby. I said, '*Bobby, I don't know what's wrong, but something's very wrong.*' And I said, '*I'm gonna keep doing the scene, but can you just have a bucket on standby? Because when I'm talking to her, I feel like I'm gonna just projectile vomit all over her.*' He was like, '*Oh my God!*' So we got through that scene and yep, while we were setting up for the next take, I lost three pounds, came back, and everybody was like, '*Are you okay?*' I don't know what it is, but I just feel like as an actor, you can't say, '*Oh, I'm sick, sorry, I can't come in today.*' No, we're on a time schedule; this is what I love, I'm so excited about this project. You have to fight through it, but I definitely had food poisoning for a large portion of the film, as did everybody else. Sometimes our lunch breaks would be, '*I'm just gonna be in the bathroom.*' Most credit should go to everybody who held it together, even though there were a lot of bathroom breaks. We were basically trying to perform and not look flustered because sometimes the actors would get sweaty in between because they were feeling so sick.

Here I was thinking one of the most difficult things was trying to work with a Bianca puppet and not laugh or something, but that's really intense that you were able to pull it all off being that sick and uncomfortable.

Yeah, but working with Bianca was so easy. She was the most talented actor on set. Because all she had to do was be pretty and be an evil hero. This is my first time working with puppets and animatronics. There's just three guys laying on the floor with their hand up a puppet's ass. You know, and they're down there sweating and balled up in weird positions, uncomfortable. But you get used to it; it's almost like they're not there. You know, they had to cut holes through planks and things of that nature so it could look like they were under the ground. For the attack scene when

I get bitten when we're on the football field, they had to set up a whole kind of plank area to make it look like it was flat ground, but they were under this thing. I was on top of a level of area with some thick grass on it so that his hand could be through the planks so that a critter could bite me.

Because if we didn't have that, you would see the puppeteer's arm doing it. So he had to come up through something to conceal that the puppet was being controlled. Which was really, really cool. And I remember being told by Keith Arbuthnot, who was one of the head animatronic actors, '*If you see sparks or if you see smoke, run.*' I thought he was kidding. And he was like, '*No, seriously, but because it's animatronic, it could explode.*' I was like, '*Oh shit, oh okay, I didn't know that.*' I really thought he was kidding. But yeah, the guys were great. And actually one of the puppeteers, he had hair exactly like Bianca. It was like blonde with a black streak. I thought, '*Wow, that's crazy.*' But yeah, Bianca, she was professional, she was a little bit of a diva. She got more makeup applied than me. But, oh my gosh, she was so cute. If I did have a critter to take home, it would be Bianca because she was really a beauty.

Do you recall how long you were in South Africa for?

I was in South Africa from the beginning of January up until mid-February. And I literally had the time of my life on my days off. I was able to explore the city and got to see some wild lions. I went to a cheetah reserve and I got in the cage with the cheetahs. I was able to have my mom out there with me. It was her birthday. So we had a nice little birthday party for her. And the friendships that I developed while I was out there, I'm still close with a lot of the cast and crew to this day. We unfortunately had two people on set who passed away. My driver, his name was Tim Bella. He passed away and one of our ADs, his name was Adrian, passed away as well and because I love the cast of *Critters* so much, I cried like crazy. I guess I kind of felt like even though I did keep in contact with everybody, you always wish you could have spoken to them one more time before their untimely passing. I would love to work with the same cast and crew again. Bobby was an amazing director, and he really was the backbone of the film and was a great captain of this ship.

Have you heard of any murmurings about another project of this caliber in the mix?

No, but I have thrown it out there that they should do a *Critters vs Gremlins* like how they did *Freddy vs Jason*. I think that that would be amazing and the cult following that both these franchises have, people would definitely come out and see that.

And I would love to have a lot of the original cast back. I would love to join them and have them come aboard because I think that's definitely something people wanna see. And I was surprised because I remember *Critters Attack!* was originally supposed to play on SyFy. I think it was in October around Halloween and I was really excited about that, but the *Critters* mini-series came out while we were shooting. It kind of ruined how the critters are back in the way that we kind of wanted to put it out.

So that was, for lack of a better word, hurtful. Because we wanted to bring it back with a big bang, but because the TV series was out and got mixed reviews, I feel like that took away from the momentum we had. And on set, even the boom operator came and showed us like, '*What is this? These puppets, these are not our puppets. Who is this?*' We were devastated and I think that, because of that, they rushed to put the film out early in the summertime.

I mean, I'm grateful that we went to Comic-Con and stuff like that, but I was really looking forward to being a part of the fright that October, that being the way the film should have premiered rather than in the summertime. And due to time restraints, some scenes were cut with Dee Wallace. I just remember reading the script and being so in love with it. But, certain things are beyond your control. So at the end of the day, you do the best that you can on set and then how they edit the film and how they put it out and how they promote it; it's beyond your control.

I do wish certain things were a little different because this film is like such a gem to me and we worked really hard on it and I think everybody did a great job. I'm just waiting for *Critters vs Gremlins*. I would love to be in that with Scott Grimes. Let's have Dee Wallace back. We need Leonardo DiCaprio to come back, you know? It should be like the *Critters* all-stars and bring those all together and we each get really great kills and stuff like that. I think people would love to see that.

Do you remember seeing *Critters Attack!* for the first time?

Yes, I remember the first time I saw it and it's really hard for me to see myself on camera because I end up saying my lines with myself. I'm like, '*No just watch the movie.*' I like to joke that it's almost like we were pregnant with a baby, and now the baby's here, and we see what the baby looks like. So, it was really fun to see, and I also enjoyed seeing it on the Syfy channel because the commercial breaks would just come at the perfect time with great jokes and things of that matter. So I think it played really well when it played on Syfy. I just wish this was people's first time seeing it and I just wish that the TV show maybe came after ours. But I'm still really proud of where it's at.

It's such a respectful, tasteful continuation of what that first one brought to all of the fans. I can tell you exactly my impression when I first watched it. I was just stunned by how great of a job that you guys have pulled off. And I just assumed that you had a really tight production schedule, but I was blown away with the quality that was able to be achieved.

They're brilliant. Also, Scott Lobdell, excellent to work with him. He was just fresh off of *Happy Death Day*. So I was a big fan of that. And I was able to read the original script with some of the scenes that were cut and thought, '*Wow, this guy is so awesome.*' So between what he did and Bobby added some things, had some rewrites and things of that nature, I felt like they made such a great team. I wish Scott was in South Africa with us while we were shooting, but I think there was a schedule conflict or budgetary issue. But ultimately, I'm really, really proud of this film even with the trials and tribulations around it. I can't wait to show it to my kids if I ever have any. I think it's a great movie, a great starter horror movie for children – you know something that's like not too, too scary but something that's also like super fun and I was surprised when we got the R-rating because we got it because of gore and, had I known it was going to be rated R, I would have taken that to my fullest advantage and used a lot more curse words.

But I thought we were going for it. And I know a lot of people with kids that told me how much they enjoyed the film. And a lot of fans of the original, even when we were at the Fantasia Film Festival, I never knew what to expect from people. It's really hard doing sequels because I know me personally, a lot of times, the original is the best installment and the sequels are kind of trash. I remember this guy raising his hand in the audience and he had a really serious face and I was like, '*Uh oh.*' And his arms were kind of folded and he was like, '*I just wanted to say I was a huge fan of the original and you know what you guys did here. You guys did a great job and this is the best one I've seen after the original.*'

I was like, '*Holy shit.*' And at the Fantasia Festival, they meow at each other. So that was a meowing moment. I don't know why they do that, but it's really funny. The whole audience would just say, '*Meow, meow, meow.*' So when he did that, I started meowing, and everybody started meowing. It was really cute.

Not surprising, Dee Wallace (center) was beloved by cast and crew alike. Dee is surrounded by puppeteers Keith Arbuthnot (left), Hansie Visagie (right), and Mike Fields (far right). (Source: Keith Arbuthnot)

REDESIGNING THE KRITES

Ever a fan of the original *Critters* and growing up on similar practical effects-laden creature features like *The Gate* and *Ghoulies*, director Bobby Miller knew how critical getting the right look of the puppets would be for the project. Before fully committing, Miller needed to firm up the design and look of the critters before departing L.A. for South Africa, though his first impressions nearly left him contemplating departing the project altogether.

"At first they wanted us to use the puppets from *New Binge*," explains Miller. I'm not sure what initiated it, but when I saw the puppets there, they were more cartoony than the puppets I grew up on. And I was like, '*This works great for what they were after, which is way more absurd and a funny kind of cartoon thing, but I don't think it works for what we're trying to do.'* And so that was kind of a big early thing. To me, the puppets are obviously so important. And I didn't want to say '*Yes*' to the movie until I knew they were gonna look how I thought they should look. So I was able to get the guys who worked on my last movie, *The Cleanse*, to do the creatures. We ended up taking photos of the original puppets and shipped them to Vancouver where they're at and they were able to, you know, and obviously add a little something different to their design but also keep it in the mold of the movies, which to me was that tonal balance. I always thought of these as gateway horror. The PG-13 gateway are movies for kids. That was the way I viewed them and that genre and it's what got me into horror – these types of movies, so I wanted them to be a little scary when you see them. If they look too goofy, I mean obviously they're critters, so you know all it takes is for them to chomp on a human for you to be like this is kind of funny. But you know, I tried my best to kind of reign that in. So that was in L.A., kind of early days, trying to figure this out."

With extreme budgetary and time constraints facing the production, the Vancouver-based effects crew at Amazing Ape would repurpose some of the already existing hero puppets made for the *New Binge* production. The puppets were housed at a warehouse while some others, including the giant critter ball, were stored inside a rural horse barn.

"For *Critters Attack!* we had a very limited budget, very limited time," says Werner Pretorius, the film's lead critter designer and owner of Amazing Ape. "And, there was a warehouse in town and they had stored all of the old critters from the TV series. I decided, '*Let's go have a look at those puppets and see what we can repurpose.*' So, we went in there and there were just like so many things there from that TV show. Some of them were awesome, some of them weren't that useful, but it was a really great place to build on. I think we got like 30 boxes worth of stuff out of there. There were definitely some things that really helped us along. It's like when you're figuring out how we're going to do some stuff that the previous folks that had done the TV show had really kind of figured out the basics of it. So we could kind of add on to that, which was great. But for the critter ball, there was this big barn on a horse farm and there it was, the big critter ball. It's just sitting there in the dust. It was pretty awesome, actually. But then when we tried to move it, it was massively heavy. We couldn't do it. Honestly, if that had rolled over someone it would have killed them. But there were actually some partially useful animatronics in some of them. The cartoony looking ones, the really cartoony looking ones. So, we stripped those out and then we kind of built the new skins to fit those animatronics and we jazzed them up and rebuilt a bunch of stuff, but we

Werner Pretorius and his Amazing Ape Productions created the Krites, although their design was a larger variety closer to those used in *Critters 3* and *4* and the *New Binge* production. (Source: Werner Pretorius)

used a lot of the original components and it saved us a massive amount of time. There were some things like the spikes shooting out of their backs, that basic rig was already built and we kind of repurposed a bunch of it. We scaled it up a little bit, repurposed what we could, built some new darts or quills for it."

Ultimately, Pretorius and his Amazing Ape crew would execute a crash course in refurnishing the previously built puppets with new skins made from foam latex just like those used in the original *Critters*, and would rely upon a South African-based effects crew to assemble and finish the puppets. In total, Pretorius's team had 5 weeks to design, acquire the previously made puppets, refit, and assemble all of the critters that were to be used on set in South Africa.

"I forget how many characters we made, but I feel like it was like 40 different critters," Pretorius recalls. "I think we had a month to build all of them, so it was an insane deadline. And it was right before Christmas [in 2018]. In fact, as soon as we finished, we literally put them into crates on Christmas morning and shipped them off to South Africa that week. There were so many things, like so many things we had to do, little things that you don't think about. It's like, '*Oh, we need scars for this. Oh, we need a wound for this. Oh, we need little baby critters that are going to get birthed out of this.*' And so we need the guys back, it's like all this stuff that just kept on coming as he was developing the project that we weren't thinking of initially. And of course, with a tight timeline, we just had to get into it. I wanted to do the best job we could, given the limitations, for Bobby, because Bobby's awesome. It was always a bit of a fight between us, including Bobby, like the creative kind of guys versus the money guys. But you know, realistically, this is not a big budget movie at all. So, whereas the old *Critters*, and definitely *Critters 2*, had pretty decent budget. We had no prep time and no budget."

To quickly educate the production team, Bobby drew upon the then-recently released Blu-ray box set of the original four *Critters* films and made reels depicting each of the previously shot critter gags and bounced ideas around about how to achieve similar effects. "There was one shot that, and it's in the behind-the-scenes of *Critters 2*, where the critter ball is connected to the camera," Bobby points out. "And I was like, '*We gotta do one shot like that.*' And we did indeed get a shot like that where the critter ball is attached to the camera, as if we're with the critters. So for me, it was important to figure out how we can play the greatest hits and also hopefully do something a little different that a new audience member could roll into this movie and not have seen the other ones and hopefully it feels right and all comes together and works."

Pretorius and crew prepared dozens of critters on short notice and shipped the puppets
from Canada to South Africa during pre-production in late 2018. (Source: Werner Pretorius)

What sets *Critters Attack!* apart from its predecessors is the introduction of a skunk-furred black and white Queen Krite, Bianca. "Bianca was supposed to be smaller than she is now," explains Werner Pretorius. "The choice was made in interest of budget and time, and just getting this thing on film, to get her done as quickly as possible. We had to scale her up and fit her to an old-school animatronic, but she didn't turn out as nicely as I had hoped. She's kind of my least favorite one, unfortunately. Bobby's concept art for her was so beautiful that it was a real shame that we steered in that direction of having to make her larger."

We had been involved on the design side, but mostly for Bianca because she was this new critter," says Bobby Miller. "That was something that I had worked with this artist on and we did paintings because obviously Warner Bros. being the gatekeepers of the intellectual property also wanted to weigh in and make sure they were satisfied with Bianca's particular design, so that had a couple more steps to it. But the other critters were pretty straight forward other than the lead critter, which had a scarred face. We went back and forth on that design, but more so just about the placement of the scarring. But the overall kind of critter look was really locked into those original movies. You know, it's funny, I had thought that it was a critter that we were basing off of *Critters 2*, but I'm pretty sure it was based off of the *Critters 3* mold. I'm not a hundred percent sure which mold they had it based off of, but it looks good to me."

Opposite: The black and white queen Krite, Bianca, makes her debut at the Amazing Ape studio. Although Miller had input on the design, it was ultimately up to Warner Bros. to approve the final look.
(Source: Werner Pretorius)

Right: Pretorius is seen here checking some wiring to one of the Bianca hero puppets, two others of which appear below.

(Source: Werner Pretorius)

PRODUCTION

Principal photography in Cape Town ran between January and February 2019 and lasted nearly 4 weeks, a fairly routine shooting schedule despite some eventual turbulent health challenges given the environment. "I actually thought it was a pretty good principal photography schedule at that point because my first movie was 20 days and I think we were able to get 20-something days on *Critters Attack!*, so as an indie person, I was like, '*Wow, I got a couple more days*,'" says Bobby Miller. "Then you hear what the older movies had, like how many days they had, and you're like, '*Ah, crap.*' But for me at the time, I felt the schedule could work and the new thing for me as a filmmaker was we had multiple cameras to shoot with. Now, that was kind of a necessity, but I've always been opposed to the notion of using a bunch of cameras because that, I think, tends to make you not make definitive choices on frames and composition, and you're just kind of grabbing coverage. But for this type of movie, it's what we had to do. So for me, it was like we had two cameras every day, sometimes three. And with the schedule we were on, I was never freaking out. And again, maybe it was just kind of going through the fire on my first movie and feeling like nobody can hurt me anymore. You know, it's just like I could do it. So really the shooting wasn't a concern until everyone started getting the stomach flu."

Nearly the entire cast and crew briefly succumbed to a wicked stomach illness, plaguing everyone from the lead actress Tashiana Washington to even crew members not on set every day. "I got really sick. I was so incredibly, incredibly sick," painfully recalls Gigli. "And then I went back to bed, probably four days after I got it. I remember seeing Bobby and waving to him and walking up to him. And like from a distance I could see Bobby like, '*Oh hell, I'm way too sick.*' And then as I got close to him, he was like, '*Ben, you need to go home. You look terrible.*' He's like, '*You don't look well enough to be here, man.*' He wasn't wrong. I was very much like, '*Dude, I gotta get to set. I gotta get to set.*' No exaggeration, I lost 10 or 15 pounds in a four-day period. It was really bad. It was really, really bad. But yeah, I was back in it shortly thereafter."

"I don't think anybody escaped that," chuckles the film's editor, Mike Mendez. "I remember Tashi [Washington] had the stomach flu pretty bad. She lost a ridiculous amount of weight in a few days time, so her outfit started to fit differently and stuff. And obviously that's a different thing to be on set and having to kind of work through that kind of malaise that you get being sick and then having to act. It's different when you're in the back room not having to get with the people that you're working with. But when you're acting, you've got the whole crew staring at you. I don't

Director Bobby Miller on location during the production's fifth day
in Cape Town, South Africa. (Source: Bobby Miller)

envy her for that. I definitely remember spending some time in the editing room with Bobby where we were both pretty uncomfortable (laughs). Thankfully, I didn't have the burden of being on set every day. They had doctors that would come in and visit us so we wouldn't have to go to a clinic or something and they would even come to the editing room. And basically they would just say, '*You got a stomach flu, just drink a lot of water, take some vitamins, and you'll be fine in like four or five days.*'"

"In South Africa there's a pretty gnarly stomach thing that hits anyone who's not South African," explains Bobby Miller. "One of the execs that was out there for Warner Bros. got it and then I got it, and then our editor got it. It was summer, so it was really hot and I had diarrhea; it was just terrible. So for me, the real setback was getting sick."

Fortunately, lead puppeteer Keith Arbuthnot and his fellow crew members escaped the wrath of the stomach illness. "Mike Fields, Raj [Mariathason], and myself were so busy trying to get shit done on other sets that we missed it," says Keith Arbuthnot. "Maybe we were running on too high an octane of fear for the bug to really get a hold of us. I think it was Raj who had one tough morning but he pulled through. The rest of us just crossed our fingers and hoped for the best."

On top of the rampant illness, the inability for the film's writer Scott Lobdell to be on set forced creative changes to be made by Miller and at times, on the fly. "I think the one unfortunate thing about this for me, this being my first director-for-hire thing and the first time I directed someone else's writing, I really wanted to be really collaborative with Scott and my first thing when I signed on was like, 'Can Scott come out to South Africa with us?'" says Bobby Miller. "I'm a big fan of Joe Dante and he would say that he would cast his writer in the movies so that the producers would fly the writer out so they could be on set. And I tried every way to get Scott there, but there was just no money to house him. And so for me, there was a missed opportunity for Scott to be with me and do those rewrites. So really, the rewrites, because when you get into prep, you're looking at the reality of the situation. So rewrites had to fall on me because there was no one there, you know. He had done his contracted work and that was it. That to me is a bummer. I've written stuff on my own and directed and it's so much work to be prepping a movie and then also rewriting at night. So I really looked forward to it and to me that was the only missed opportunity - not having his brain out there too."

The rapid, no-break pace in shooting and the local crew's usage of the Canadian-made hero puppets for the first time offered plenty of challenges, including short circuiting animatronics and near catastrophic small-scale fires. "Early on with the animatronics, I remember with Bianca, at one point she just started smoking," Bobby Miller says. "You know, because the mechanics are so fine and small that when you run them too long, they just start smoking. So that was like introduction to animatronics for some of the crew on day one or two, when she started smoking. There's one scene actually in the parking lot, a night scene at the sushi restaurant, where the one critter on the trash can was smoking. That was actually the animatronic that was smoking. I wish we had the outtake of this because the puppeteer was inside the trash can and it started smoking and it got very hectic for a second."

Despite a rampant stomach flu ailment affecting many of the cast and crew, puppeteer Keith Arbuthnot and his colleagues largely dodged the sickness and continued to perform in the trenches unimpeded. (Source: Werner Pretorius)

BRINGING IT ALL TOGETHER

Critters Attack! not only introduced the new gendered Krite queen, Bianca, but the effects team incorporated more gore and goop when the Krites were killed in an endless array of kill shots, setting it apart from its predecessors. But the crew was also adamant about paying homage to the original Chiodo brothers's giant critter ball design, an accomplishment not lost on any of the cast and crew.

"One of my most memorable and proudest achievements was the team working with the giant critter ball," says Ben Gigli. "There's a close-up on the critter ball, you see all of those moving little critter faces, like, everything and the way that they did that was super fucking clever, like huge props to our amazing puppeteers and VFX people. We had the giant inflatable critter ball that was literally like an air bladder with a critter skin over it. You'd just inflate it until it was like 10 to 12 feet in diameter. You'd then bounce it down the street and there was usually one person running behind it rolling it like a giant bowling ball. I think some of the critters's eyes lit up, but otherwise they were kind of static. And then the way you do the close-up with all the critters on there is they built this rectangular wooden frame that was like 8 or 9 feet long and 5 feet wide, and they made a critter skin on it. But in this critter skin are a bunch of fully articulated critter puppets. The puppeteers would lay underneath this wooden frame and move the critter puppets. And then they mounted the camera on a kind of rail and they would run the camera over the wooden frame of the moving critters and they would intercut it so you have this kind of editing illusion of the ball rolling in super close-up. Here's all the critters moving, and na, na, na, na, na. That was one of my favorite kinds of clever visual effects, actual visual effects moves that they did."

"Working with the giant critter ball, obviously it's a big undertaking," recalls Bobby Miller. "There's a ton of critter pelts on that thing. Apparently, Warner Bros. had shipped vintage pelts; these were like original used critters from the 80s, that we had access to. I was joking that this was a very eco-friendly shoot because we were repurposing all these old critters. And I thought it was them giving me a line at first, like, 'Oh, we're sending you these old critters.' But then we got the shipment and these are old, these are definitely well-worn, aged critters that were on that thing, so that was kind of cool to have the old guys on there."

The cast and crew assembled at the university the night of the giant critter ball shoot, which was set to take place in the early morning hours around 2 a.m.. Much to the crew's surprise, the sequence mostly went off without a hitch. "We didn't have any trouble with that giant critter ball going down the steps," says Bobby Miller. "I mean, it was a little scary, I'll be honest. It's like, we were shooting it super early in the morning, everyone's a little blurry and you hope everything goes well, but we didn't have any issues with the critter ball, thankfully. We started shooting and I remember just, I don't know if I was emotional, but the first time we rolled the critter ball, the group shot, it was just so much joy on set. Even older guys who were crew on the movie were just like, 'Hey can I throw a critter ball into the shot?' I turned everyone into little kids and I just thought it was so beautiful. We're all out here throwing hairy basketballs into frame and there's this one guy, one of the camera guys, a very respectable older gentleman. One day, we were shooting that stuff in the parking lot where there's a big massacre outside the sushi restaurant and he just grabbed a piece of fur, put it on his hand, and started waving it around. There's like this one piece of fur that flies into the frame. He really got into it and was just so excited to be a goofball with us. It's those moments where, as hard as everything is, you see people turn back into kids. That's what it's really about. And I saw that multiple times throughout the movie. And that's the stuff you do it for, man."

Although working with the giant critter ball proved uneventful in technical terms, the much more straightforward climactic shot of the critter ball's explosion and slime slamming into the film's heroes turned into a nightmare. "We did have issues with the last shot of the movie because I wanted the survivors to be drenched in goo for the final shot like the end of Peter Jackson's movie *Brain Dead*," says Bobby Miller. "Bless their hearts, they were really great guys on duty for this stuff that night, but just about nothing, like barely any of the goo we had prepared, hit the actors. We had no time to do another take. So off-camera, I ran in and smeared goo on Tashi's face. I was like, '*I'm sorry I gotta do this but I just need some goo on you for this end.*' I think that was one where it didn't work out as planned. They had buckets of goo and launchers of all sorts, and I don't know what happened, but we just didn't nail it. I was like bracing the actors for it, '*This is gonna be gnarly, da da da,*' and that was one of those things where I was just like, '*Oh man, that didn't work out.*'"

Opposite: Ava Preston and Bianca on the set of *Critters Attack!* The overly large design of Bianca became a disappointment for designer Werner Pretorius, who felt the character should have appeared smaller in stature compared to the other Krites. (Source: Keith Arbuthnot)

BRINGING THE KRITES TO LIFE
An Interview with Keith Arbuthnot

(Puppeteer, *Critters Attack!*)

When I think of *Critters Attack!*, it reminds me of the nostalgia and family oriented tone captured in the first *Critters*...

Yeah, they nailed the tone. There's some things that we really would have loved to have done, but at the same time, we were lucky to get what we did. We had 29 days, and that doesn't include the weekends, so we were around the 20-day mark for getting it shot. And they had no money for extra days or reshoots or anything else like that. I know that they snuck a few in. I think they were able to negotiate like five or ten days after that for bits and pieces, but, you know, for the most part, that's all they had. My God, the money that they saved shooting in South Africa too was astounding. It was an ultra, ultra, ultra low-budget. Because one American dollar is worth ten in South Africa, so they saved a fortune by shooting it down there. And of course, half the crew wasn't paid, well, they weren't union wages, I'll tell you that. And half the crew, I think a number of the crew weren't actually even being paid. I think they were just being utilized. I don't know how they paid them. But yeah, it was beyond a shoestring budget and I don't think they expected it to be as good as it was in the world.

Opposite: Crew members prepare to roll the giant critter ball, a favorite gag among the film's cast and crew.
(Source: Keith Arbuthnot)

It's one thing to shoot over the course of 20 days, but you guys had creature effects, child actors, night shooting, and being on set in Cape Town. How did you pull it all together?

If it wasn't for the fact that Werner [Pretorius] was able to design three brand new characters for the film and also have access to past creatures that he could rebuild from, we might not have pulled it off. And really the fantastic crew that I got to work with, Mike [Fields] and Raj [Mariathason] in South Africa and the local makeup FX shop down there. Mike's an amazing builder and performer. He's been at this a long time. He knows what he knows about this shit and I love working with him. He's a no-nonsense what-do-I-gotta-do kind of a performer. Mike and Raj are just absolute rock stars. If it wasn't for the two of them and the South African crew, who really opened up their shop to us and let us in there to make a mess, we would've been screwed.

Honestly, we were rebuilding those characters right up until the day we finished shooting. It would not have happened with limitations like that, if it wasn't for the fact that Mike, myself, and Raj are all builders. If you just sent puppeteers down and said, '*Here's your critters*,' there's no way. They would have looked at them and said, '*These things don't work*.' But with Mike and Raj, you know, we've worked together on a lot of things in the past. You get a bit of a shorthand with the team after a while, which is invaluable. And if something was going wrong on set, we would just give each other a look, and we would step in and swap things out. Raj would run back to the truck and start rebuilding or refitting something and then run back to set and hand it off. Production would just keep rolling on a lot of times and didn't even realize stuff was happening behind the scenes. For any other production they would have just stopped. It was nuts. It should not have happened. It should not have come together as well as it did. But there was the right amount of '*Let's do this, let's make it happen*' and teamwork from everybody involved. I can't speak highly enough of the South African guys. I don't think they've experienced anything as crazy or impossible as that before. So they probably didn't know that it wasn't supposed to happen. There were a couple times that the critters actually caught on fire because we had no access to, little or no access to all the hobby shops that were down there.

Things would be on fire and they would go, '*Oh my God, shows over*.' And then we would run off, fix it and come back and they were like, '*Oh, wow, okay. So I guess this is normal*.' It's like, '*Don't get used to that, guy. It's not fucking normal*.' It should not be this way. It should be, you know, in a perfect scenario, we would have like the original *Critters* films of the good old days of monster building in the past, where you have days, weeks, or even months to build and rehearse and put stuff together. You know each and every shot that the guys had come up with all those gags years ago, you know, they had access to everything in advance and test puppets and test sets and they were like, '*Okay, now here's this set we're using for this and we've got holes cut in it all over the place for putting the puppets and for hiding performers*.' You'd think we'd be getting better at it now, but unfortunately, a lot of productions are just like, '*Get in there, why are we seeing the puppeteer?*' Well, because you didn't build a set to hide a puppeteer, so right now you're going to have to green screen them out and that'll cost a fortune. '*We can't afford to wipe out the performer*,' they say. It's like, '*Well dude, then you should have talked to people months ago about how to put this together*.' Unfortunately, that's kind of the real world now, but technology's catching up and with the right VFX crew nowadays – you can literally have a puppeteer sitting right beside a puppet on set and shoot it. And fairly cheaply wipe him out of the shot, but it's still cheaper just to do it right the first time.

Would these effects still look better practical?

Absolutely. I'm a bit of a purist that way and I feel practical effects have a sense of weight, a gravitas that comes across. The actors have something that they can focus on; they're not staring off into the distance at a little tennis ball that doesn't exist. Practical will always win out as far as I'm concerned. The new way of doing things is augmented with practical effects but we're not there yet where actors and imaginary, invisible creatures can interact in a scene convincingly. We just aren't there yet and actors aren't even trained for it.

In terms of the puppets, from a technical standpoint, were they prone to breaking down in any certain way, or was it just a host of different problems arising from working with them?

The thing is, Werner had less than a month to design, build, and rebuild the ones given to him by production from that other show [*New Binge*]. Those puppets were designed with programmable servos. The difference between a programmable servo and an analog servo is a programmable servo can have its limitations set within the puppet. Afterward, you can puppeteer all you want with it and the servo will do what it's designed to do as far as left and right or up and down movements are concerned. It takes the onus off of the puppeteer, in a way. With analog servos, you have the freedom with which you throw it in, meaning you set your remote and signal for it, and then adjust from there. It's a more manual type of operation. For the limitations on analog servos, you can put a certain amount of limitations on that from your controller, but for the most part, it's just plug-and-play.

The biggest problem with programmable servos is when one blows or burns out, you have to pull that sucker out of the puppet and put a new one in. You also have to pull out your PC and program its limitations from its minimum to maximum movement all over again. You can't do that when you've got a shooting crew sitting around and everybody's wondering what the hell's happening and why the signal is only resulting in the blinking of one eye. They tend to think that we can just take the puppet back to the shop, fix it overnight, and bring it back. The reality is there is no doing that. You've only got 18 days of shooting to do and one puppet to do it with. So you peel the head back, you yank out the servo, you put a new one in, and you plug it in and you go. We ended up tearing out all of the programmable servos when we got to South Africa and replaced them all with basic run-of-the-mill analog servos that we could get locally and brought everything that we could stuff in our luggage when we left. Thankfully we did because it saved our bacon more often than not.

The other thing is, when working with analog servos, you don't need a PC to program the damn servos. I'm a Mac guy and Mike's also a Mac guy. We're all Mac guys; we're all fucking artists. Giving us a PC to work with, which thinks like a robot, was a bit of a challenge there at first. When it came right down to it, Mike, myself, and Raj agreed that we couldn't have too many challenges ahead of us and that's when we tore out those programmable servos and went back to basics. Once we did that, everything moved pretty smoothly. One of the other challenges with puppets is that they weren't built by puppeteers. They were built by engineers who thought they knew how to puppeteer, or knew what a puppet needed to do. This is fairly common. You've got this thing that looks good on paper or in a digital file, or a CAD design, and then a puppeteer comes along and says, 'Well, that's fine, but where am I going to put my frickin' hand?' Or 'Where am I going to put both of my hands?' Or 'How does somebody else help me puppeteer this?" That's kind of an ongoing issue with most of the puppets that we're building nowadays. However, the sooner you get a puppeteer involved with the build, the better the performance will be in the end.

Engineers will walk in, look at something, and go, 'Okay, pretty.' And I cut a hole in the side of its head so I can get into it. And then the engineers and builders look at me shocked and say, 'Oh my God, no, I spent 2 weeks putting hair on that thing, no.' So that was one of the challenges with the puppets; they were not designed to be manipulated easily. Again, thanks to my garage and the shop team in South Africa, we were able to tear the puppets apart and rebuild them as we needed to.

In terms of puppet designs, the Chiodo brothers mentioned that in the first *Critters* movie, their design flaw was that they had built them way too small. Of course, by the second one, which had a much longer schedule and a much larger budget, they said the one thing that they did right away was enlarging the puppets. With your experience, would you describe the puppets you had to work with as being the proper size, or did the size used impact your puppeteering abilities?

We had three or four different sizes of puppets to work with. We had some of the Chiodo brothers's puppets that were deep background puppets that were old and crusty. We ended up squibbing and blowing some of those up. We gave those to the FX guys and said, '*Here, enjoy.*' Those particular puppets were two different sizes. Most of them ended up being squibbed and blown up because it was difficult to get a hand in there and they were in such bad shape. The next puppets were the ones that Werner had gotten from the other show [*New Binge*], and they were fine but not built to be puppeteered. We had to rip their guts out to get inside of them. Then we had the ones that Werner built that were larger, even more than the other show [*New Binge*]. Once we were able to refit them to get inside, we were able to get some pretty good stuff. So that was good. We were lucky with working with Bobby because he was so easy-going and supportive about what we needed to do to get the shot. It made it a bit of a dream that way.

I think we were able to really coordinate and work together well. I love working with Bobby. I'm still down working with him again in a heartbeat. And he would say, '*Well this is what we got from the script, how are we going to do it?*' Then we would do a rehearsal, or even practice the day before if we were lucky, and take a look at it and huddle up where we would all discuss what could be done movement-wise with each of the puppets to refine the movement in that particular shot. If it wasn't for Bobby being as easy-going as he was, there's no way we could have finished the film the way we did. It was a real blessing to be able to have him be as open-minded as he was.

You were responsible for bringing life to the puppets among many other things, but Bianca was kind of your puppet, right?

Well, the way things ended up, we considered doing that, having me as the primary puppeteer for Bianca. It's common a lot of times on shows that we have a puppet that each puppeteer will take ownership of and develop a character around. But on *Attack!*, because of the challenges that we had with time and shooting and whatnot, it ended up with me mostly puppeteering at the same time as well, not just doing Bianca. I ended up doing animatronic puppeteering for all the puppets and Raj and his team would get down and dirty and do the physical manipulation. Occasionally we had to pull out another remote to operate the hero puppets for their facials and stuff, but a lot of them were cutaway scenes and it was rare if ever we had villains and heroes in the same shot. It was easy for me to just swap out the controller and have Mike jump into the other puppets and get himself underneath something to make them work. Bobby and I would then talk through the shot and coordinate things as the day went on. A great thing Bobby did was being very open to just taking the puppets and the other camera and shooting some cool shit while I was working with human actors over here, and then seeing what extra coverage that Bobby shot could give us. I think had we not done that, we would not have been successful in getting all of the coverage needed for that particular day. There were a lot of times, especially throughout the last two weeks of production, when Bobby needed to go into the set next door to shoot the dialogue, get extra coverage of the actors, and whatever additional scenes were needed.

Raj, Mike, and I were given free rein to get all these other bits and pieces with the puppets. They set up a monitor so that Bobby could watch what we were doing. Bobby would use a radio to provide feedback to us and would say things like, '*That's fucking hilarious, do more of that.*' Or, '*Hey, can we get something else.*' That part of the teamwork effort was fun for everybody and having that little second unit with the other camera guys made it more fun because otherwise they would have just been sitting around shooting talking heads with actors. Meanwhile, they were over on the other side with us just having a freaking great time. There were a few times they'd come over to our set and say, '*Guys, you're having way too much fun. Honestly, you need to stop laughing so loud because we're hearing you next door.*' For instance, I know it happened in the scene where the critters are just rampaging through the mall and outside the sushi shop.

And all those scenes, such as the sequences where you see the critters rolling through the shops and then you see them fighting over a bone and then chewing at a skeleton out of nowhere, were all derived from us just playing around. When Bianca shows her darker side and you start seeing critter pieces flying everywhere was shot the same way. That was us messing around. Bobby would say, '*More, more, more!*' That kind of stuff made it worthwhile for Raj and the rest of us. I can't say enough good stuff about the local makeup effects guys. They had their own shit to deal with but they were a big help and major kudos to them for jumping in there and working with us whenever they could. The same goes for the visual effects guys, they were super cool.

The aspect of having to rely upon local crews, that's another step into the unknown, right? Because you're working in a third-party location with crews you haven't met before…

In a lot of ways it did all work out. I mean, it wasn't perfect. I would have loved to have had more time to work with the guys and learn from them and get into their groove. A big reason that this stuff is shot in South Africa is not only because it's cheap, but they're problem solvers on set, which reminds me of how Canadians tend to be on productions. The American crews have had too much time and too much money and in many cases, they have a very specific set of expectations of what they need to do in order to do their jobs. Don't get me wrong, the American crews are the pros. They know what they're doing. They've been doing it forever. It's their sandbox. They invented it, right? But Canadian crews and the South African crew on *Attack!* were a lot like Canadians in that when a challenge came about, we felt that anything was possible to overcome it. If it wasn't for that can-do attitude and the let's-learn-from-each-other mindset, I don't think it would have happened. I would go back to South Africa in a heartbeat if I could work with those guys again.

I wonder if by having just a little bit more of a budget, *Critters Attack!* could have been a much different project. Maybe it could have enjoyed a bigger and longer-lasting legacy than it ended up getting.

I think it could have been much different. Some things about it forced it, or maybe pigeonholed it, into the low-budget, if not ultra-low-budget category that it ended up being placed in. If it had just a little bit more funding, a little bit more love from the producers, and a little bit more faith in what it could have been, *Critters Attack!* could have resurrected the entire franchise. I imagine it would have entailed about 10 more days of shooting. The kids were gelling; they were having a great time getting to know each other and working together. If we had a couple more weeks of prep, so many of the bugs would have been worked out and we would have had more stuff for the kids to play with in regards to the puppets. In my opinion, there's always room for more.

I think it still shocks many people that *Critters Attack!* ultimately received an R-rating, which is bizarre. The other installments were all rated PG-13 and the second one even had some nudity. Slapping an R-rating on this project just seems wrong.

I don't think I realized that, Matt, but you're right. A PG-13 rating because there's nothing besides maybe a little bit more blood or whatever here or there, but there's no reason why that shouldn't have had a PG-13 rating. If they could have edited it differently maybe... I know sometimes the ratings reviewers or whoever will say, '*It's this scene, you lose this scene, you get your 13 back.*' Or '*It's this shot, let's work together, how can we get it knocked down to 13.*' I'm surprised that they weren't able to negotiate that but it probably was more of a time crunch schedule issue than anything else.

You had mentioned earlier though that this was not the first project you had worked with Bobby, right? Did you work with him on *The Cleanse*?

Yes, I worked with Bobby on his film *The Cleanse* and I built some of the creature effects used for the final scene where the creature melds together with the other creature and it crawls out as this abomination of two monsters linked together. I put the animatronic for that together with Masters FX. Bobby, even on that one, was super cool to work with and easy-going. He kind of had to be, again, because no money, no time.

Looking at all the challenges that you guys faced and really kind of pulled out the adaptability card to overcome these issues and make sure everything was successful, was there anything that stuck out to you looking back that was a particular challenge or obstacle that was overcome or an instance you were fairly proud of?

I think one of the reasons why it's one of my favorite projects over the past several years, you could even say 10 years, is that there were so many challenges that we had that we did have to get a green light to play with and do it. Overall though, I enjoyed it. One of the challenges that worked out well – it's one of my favorite stories from it – is the scene when the camping guy gets attacked by the critters and they're eating him in the jungle or the forest. There's a whole team of critters just going at him. We sort of threw that together. We talked about it with the special effects guys a couple of days before. They asked how we could do something like this. We said, '*If we have a platform built big enough to have two puppeteers underground, then we can put the platform over top, we can lay the camper on top and put some sod or whatever on top, and then we could film it with them with their arms coming up and out.*' They decided to give that a go. On the day this shot is set up, we used a 4'x8' piece of plywood to create a makeshift platform and they threw it all together and then we looked at it and they wanted more puppets. Then we said, '*Okay, let's throw another puppeteer underground.*' So we engineered it all underground. Now remember, it's under these one-foot platforms, right? And as we're laying these pieces of plywood over the top of the guys, the local crew are shoveling dirt on top. I had to step in and say, '*Whoa, whoa, whoa, slow down guys, you're burying them alive.*' The dirt was falling on them.

As we were sealing it up and just before the last piece of plywood went on top, I stopped and realized they had a woman on set who was there to catch snakes, specifically venomous snakes. It occurred to me, and I said to the puppeteers, '*Are you guys allergic to snakes?*' And Raj looks at me with big eyes (laughs). But ultimately Raj and his guys were determined and said, '*Let's just do it.*' So we threw them down in this pit, and of course, we were running out of time because that's what happens. We threw them down in there, put on the plywood, and then dressed it all up with whatever we could find for greenery. We shot it and it looked awesome with all these critters just chewing away on this guy and the actor was fabulous too.

All things considered, we should not have been able to get that shot within the time that we had and as good as it was, without rehearsal, without proper planning, and without an experienced crew of people who were ready to do it. I mean, it was a bit. After we got the shot, they had to run off and catch another shot before the end of the day. So the camera crew just basically packed up and went on to the next location. Most of the crew went with them too but I'm standing there with two or three other guys. I look over and ask, '*I need some help picking these guys up and out of the pit. Anybody? Anybody?*' And I realized there's only me, the assistant camera guy, and one of the ADs that speak English and meanwhile, these other guys can speak very little English. I turn to the biggest guy I can find on set because he's standing there with a broom and a shovel and I'm thinking – '*THAT guy will get my people out from the pit and unbury my guys as quickly as anybody.*' We've had people underground for at least an hour and a half at this point. I said to him, '*Okay, I need you to help me undig my guys.*' So he gets right in there and in what looked like two heaping scoops of dirt, he reaches down to the plywood and tears it off, single-handedly. The other guys start to see what's going on, just in shock. It was freaking hilarious as we pulled them out. The guys climbed up and out and asked, '*Where is everybody?*' '*They're over on the other side already. It's just us, baby.*' (laughs) That was a great night.

If it wasn't for everybody pulling together, we wouldn't have gotten it. Having an actor that was a big '*Yes-let's-do-this*' guy, having a crew that was like, '*Just let's get her done,*' and having puppeteers that weren't princesses and were happy to do what it took made it come together. There were a few other nights too that were freaking awesome, that just happened because everybody said '*Yes.*' Like the scene where Bianca loses her shit at the university and puppet pieces are flying everywhere. The university being so cool about letting us destroy their laboratories, that helped.

That ending sequence at the university and the soccer pitch, that was the same location, right?

Yes, that's correct. The university deserves kudos on this thing too. I have no idea how they were able to get a functioning university to say 'Yes' to allowing a low-budget film crew to go in there and do what we did. But the fact that they did end up giving the production a level of quality that it easily couldn't have had. The shot where Dee Wallace is showing up in the golf cart, for instance. It was this great long shot of her coming down the field and meeting up with the rest of the team. It just gave this opportunity for Bobby and everybody else to get in there and fill the shot with as many angles as they could to make it look like critters were coming from all over the place. That was awesome to be able to do that. The local makeup effects team that was there was excellent. They had been working for weeks on these rolling critter ball yokes and stuff like that that they were finally able to use. The effects guys had rigged up all these fantastic exploding critters. It was fun.

Do you remember seeing *Critters Attack!* for the first time?

I do. I got to see it early because Bobby and the producers had asked me to go to Comic-Con that year [2019]. So that was a treat. I was able to sit down with my girlfriend and a couple of other friends and Mike and Raj and say, '*Hey guys, we got a first run copy*.' Unfortunately, I wasn't able to be in the same room as Mike and Raj, but I was able to sit down with my girlfriend and I think one other friend. It was something special for all of us to be watching it in a theater setting. There was a sense of accomplishment there that I hadn't experienced in a while for a lot of reasons. I think the first reason is that a lot of the stuff we did ended up on camera and incorporated into the final edit. Mike [Mendez], the editor, was also great to have on set. He was there for like a week or so but he was editing on the fly the whole time. If it wasn't for Mike being in South Africa and throwing ideas around and whatnot and us knowing what it was that he did, I think that there would have been some shots that we wouldn't have gotten. The shots would have been missed because having him there, he was able to express to us the kinds of things that he was hoping to see and I think we worked well with them to get them where you needed. The most rewarding part of it was seeing that most of the stuff we did ended up in the final film.

That's awesome.

Mm-hmm. I'd work with those guys again. The camera crew and special effects makeup guys down there were all great. They did *Mad Max: Fury Road*, by the way. Their team worked heavily on *Fury Road*. I think it was just before *Attack!*. They had just been up in Johannesburg building bodies to throw off trucks. I think they end up working on *Raised by Wolves*. It was being shot there at the same time. And the special effects team, not to be mistaken with the makeup effects guys, but the special effects team, those guys had come back from Tunisia and England where they had been working on the final season of *Game of Thrones*. So those guys had a crazy experience. The *Black Sails* was a series about pirates that was shot down there too. The camera crew had come from *Black Sails* and a few other things. They all knew their stuff. The costume department had worked on *Fury Road*, *Black Sails*, and *Outlander*. They used South Africa as a location for the Bahamas. It's an amazing talented group of people. It's kind of like the Canadian crews here have gotten big in Vancouver. I mean, Vancouver went from being a membership of maybe 2,000 to approximately 5,000 or 6,000 crew members now. But the South Africa crew, I love the way it was when we walked on set for the first couple of days and everybody was like, '*Hey*,' high fives, and '*Great to see you at the party last week*' and '*Did you see what they did with our stuff on* Outlander?' It was that type of shorthand with all of them and the camaraderie and the familiarity between each other really helped with the project and it also gave everybody permission to just do their jobs and to do the best they could. Some nights were tough in regards to frustration, but mostly in the sense of wishing we had more time, money, and sleep but everybody was pretty cool about getting to work together and getting stuff done. I saw the makeup girls help in the costume department. I saw the costume department jumping in at work with makeup and special effects when they had to. I'm not saying that doesn't happen with the bigger shows with more money, but there is more of a sense of '*It's not my job, right*' on those bigger shows. But for the local guys in South Africa, there was still a feeling of family, which made things work.

POST-PRODUCTION

Benefiting the production was the presence of editor Mike Mendez on location in South Africa. Mendez, a Los Angeles native and filmmaker in his own right, inadvertently became associated with *Critters Attack!* through a connection with a notable *Critters* franchise alumnus. "I actually, through a roundabout way, got onto this because of Mick Garris," notes Mendez, "which is funny, because I don't think he even knew that it was a *Critters* project. I had edited *Nightmare Cinema* for Mick and Joe Russo, Mick's producer on his podcast *Post Mortem,* knew Bobby and they said they needed an editor that was good at comedy and horror. They wanted to hire someone locally and that was something Bobby really fought for, but not knowing me – actually maybe he regrets it (laughs). Bobby really wanted an editor from L.A. and wanted to fly the editor out to set. And so for me, it was awesome. South Africa is a trip. It's a beautiful place where the dollar goes very far. And for the most part it was really nice. I actually kind of think the South Africa part almost overshadows the production part because it's just so unique and it was such an experience working with an African crew. It's a part of the world I haven't experienced before and really got a lot out of being there."

To maximize the most out of the lightning-fast 2 weeks dedicated for post-production, it was crucial that Mendez cut while principal photography was still underway. Perhaps a blessing and a curse, the rapid pace left the production without the ability to test different cuts of the film in front of audiences.

"The funny thing that happened was we had a shorter cut that was a little, I thought, funnier," Bobby Miller explains. "There were a few bits that we thought were great and Mike Mendez was a joy to work with. I think we were working toward something that was a little shorter, that Warner Bros. loved, but Syfy wasn't on board with. There was a tighter, funnier, slightly funnier cut. Again, who knows though, if you had more time and you put it up against an audience and those bits don't play that you thought were funny, then they'd go anyway. So you really don't know. But I would have liked the opportunity to play with that a little longer."

"I would think that it's usually 4 weeks for the director to get his cut, and then it goes to the network and whatever, or the producers, whoever's involved," explains Mendez. "And then we start probably in another four weeks from there, going back and forth and trying to do it. So basically that eight-week period was kind of condensed into three to four weeks for us on *Critters Attack!* That's part of the reason that as soon as they'd shoot something, I'd start cutting it. So in

Editor Mike Mendez and his Krite companion working hard inside the editing suite in South Africa.
(Source: Mike Mendez)

some ways, I had that extra time. I also had a wonderful assistant over there. Their whole post setup was great. My assistant would digitize everything in the morning and by the time I got there I had all the stuff from yesterday, and so I started cutting away and trying to get ahead. But it was fine. I think I visited the set probably three times. I got to see Dee Wallace. I got to see the main puppets and meet the team and everything. It was great. Once we wrapped, Bobby joined me in the editing room and we just kind of hashed it out for the next three very intense weeks. I think they might have given us an extra day or something like that. But it was this really ridiculous timeline that it was something about, '*Oh, the DVD department of Warner Bros. needs time in advance to market it*' or whatever. So they needed it for like seven months before it came out or something. It was really, really intense, especially considering the time crunch. And then I did another movie for Blue Ribbon and it had the same kind of time crunch."

Accompanying Mendez and Miller in the editing room was a full-sized Krite hero puppet delivered to the suite by puppeteer Mike Fields. Mendez affirmed that besides a few longer editing sessions, the overall post-production efforts unfolded smoothly and straightforwardly. However, the cut's receival of an R-rating took nearly everyone by surprise.

"It's rated R, which was never my intention at any point," says Bobby Miller. "I guess, if I could do it all over, I'm assuming it's all the blood in the movie. I guess I was under the impression, because we're not, I mean it's relatively cartoony, I thought that this was PG-13. And I remember when *Bloody Disgusting* reported the rating of the movie, '*The new* Critters *is rated R.*' I was like, '*Ah shit.*' People are going to think this is us doing a gritty reboot. It's going to have Dee Wallace cursing and everything else. I felt like the rating did us a disservice because in my mind we were doing that gateway-horror-teenager movie. Nothing would have pleased me more than some kid flipping through SyFy or at Walmart seeing the Blu-ray or whatever and getting hooked into horror through this movie. So for me, I never wanted it rated R. And actually when we got that rating, I said, '*I'll recut the movie,*' but because we had no time, we already didn't have enough time to cut the movie, there was no way Warner Bros. was going to give me time to then work with the MPAA on the rating. If I could do it over again, I would have made the gore more or less just green goo. The ratings to me are so mysterious. I think that one gory shot of them getting birthed probably would have been cut, but I would have loved to know what really pushed this into R because it was never my intention to make an R-rated *Critters* movie. If we wanted to do an R-rated *Critters* movie, that would have been a totally different approach. I would have been like, '*Well, we can't have kids in this movie.*' We have to really go and make a gnarly R-rated *Critters* movie. The UK, I thought, labeled it correctly. They called it, because they have like a rating of 15, I think. I think they have it in between PG-13 and R and when I saw their rating come out I was like, '*Okay, they got it.*'"

"It feels like what constitutes an R-rating, especially in regards to violence, the kind of subjective nature of some of it sure seems to have shifted a little bit over the decades," posits Ben Gigli. "You know, it's just like, there's no way that *Critters Attack!* gets an R-rating in 1992, you know? We were always of the mindset that this is all pretty puppety and silly violence. There's some blood and gore, but also like, '*Come on, look at these puppets.*' You can't possibly take it that seriously, but it ended up with the R-rating, much to our surprise. That's the whole joke, where it's like you can you have this two-hour long movie where the hero kills 500 mujahideen or whatever with a machine gun and machetes and tomahawks and as long as you never see a drop of blood, you're fine, it's a PG-13. The minute you see a nipple or a butt, it's an R-rating. That's 1988 in a nutshell. 30 years later, it's like, '*Okay, well, maybe all the violence is the thing that we shouldn't be showing kids so cavalierly.*'"

The grusome splatter effects in *Critters Attack!*, which included these "meat" effects from Werner Pretorius and his Amazing Ape crew, were partly responsible for the film's unexpected R-rating. (Source: Werner Pretorius)

RELEASE AND RECEPTION

Critters Attack! premiered at the Fantasia International Film Festival on July 13, 2019 in front of a live audience and enjoyed initial praise upon its debut. Warner Bros. Home Entertainment released the film on DVD, Blu-ray, and via streaming platforms on July 23.

"The first time I saw it with an audience wasn't while we were working on the movie to see how it played, it was at Fantasia in Montreal, and it played like gangbusters," enthusiastically recalls Bobby Miller. "We were really pumped on it and Warner Bros. was awesome throughout the whole thing. I'm really thrilled with what they did with the Blu-ray. They were super open and did some behind-the-scenes stuff that I thought were really well-produced for such a tiny budgeted movie. I was really happy with the way they handled it and the release. We went to Comic-Con with actual critters and posters and stuff. I thought Warner Bros. did a great job."

Though the soft release in July resulted in initial positive reviews, *Critters Attack!* would premiere on the Syfy channel on 19 October the same year. To mark the occasion, Bobby hosted a live watch party at his L.A. home with many cast and crew members in attendance, including Mike Mendez, Scott Lobdell, and Tashiana Washington.

"Scott came over to my house when it was premiering on Syfy and I'm sure that screening for him was interesting because there's stuff that got cut that he's probably seeing for the first time and there was like no communication about it beforehand," Bobby somberly recalls.

"I don't want to sound bitter, because I'm 100 percent not bitter," Scott explains. "I think it seems like a fun movie, and the people that watched it seemed to enjoy it, so that's great. I saw the first 20 minutes at Bobby's screening party, and then I snuck out the back. I haven't seen the rest of it. It looked entertaining, but when you're in that experience, all you're doing is watching and being like, '*Oh wow, that could have been so much more.*'"

"It's always difficult when you work on something and when you see it for the first time with an audience, because it's hard to take a genuine look at it," notes Mike Mendez "I do think it's one of the better *Critters* sequels overall and I think everybody did a great job. I think you want perhaps a little more critter action, but this is the problem when you're doing these kinds of smaller films. I think all the critter action we want is difficult to pull off on these budgets, but overall, I think it came out really well."

Critters Attack! director Bobby Miller attends Comic-Con with a special guest. (Source: DepositPhotos)

Unfortunately, the release of *Critters Attack!* followed *New Binge,* which aired on the horror streaming service Shudder on 21 March, 2019. The lackluster micro-budget *New Binge* series sucked the air out of what was otherwise a joyous moment for fans celebrating the return of *Critters* installments. With its reliance on shoddy visual effects, cartoonish Krites, and a deranged sense of humor, *New Binge* offered an entirely different viewing experience and obliterated any remaining expectations or interest by the time *Critters Attack!* was released in July. "The simultaneous or very near release of *New Binge* and *Critters Attack!* was unfortunate and it created confusion around both of them, to be honest," Gigli contends. "There was a delay with *New Binge* that kind of pushed it into our world. But in the case of *Critters Attack!,* we had a really specific timeline that we had to stick to because of the nature of SyFy's need within a specific window and Warner Bros. Home Entertainment to release within a specific window as well."

Whether still bitter about being duped by *New Binge,* critics soured on *Critters Attack!* and the SyFy release of the film in October did little to garner additional momentum for the franchise, scuttling any ideas about additional installments. Despite those misgivings, director Bobby Miller remains upbeat about what he and the crew achieved. "As far as I know, it did well for Warner Bros. and everyone was happy," he says. "But unfortunately, I think that department of Warner Bros., Blue Ribbon, I don't know if they're still going with the pandemic and everything, I know a lot of the people I was working with are no longer working there. When we made the movie, there was this energy around these old IP projects as there could be more stuff like this. There was this momentum and then it just went away. We were all excited at the time – we thought we were going to kind of kick start this effort, like what other weird things can we make? Ultimately, that didn't happen. But Warner Bros. was great and I'm really happy with what they did with the release and everything."

Previous Page Spread: voice actor Steve Blum, director Bobby Miller, actress Dee Wallace, lead puppeteer Keith Arbuthnot, and actress Tashiana Washington at Comic-Con 2019. (Source: DepositPhotos)

Safety officers had their hands full on location in Capetown.
(Source: Keith Arbuthnot)

IN MEMORIAM: BRIAN MUIR

The making of *Critters* would never have happened without the original story and script written by Brian Muir, a prolific writer, artist, filmmaker, and film enthusiast who sadly passed away from cancer complications in 2010 at the young age of 48.

A rare glimpse at a young Brian Muir (left) and his sibling Bradn (right) growing up in West Linn, Oregon. (Source: Charles Austin Muir)

Brian Domonic Muir was born in West Linn, Oregon, on 20 January, 1962 and became the eldest of his three siblings: two brothers and a sister. At a young age, Brian took interest in various art forms and found himself drawing, sketching, writing, and yearning to make movies. His early tastes were centered around the sci-fi genre, as he regularly viewed television programs such as *The Twilight Zone*, *Outer Limits*, *One Step Beyond*, and *Star Trek*. Brian also consumed copious amounts of literature, whether it was sci-fi, "pulp fiction," horror tales, or comic books and became a virtual walking encyclopedia of all things related to cinema, literature, and popular culture. Charles Austin Muir, one of Brian's cousins, despite being 9 years younger, watched with fascination as Brian took to learning his craft and honing his talents.

"Brian was always very driven," explains Charles. "He wanted to do movies. He was drawing a lot. And he was always writing. But he had a vision, he even started a production company, and his middle name is Domonic, and so he called it Domicade. And it was *way* ahead of its time for a kid to be thinking about something like that. He had this workflow from a young age that was insane. Way before computers and learning how to do file structuring and naming and all that sort of like archiving and how to organize all your stuff. I mean he had this habit of taking meticulous notes. If he drew a picture for instance, he would write background notes on every little thing, explain what was happening in the picture and what would happen next. He always had extremely detailed notes on everything he worked on."

As an adolescent, Brian began experimenting with filmmaking while in 7th grade, shooting Super 8mm shorts with his friends around their town of West Linn. In one example, Brian directed a 20-minute short titled *Something's Wrong* in 1979, based on a screenplay written by Brian and his friend Robert Epler, that took its inspiration from the horror anthology classic, *Trilogy of Terror*. "He had done a lot of short films in his youth that were pretty funny," remembers Brian's friend and fellow Corman-era colleague Pat Rand. "He did one called *Traffic Vigilantes*. It was exactly like you think it would be, these hardcore vigilantes, but if you violate a traffic rule, they're really coming after you (laughs)."

In September 1981, Brian departed West Linn for a new life in Los Angeles with dreams of making it in the film industry. Earlier that same year, Brian had completed a draft of *Critters*, though it would not see the light of day for a few more years. A young Brian Muir's hopeful entrance into the film industry took shape under the banner of Roger Corman's New World Pictures where Brian started out in the mailroom before becoming a production assistant on sci-cheapies such as *Time Walker* and *Android* while later serving as a camera assistant on *Space Raiders*. "Brian and I had met while working for Roger Corman," explains Mark Pritchard. "I had started working for Corman in 1979 as a set carpenter and Brian had come on as a production assistant not long after that. We both had offbeat styles of humor and I would see him hanging around the sets after he had completed his day [worth of work], so I knew he was someone who was really into films. We became fast friends. He had been writing even way back in his production assistant days. As far back as I remember he was always writing."

With budding relationships with like-minded Corman regulars like Rand, Pritchard, and Stephen Herek, the idea to pitch their own script to Corman came to fruition. Brian suggested taking a look at his completed *Critters* script, a sci-fi horror film that shared sensibilities with what Corman's studio was putting out at the time. "Brian was really excited about getting *Critters* made," remembers Pritchard. "He was very excited. That was the first time he had gotten an option or sold one of his scripts. It was a big deal for him."

Brian Muir's enduring love for filmmaking inspired him and his close friends like Robert Epler (right) to write, produce, direct, and act in homemade short films shot on Super 8mm during their adolescence. (Source: Robert Epler and Charles Austin Muir)

Around this same time, Brian and Pritchard began their 2-year run producing their own cable access show *Two Guys Who Watch Movies*, which ultimately aired 21 episodes, four of which included short segments and interviews about the making of *Critters*. Larry Bock, Stephen Herek, and storyboard artist Len Morganti all made separate appearances prior to the April 1986 release of *Critters*, and a fourth episode included Brian and Mark's review of *Critters*.

Back in West Linn, Brian's large and extended family shared in the excitement of *Critters*. "At some point I knew that *Critters* was getting a theatrical release," reflects Charles Muir. "My parents, other relatives, and I sat and watched Siskel and Ebert's review of *Critters*, just waiting for them to get to the segment, and then it was like, '*Oh my God, they gave* Critters *a really good review.*' Siskel and Ebert were some of Brian's favorite critics. So at that point, we were all excited. And then a bunch of us, all this extended family, we wore these goofy *Critters* pins and went to this screening and everyone was cheering when Brian's name came on. But one of our relatives, they actually saw it like a week or a few days before during a screening with a different ending."

Of course, *Critters* went on to enjoy commercial and critical success, both at the box office and on the home video market, but Brian's standard one-time payment contract as the film's writer left him without royalties, residuals, or financial security. Unbeknownst to many at the time, Brian was also battling cancer and had fallen ill in 1986, one of three bouts that Brian would struggle with during his lifetime. The success of *Critters* boosted the career of director Stephen Herek and undoubtedly served as a critical win for Bob Shaye and New Line Cinema. Herek, editor Larry Bock, and cinematographer Tim Suhrstedt soon reunited on Herek's next and unexpectedly successful film, *Bill & Ted's Excellent Adventure*. Muir, left out of the loop, struggled to land the next big gig and his once strong relationship with Herek waned. Eventually, the pair fell out altogether.

"Even with the success of *Critters*, Brian's career didn't really take off," recollects Rand. "I actually worked on *Three Musketeers* that Steve [Herek] did, we hung out for a long time. After *Three Musketeers* we kind of fell out. We all kind of thought he went Hollywood. I think he would kind of admit to that (laughs). It's easy to get caught up in fame and fortune as so many people do. And Brian and I were just kind of doing our work and trying to get ourselves going."

Critters eventually became a mere memory for Brian, a topic he rarely discussed publicly or privately. Never a fan of sequels, Brian's interest and participation in the *Critters* franchise never materialized. The lasting negative financial aspect of his original contract's one-time payment, lack of follow-up opportunities, and his falling out with Herek left Brian disinterested, if not somewhat piqued, about *Critters*, though not to suggest Brian remained bitter or despised his participation in the cult classic.

"We didn't talk about *Critters* much after the fact," recalls Pritchard. "We never did a post-mortem or hosted a discussion about his overall feelings of the film after it was made. I just let him talk about it as much as he wanted to or not. Oddly, he and I didn't really talk about it all that much. He talked about it more in the beginning."

"Brian never really talked about *Critters* with us, but we became friends later on and in all that time, we almost never talked about it," says Charles Muir. "In fact, here's the first time my wife, I've been with her for 33 years, first time we met was in 1990, and we were at a family reunion at a pizza place and I introduced Brian to her and the first thing she says is '*Oh, you wrote* Critters, *I love* Critters!' But he just kind of looked at her and went, '*Oh, yeah, thanks.*' And then just started talking to someone else and she just went, '*Oh,*' and got deflated."

Following *Critters*, Brian was rumored to have been offered a perhaps short-lived opportunity to write a sequel to *Gremlins*, which did not pan out, but maintained a presence in Hollywood, serving as an assistant editor on *Twice Dead* and *Book of Love*. Brian eventually wrote the English version scripts for dubbed versions of Asian action films in the early 1990s, but eventually became a regular at Charles Band's Full Moon Entertainment in the early 2000's writing screenplays under the pseudonym August White, of which 17 were made into feature films. Brian was also commissioned to write several screenplays (yet to be produced), and often helped friends and colleagues in the industry, such as *Critters's* second unit director Mark Helfrich, revise and enhance dialogue for scenes in films like *Stone Cold*, *Action Jackson*, and *I Come in Peace*.

"Brian is the only person I know who *never* took a side job," says Rand. "He just wrote – and he lived like a pauper a lot of the time, but he just wrote and he wasn't going to compromise that. He thought it was going to take away from his ability to write; I had such admiration for him doing that. The rest of us were like, '*We've got bills to pay, I'll take another job*' (laughs). But Brian had written a lot of things, most of it was very funny, and very dark. He was a great writer, he really was. He was prolific in terms of his writing and the volume of his output."

Brian's diverse range of interests and impressive output were not restricted to sci-fi and horror, he also had deep interests in the pulp-era's detective yarns, mysteries, and fixated on blending genres, like sci-fi westerns or horror-westerns. At his core, Brian was a *writer's* writer; creative, innovative, and dedicated. Besides screenplays, Brian also devoted his time to short fiction and novels, including his wickedly entertaining debut sci-fi novel *The Outcasts*. "I think his sensibilities changed over the years," explains Shane Bitterling, one of Brian's best friends and fellow screenwriter, thoughtfully. "When he was a younger guy, it was kind of sci-fi all the way. As he got older, I knew he wanted to do a western that Tom Callaway was going to direct. Never happened. That was called *Corpse in the Saddle*. Brian had a file cabinet, or a couple file cabinets that were full, and a huge chunk of it was all this material over the years from *Corpse in the Saddle*. So there were multiple versions of the script, there were notes, there were conversations, just everything you could think of. Sadly, that just didn't happen, like a lot of the things that just didn't happen. But I know he really wanted to do that for a while and to work with Tom in that way. He loved horror and that's what he wrote to get, I mean that paid the bills. In the later years, he really kind of focused on like the murder mystery type stuff. He was doing short stories, a lot of prose fiction. He sold a couple of stories to *Ellery Queen*, which was a huge deal. They were so hard to get into and I know a lot of big, what I would consider A-list writers, tried to get into *Ellery Queen* and could not. And he did several times. But he had a novel that he was trying to get published through *Ellery Queen* which was a recurring character in the shorts. He was really into that. Those were sort of very *Murder, She Wrote*, suspense, light type things, but some of his short stories for other publications would kind of bend into the horror genre a little bit. But he was kind of all over the place. He loved so many different things and I know people wear kind of a badge of pride, '*Oh I'm a horror writer, I'm a this writer, I'm a that writer.*' He just wanted to be a writer. I don't think he could be pigeonholed, which is kind of a great, bad thing when you're trying to market, or trying to market *you*. His book *The Outcast* was kind of a mix of everything. It was sci-fi, horror, also very sweet, fun stuff, and comic books. He loved it all."

Corpse in the Saddle is but one of many (sadly) yet-to-be produced projects Brian had written. Brian had also collaborated with the Chiodo brothers in the mid-2000s on a potential film project titled *Santa's Little Helper* about an evil elf. Charlie Chiodo rendered various designs and the Chiodo brothers were set to create a puppet version of the elf character as well as a skeletal/bone raccoon puppet. Actor Tony Cox was considered for a role in which he would play

A prototype movie poster for the yet-to-be-made *Corpse in the Saddle* is a testament to Brian's meticulous planning and endless well of creativity. Artwork thought to have been rendered by Brian's friend and storyboard artist Len Morganti. (Source: Charles Austin Muir)

the costume version of the evil elf. "He was trying to get that off the ground," says Edward Chiodo. "He came close, but then he got sick. It was going to be Brian's directorial debut and we were going to do the puppet effects for him. But there was another project, one of my favorite Brian Muir projects, and it was about a producer wanting to make a dinosaur movie, a low-budget dinosaur movie. He couldn't afford expensive dinosaur effects, so he built a time machine, bringing a movie crew back in time to shoot it on location. And then there's a mishap and the time machine gets damaged and they can't go back. So you've got the movie crew trying to survive the age of dinosaurs. It's just a funny premise."

Brian's long bout with cancer – first with Hodgkin's disease and then lung cancer 25 years later – came to a crescendo when he was diagnosed with a brain tumor, a tragic turn of events that slowly but steadily eroded his physical capabilities by the summer of 2010, but failed to diminish his spirit or determination to continue writing. "I have a tray of his that was passed on to me where it just says, '*Don't just sit there, write,*' and he had his routine," attests Charles Muir. "My wife saw that because she took care of him for a week as he was getting really ill. But even right toward the end, he had his routine. And he was going through cancer treatment. He couldn't even taste coffee anymore, but he would still have his coffee because it was part of his ritual. He was going to sit there, and he was going to write and he finished a fourth draft for a fourth novel and a script for Charles Band at Full Moon with a brain tumor."

"He got so bad toward the end, but he just wouldn't admit it," a somber Shane Bitterling says. "I had the key to his house, and I was there every day, bringing him food or doing his errands and that type of stuff. So this one time, my mission was to find him crutches. He wanted crutches. But by the time he actually needed crutches, he really needed a wheelchair. So I had to change my mission. I walked in and he was sitting on the floor and I said, '*What the hell are you doing?*' He's like, '*Oh, I just dropped something down here and I'm looking for it.*' I go, '*Bullshit, get up on the couch.*' And he couldn't do it. He just didn't have the ability to pull himself up because of the havoc being caused by the brain tumor. I was taking him to all of his appointments and everything at this time and it got to the point where I'd wheel his ass out in a wheelchair to the car and then I'd have to pick him up to put him in the car and everything. And he was always wearing sweats at that point. And I'm like, '*I don't know how to lift you. I'm not sure what to do.*' So I was asking one of the doctors, I'm like, '*How do I lift him?*' So they showed me this whole kind of process on how to do it. But going in there, he kept slipping because he was a good four or five inches taller than me and he was skinny and lanky and I didn't want to hurt him. But we were kind of doing this move where he put his arms around me facing me. I would hold him up by his inner thighs and his butt. It really looked precarious. We looked like lovers (laughs). We kept slipping. So he was slipping as I was going across the parking lot and I ended up carrying him by his waistband like a fucking briefcase. And his legs were just flopping. He was like, '*Jesus Christ!*' And I was just like tugging on him. I was just like tugging on, and his head was kind of swinging around in front of me and everything. And I got the door open to the place, I walked in, all these nurses were just staring at me, he goes, '*Yeah, can't you tell he's my best friend?*' (laughs). He just always had those like zingers that were so perky, and I was like, '*You're just a big meat bag and I'm trying to figure out how to lift you up. Can you have one of the doctors show me how I'm supposed to lift this asshole?*' (laughs) But that was us 'til the end, he was such a great guy, always funny, still cracking each other up even though he was going through all of this horrible shit."

Brian passed away from complications related to his cancer and brain tumor on 19 September 2010 at the Norwalk Community Hospital in California. An endlessly creative, talented, and brilliant writer's life cut heartbreakingly short at the age of 48. With Brian's untimely passing, few could imagine his unexpected parting love letter to the *Critters* fanbase.

Even while ill, Brian never lost his sense of humor and maintained his disciplined writing regiment while contending with a debilitating brain tumor. (Source: Charles Austin Muir)

Several years before Brian's death, the Aero Theatre in Santa Monica hosted a revival screening of *Critters* on 35mm. In fact, the reels to be used for the screening were the only ones left in the Warner Bros. archives. The rare occurrence of seeing Krites on the silver screen loaded the theater to capacity, and Brian and many of his close friends, including Shane Bitterling and Jeff Burr, were in attendance. Within a few minutes, the shocked audience watched on in dread as they slowly realized that every scene – in fact, every frame – that contained any visual or special effects had been removed from the print. The jocularity of the audience soon turned to disappointment as devoted fans walked out in disgust; bewildered staff handed out refunds. Though Muir found the event comical at first, he later spent years trying to solve the mystery of the missing frames and the culprit behind what became known as the *Critterless* screening. Never again would *Critters* enjoy a revival screening for the rabid new generation of fans as Warner Bros. had no additional prints of the film.

After Brian's passing, friends and family members took turns sifting through his belongings and artifacts. Shane tackled the daunting task of clearing out Brian's densely packed and cat hair-smothered closet crammed with comic books and t-shirts. Tucked behind various editing equipment, film projectors, and boxes stuffed with books sat a large, hefty box. Upon closer inspection, the box had been shipped to Brian years prior by Bob Murawski, a fellow friend and well-known film editor who won an Oscar (along with his wife and editing partner) for *The Hurt Locker*. Murawski, a co-founder of Grindhouse Releasing, a film restoration and distribution company that specializes in cult classics and European horror films, had acquired a complete version of *Critters* with both endings and shipped it to Brian in 1996.

Murawski arranged a special screening of *Critters* at the New Beverly Cinema in Los Angeles, this time hosted by Bitterling in Brian's honor. The print was donated back to Warner Bros., where it would later be restored for the 2018 Blu-ray edition. The Mahoning Drive-In Theater, a longstanding drive-in theater tucked in the Pocono mountain range of eastern Pennsylvania, held a remarkable screening of *Critters* in June 2021 during the dog-days of the COVID pandemic, attended by hundreds, with a special guest appearance by the Chiodo brothers. The print used for the screening? The long-lost box of reels from Brian's closet – his one last romantic gesture to *Critters* fans everywhere. "The screening of *Critters* at the Mahoning was only possible because the creator had the only known complete trans-center reel sitting in his closet for over a decade," Charles Muir proudly asserts. "It's just crazy. It was Brian's gift to the fandom all over again."

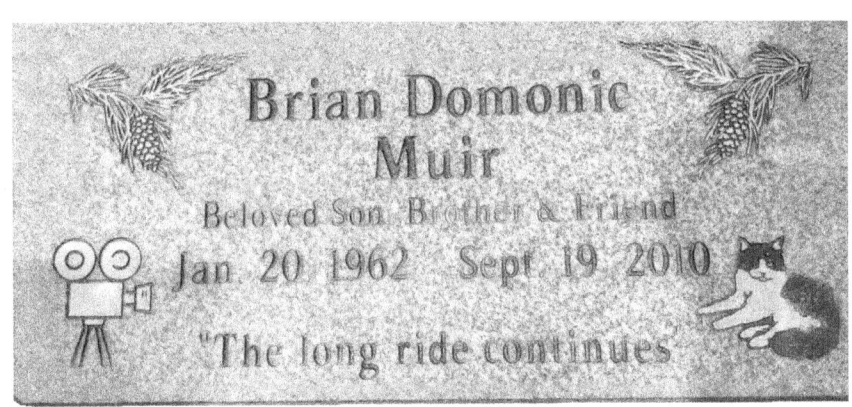

A Note on Sources

Most of the research for *We're Here for the Krites* consists of original interviews with cast and crew members conducted by the author, as well as original production notes and early screenplay drafts. However, some previously published works cited throughout were also relied upon, as were several noteworthy texts meriting additional attention.

First and foremost, the featurettes and audio commentary tracks on the *Critters* collection from Shout! Factory proved invaluable, particularly *They Bite!: The Making of Critters* documentary. Coverage of *Critters* and *Critters 2* found in *Monsterland* 7 and 12, *Fangoria* 51, 54, 73, 74, *Starburst* 141, *Gorezone* 2, *Starlog* 272 was very insightful and *HorrorHound* 88 also provided a wonderful roundup of the *Critters* franchise and its universe of collectibles. Credit is deserved for author Jim Knipfel for coining the phrase "monster comedy" in his great *Den of Geek* article, "*Critters* and the '80s Golden Age of Monster Comedies."

In addition to these great resources, several books are also worth highlighting. *Critters: Devoradores del espacio exterior* (2020) by Octavio López Sanjuán, is a critical work, whether you can read Spanish or not, it's a beautiful rendition worthy of your time and attention. The official biography of Mick Garris, *Master of Horror*, written by Abbie Bernstein, provided rich context to Mick's career and his approach to making *Critters 2*. I also found Bruce G. Hallenbeck's *Comedy-Horror Films: A Chronological History, 1914-2008* entertaining and is the literary source for claiming the "Kelly-Hopkinsville (Kentucky) goblins" episode in UFO lure as the inspiration for Muir's original extraterrestrial storyline for *Critters*, though unfounded.

About the Author

Matthew C. DuPée is the author of *A Scary Little Christmas: A History of Yuletide Horror Films, 1972-2020* released through McFarland Books. Brought up on a steady diet of classic and contemporary horror films in the early 80s, Matthew eventually attended Point Park University and graduated with a degree in film and video production in 2002. He has also written for *Rue Morgue, Morbidly Beautiful, Offscreen*, and *Bright Lights Film Journal*. He lives outside of Annapolis, Maryland with his wife, two children, and beloved Chihuahua-pitbull, Bella. Matthew continues his research into cult film history and is working on several additional projects, including a book examining the fascinating story behind the making of Albert Pyun's post-apocalyptic rock-opera, *Radioactive Dreams*.

Acknowledgments

The literary endeavor of writing a book manuscript is certainly a testament to one's creativity, abilities, and passions surrounding a particular topic, but it's also a grueling exercise in discipline, patience, and humility. This literary journey, while romantic in terms of uncovering those rare sources of primary information and the ability to speak with various Hollywood legends, could not have been possible without a profound level of support and assistance from very kind and generous individuals.

The Chiodo brothers, Bradford Plows, Chris Biggs, John Naulin, Anthony Doublin, Jene Omens, Frank Ceglia, Mark Helfrich, Larry Bock, Hilarie Roope, Kevin Thompson, Lin Shaye, Jeremy Lawrence, Dee Wallace, Tim Suhrstedt, Barry Opper, Rupert Harvey, Dwight Roberts, Dodie Pettit, and Daniel Griffith of Ballyhoo Productions graciously provided their keen insights and shared personal, often times rare photographs for the book; I thank you all. I would like to thank Mark Pritchard, Brian Muir's co-host of the cable access show *Two Guys Who Watch Movies*, who patiently dug up rare archival footage of several episodes of the show that featured Brian and Mark discussing *Critters* with director and co-writer Stephen Herek, editor Larry Bock, and storyboard artist Len Morganti, a gesture for which I'm eternally grateful. A special thanks is owed to Clay Bush (Greenbush), who not only provided information about his cameo in *Critters*, but also arranged for his father Billy Bush (Green Bush) to speak about his acting career and his role as "Jay Brown" in *Critters* all of these years later. A nod to both Scott Grimes and Billy Zane, both of whom I spoke to during the writing of this book, though formal interviews were never made possible.

For insights into *Critters 2*, I owe much gratitude to the Chiodo brothers, Barry Opper, Allan Holzman, Mick Strawn, Liane Curtis, Lin Shaye, Brafford Plows, Ans Ellis, Dwight Roberts, Charles Bornstein, Chris Biggs, Kevin Kernohan, and James Belohovek. Keen insights into the making of *Critters 3* would not have been available if it weren't for the generous time and recollection provided by Kristine Peterson, Katherine Cortez, Geoffrey Blake, Tom Callaway, Barry Opper, Rupert Harvey, Mark Ordesky, Edward and Stephen Chiodo, Frank Ceglia, Deborah Galvez, and Terry Stokes. Additionally, David Witz provided historical documents detailing the daily schedule and production notes for both *Critters 3* and *Critters 4*, for which I am eternally grateful. A heartfelt thanks to my friend Paul Salamoff who meticulously kept an archive of his fabrication work on *Critters 3* and *4* and spent valuable time and energy scanning his photographs and personal invitations to the wrap party and cast and crew screening and provided great insights into the production of both *Critters 3* and *Critters 4*. Although our schedules never worked out, I appreciate the time provided by Aimee Brooks who acknowledged that *Critters 3* remains a project dear to her heart. I would also like to thank Kevin Lane for his introduction to Anders Hove who kindly spoke about his experience on *Critters 4*.

For *Critters Attack!*, I am indebted to Bobby Miller, Scott Lobdell, the legendary Mike Mendez, Ben Gigli, Tashiana Washington, Dee Wallace, Werner Pretorius and his Amazing Ape Studio, and Keith Arbuthnot for all of their generous time, patience, and personal photographs. An extra huge thanks is owed to Mike Mendez for his powerful assistance in arranging connections with other creative forces behind *Critters Attack!* and the *Critters* universe in general. The *Critters* Rehatched Facebook group also served as a wellspring of inspiration and proves just how rabid a fanbase the *Critters* franchise enjoys, thanks to Chris Lacks, Sean Beard and their team of admins for keeping the group alive and nurtured.

A heartfelt thanks is also owed to Charles Austin Muir, Brian Muir's cousin and stalwart advocate of Brian's legacy, who provided deep insights into the lovable, caring, and brilliant mind of Brian as well as numerous photographs and patiently answered dozens of follow-up questions and musings over the past 2 years. I am humbled to call Charles a friend. And thanks to Brian's closest friend Shane Bitterling, who, like Charles, upholds Brian's admirable legacy with considerable enthusiasm and respect, as well as Patrick Rand, who was extremely generous with his time and candor.

I am forever indebted to the infinitely talented Natalie Tomaszewski for her herculean editorial efforts, which truly enhanced every aspect of the manuscript and can be felt on every page. Much praise is also warranted for George Todoroff, the talented artist responsible for creating the book's brilliant and mesmerizing cover art. Thank you, George.

I also owe a debt of gratitude to those who provided copious support and encouragement throughout my time researching and writing this book, including author and the owner of Harker Press, Dustin McNeill, a true beacon of inspiration; filmmaker and owner of Poltergeists and Paramours, Ama Lea; filmmaker and author Mike Lombardo; Jay and Jeff from the *Horror for the Holidays* podcast; Kevin Lane from the *Spill Your Guts* podcast; author Michael Crowl; and Amy, Christine, and the team at Third Eye Music and Video in Annapolis, Maryland. My dearest friends from AlethalWeaponArt, Aletha Boldon and Marissa Schmidt, and the wonderful Abbie Nesbitt, all served as muses during this project and I can't thank you all enough. I'd also like to to thank Jake "the Bloodhound" Cowan, Stephanie Barngrover, Chris Holbert, Jamie Layne; Rich "King Richard" Reed, DJ Orme, Sara Kirkpatrick, Darin Warner, Alex and Char Spring, Matt Kimsal, Matt Cantu, my cousin Robyne and my beloved Aunt Beth for their interest and enduring support. A heartfelt thanks to my family: Laura, Molly, and Jackson, who afforded me the time to watch and rewatch the *Critters* franchise on loop and espouse random franchise facts like a babbling lunatic for 2 straight years.

Learn more at

HarkerPress.com